COHOUSING
FOR LIFE

COHOUSING FOR LIFE

A PRACTICAL AND PERSONAL STORY OF EARTHSONG ECO-NEIGHBOURHOOD

Robin Allison

MARY EGAN PUBLISHING

Published by Mary Egan Publishing

This edition published 2020
© Robin Allison 2020
The moral right of the author has been asserted

MARY EGAN
PUBLISHING

Designed and typeset by Anna Egan-Reid
Produced by Mary Egan Publishing
www.maryegan.co.nz

Printed in China with soy inks

ISBN 978-0-473-51517-1

CONTENTS

EMBRACING COMPLEXITY

We live in a world of ebb and flow; of breathing in and breathing out, of night and day, summer and winter, growth and decay. No state exists without its opposite; it is the flow from one to the other and back again that gives us the rhythm to our lives. Yet so often our attention is drawn towards the extremes, the polar positions of black and white, right and wrong, yes and no – as though they were the only possibilities.

The overriding theme of this book is both/and: acknowledging the simplified duality that largely governs our Western thinking, while exploring the much more interesting, dynamic, alive terrain between the polar positions, and embracing the complexity and the flourishing frustrating chaos of life. In almost every area that I can think of, the juice is in the interplay of difference, the creative space where a variety of conditions exist, where there is uncertainty and room to move, to dance, to learn.

In permaculture the meeting place of two states or ecosystems is defined as 'the edge', and edges are encouraged as places of maximum abundance and productivity. Mutual interaction between the different states allows combinations and possibilities not present without the overlapping.

The creation story of Māori (the first peoples of Aotearoa/New Zealand) relates how Papatūānuku (Earth mother) and Rangi-nui (Sky father), balanced but opposite in their strengths and attributes, lie together in a locked embrace. Their children, living in the cramped darkness between them, forcefully separate their parents to create space and light, the productive edge where all the diversity, complexity and life of the natural and human world can flourish.

We inhabit the edge between land and sky, between past and future, memories and dreams, the echo of what was and the whisper of what is to come. The edge is not a narrow line that divides, but a zone within which life happens. The edge is the place of connection. In between black and white is a glorious rainbow of possibilities.

There is a saying in the cohousing movement, that cohousing is the most expensive personal growth course you will ever do.[1] And it's true! Working together on a huge, complex, challenging project with a diverse range of individuals, with their own personal stressors and circumstances and varying degrees of self-awareness, can push buttons we didn't know we had and requires us to bring as much patience, goodwill and generosity as we can muster.

This book is my personal story of the founding and building of Earthsong. There are the facts of course: what happened and when it happened. But every one of us who has been part of the creation of Earthsong will have their own experience, their own recollections and understandings of that journey.

There is an edge here between privacy and honesty, confidentiality and transparency. This is a story of community, relationship and group endeavour, and it involves many people working together – and occasionally at odds. I have striven to keep the balance between acknowledging the contributions of others, respecting others' rights to privacy and writing my story as honestly and bravely as I can.

I have always been curious about the spiritual dimension of being alive. The closest I have come to the meaning of life is that I am one small but vital part of a huge, complex, alive and wonderfully diverse whole, which – for shorthand – I call Gaia.[2] And far from that making my choices irrelevant, it makes them matter more. How can I live my life in a way that contributes most to the flourishing of Gaia?

All through this long journey towards Earthsong it has felt like the right thing for me to be doing, the highest and best use of who I am, my skills and experience, my privilege and opportunities. In some ways it didn't feel as though the impetus came from me: I have been a conduit for something that Gaia wanted to happen, and I had a deep knowing that it was important.

I have also constantly remembered (most of the time) that the journey was worth doing for its own sake as well as for the destination; that being part of a group of people working on such a project together was extraordinary. Even through the hard parts, and even if the project hadn't achieved fruition, that experience was gold.

We are all on our own journeys, and sometimes it is useful to have maps. Your journey will be very different; with different weather, the terrain changed in different light; with different companions and tools in your backpacks. By mapping the territory I travelled I hope to give some sense of direction, but you will need to be alert, agile and use all your senses, willing to take a different path if need be while still with your eyes on the mountain, the destination.

No project comes out of nothing, springing into life fully formed. Ideas are the soup we swim in, and it is what we do with the ideas we have access to and the circumstances we find ourselves in that is the dance of our individual lives. There came a time in my life when I started to recognise that everything I had experienced up to that time contributed to who I was; all the various random threads wove together to become the fabric of me, from which I could then fashion the garment of who I could become.

When I look back, I can see some of the threads and circumstances which contributed to my journey towards Earthsong. I hope that making my journey visible helps you to imagine your own journey, your own contribution to our collective good. If someone like me, with the usual quota of strengths and vulnerabilities, clarity and blind spots, tolerance and stubbornness, can do it, then so can you.

INTRODUCING EARTHSONG AND COHOUSING

1

THEME

Opening night of the Earthsong Winter Hui

Once it is dark the drumbeat comes, distant at first but steadily growing stronger, calling neighbours from their homes. I grab my warm coat and hat against the winter chill and join the group, anonymous in the dense black night. Gathering others as we go, we walk down the path to the meadow above the pond and form a large circle on the grass.

One neighbour steps forward. 'We've come to the darkest time of the year. But there is hope. Mātāriki has been seen! New light has sprung forth! Will you children help me find it?'

The kids surge forward towards the dense grove of trees beside the meadow. Muffled squeals of excitement are heard as they find the lit candle, safely housed in a large glass jar. The children return to the circle of adults, carefully carrying the jar, and go from neighbour to neighbour lighting a small candle for each.

The return procession down the path to the common house is full of candle-light and music as whistles and shakers accompany the drum. The oldest and

Opening night of the Earthsong winter hui

youngest residents at Earthsong, an eighty-two-year-old woman and a three-year-old boy, lead us into the common-house large room, and together they crouch to light the fire with their candles. We stand in a large circle in the heart of our community, looking around at each one in turn, appreciating each individual and the diverse community we make together.

After supper, chairs are set up for our annual slideshow. One by one, photos from our childhoods are shown, and names are called out as we try to guess which neighbour each one depicts. Each photo is followed by another in which the neighbour recreates the original with their adult self, to much hilarity. At the end of the evening I walk across the common green to my home nestled beside others, warm with camaraderie and belonging, at home at Earthsong.

EARTHSONG ECO-NEIGHBOURHOOD

Turn off busy Swanson Road in the western suburbs of Auckland, New Zealand; leave your car in the carpark to walk between clusters of houses into the heart of this suburban community, and you find yourself in an oasis of calm, beauty and abundance. The noise of the busy street recedes to a murmur, and you start to hear the birdsong. The air feels fresh, and your nose wakes up to smells of flowers, leaves and earth. Neighbours stop for a chat on the path, while children race past, engrossed in their own game.

This is Earthsong Eco-Neighbourhood, home to sixty-nine adults and children in thirty-two homes nestled amongst gardens, paths and a village green. The founding vision, still strongly held by residents today, has three equal components: sustainable design and construction, respectful and cooperative community, and education by demonstration. We are relearning the skills and benefits of belonging to a community and rebuilding a healthy interdependence with each other and with earth.

Residents range from babies to older adults, from singles to families, from bus drivers to midwives to university professors. This diversity brings a real strength, because our differing needs, skills and contributions can complement one another. Older people often have more time, more patience and huge amounts of wisdom, and many cherish having children in their lives. Younger adults can handle more of the physical tasks but being a parent of young children can be relentless. How wonderful to hand the baby over to a surrogate grandparent, for a few minutes or longer. How wonderful for an older person whose own grandchildren live in another country to hold the baby or read to the toddler.

Knowing your neighbours and helping each other out is not a new idea – our forebears took that for granted. From borrowing a cup of flour to minding a child or watering the garden when a neighbour goes away, good neighbourliness is all about feeling connected with people and valuing the sense of belonging which that brings. Knowing and being known by your neighbours is the best security there is.

As an intentional neighbourhood, Earthsong goes further than this. We have built a rich lifestyle of shared events, from meetings to manage our shared land and resources, to regular common dinners, to our annual winter Mātāriki hui weekend of community sharing, feasting and playing. Cooperating with neighbours often means having fun together or learning new skills. Working alongside neighbours on a cooking team or a working bee in the garden is a great way to build the social glue of relationships that maintains community.

Common dinners

It is Thursday, and Team C's monthly turn to provide common dinner for the community. As Head Cook this month, I've planned the menu of spinach and feta filo pie (with a non-gluten and non-dairy version for the 'specials'), fresh tomato sauce, baked potatoes, and a green salad from the Earthsong gardens.

Serving common dinner

I've emailed the menu to residents and bought the ingredients from local organic retailers.

The five Team C members arrive in the common-house kitchen from 3 p.m., and we spend several busy but enjoyable hours chopping, stirring, chatting and laughing as the dinner takes shape. At 6 p.m. we set the food out on the servery and ask one of the children to run around the paths with the bell to call our neighbours to dinner. Neighbours line up and are served a plate of steaming food, and as the last stragglers arrive, applause breaks out from those already eating to acknowledge the efforts of the cooks.

We serve ourselves last and eat with our neighbours, before returning to the kitchen to do the dishes and clean up. It's several hours' work, but often a lot of fun. After the meal I tally up what we have spent and divide it by five; the five team members pay the full cost of the meal.

On the other seven Thursday and Saturday nights in the month, another team prepares dinner. At 6 p.m. I hear the bell, amble up to the common house with my drink of choice, and am served a delicious, home-cooked, organic and seasonal meal. I sit at a table to eat with some of my very interesting neighbours, and go home when I choose, without doing the dishes or paying for the food. There is no obligation or worry about offending a host by leaving too early or staying too long.

Common dinner nights are the heartbeat of our neighbourhood, the regular gathering of nourishment and camaraderie that reminds us we are part of a community.

Earthsong was developed by a group of ordinary people who wanted to live more sustainably and with a strong commitment to cooperative neighbourliness. Launched at a public meeting in 1995, the project grew as people joined and worked together over several years to develop effective group processes, to set up the legal and financial structures, and to agree on what we wanted to build. In 1999 we purchased an old organic orchard, then worked with consultants to design the neighbourhood, and contracted with builders to build the houses in stages over eight years. While the first residents moved into their homes in 2002, it was 2008 before the last homes and site works were completed.

From the beginning, our Vision Statement has described our overarching purpose and main priorities. It is the bedrock upon which our community was built, keeping us focused and aligned to our agreed goal. Earthsong is based on the twin

Earthsong Eco-Neighbourhood

principles of cohousing and permaculture, with three aims that can be seen as a three-legged stool. All three legs – environmental sustainability, social sustainability and education for sustainability – are of equal importance to the stability of the stool – and indeed to a flourishing planet.

Earthsong Eco-Neighbourhood Vision Statement

**Our vision is to establish a cohousing neighbourhood,
based on the principles of permaculture,
that will serve as a model of a
socially and environmentally sustainable community.**

Within this vision, our aims are:
- to design and construct a cohesive neighbourhood whose layout, buildings and services demonstrate the highest practical standards of sustainable human settlement;
- to develop and foster a living environment which uses clear communication, decision-making and conflict-resolution guidelines that promote tolerance, safety, respect and cooperation;
- to assist in education and public awareness of sustainability by demonstrating and promoting innovative community design and environmentally responsible construction.

With thirty-two homes on 3 acres (1.2 hectares) of land, Earthsong is a medium-density suburban neighbourhood. It's a short walk from Earthsong to the shops, library and community facilities, bus stop and train station of our local suburban centre. But these are not houses dotted along a suburban street; they are houses in a garden, surrounded by old fruit trees and lush new plantings, in balance with the natural environment.

At Earthsong cars are parked along two edges of the site, and from there pedestrian pathways wind between gardens and community space to individual homes. At the heart of the neighbourhood is the common house, our much-loved community building owned jointly by all the householders and providing shared spaces including the large dining/meeting hall, sitting room, large kitchen, children's and teenagers' rooms, guest room and shared laundry.

The main path loops through the centre of the site in a large figure of 8, connecting the common house at one end with the pond at the other. From the main path, smaller paths lead to clusters of two-storey attached dwellings, all with good north-facing solar access, and stepping gracefully down the natural slope of the land to the central path.

Elements that contribute to environmentally sustainable design are described in more detail in Chapter 9, from location and site design, to buildings, materials and provision of services. Chapter 11 brings together the key stages and structures of the Earthsong development journey, including legal structures, financing and managing construction.

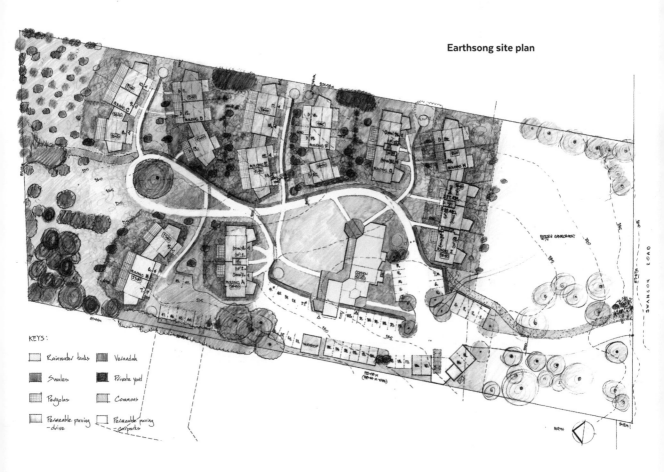

Earthsong site plan

KEYS:
- Rainwater tanks
- Swales
- Pergolas
- Permeable paving – drive
- Verandah
- Private yard
- Commons
- Permeable paving – carparks

Permaculture (**perma**nent agri**culture**) is the conscious design and maintenance of agriculturally productive ecosystems which have the diversity, stability, and resilience of natural ecosystems. It is the harmonious integration of landscape and people providing their food, energy, shelter and other material and non-material needs in a sustainable way. MOLLISON (1988, P. IX)

Social sustainability has always been equal and complementary to the environmental goals at Earthsong. Robust social infrastructure, though less visible than the architecture, continues to underpin the neighbourhood. Alignment to a strong shared vision (Chapter 3) and clear membership, governance and decision-making systems (Chapter 5) have been key elements in the creation of Earthsong, and provide the stable framework for our ongoing community life. Good neighbourliness is also supported by good design (Chapter 7).

Social sustainability includes diversity and affordability, and renters have always been welcome as residents and equal as members. While house prices are comparable to those in the surrounding area, at Earthsong they include many common facilities and low-energy, non-toxic, sustainable houses. Running costs are much less than for a standard house due to design, materials and efficiencies of community-scale services, covered in more detail in Chapter 9.

Of course, there are irritations too. Ongoing management of shared areas requires time and effort to understand each other and reach agreement, and as is the case with any group of people there are occasional conflicts that need to be worked through. Group dynamics of power and leadership occur in any large project, and these are explored in Chapter 13. Learning to work together and to make decisions for the common good is challenging, and hugely valuable in learning to rebuild *interdependence* in our individualistic world.

The third leg of our vision stool is the strong motivation to trial and demonstrate a more sustainable urban neighbourhood model. It is a powerful experience to walk around a neighbourhood designed for people and nature alike; to touch the solid, natural materials; to smell the fragrant timbers and natural oils; to sense the atmosphere of peaceful engagement. Regular public tours and a wide range of tours by request give visitors the opportunity to experience this different form of housing, and many people from all sectors of society find that visiting Earthsong is an inspirational experience.

The common house is part-owned by our educational charitable trust, the

Earthsong Centre Trust, and is a venue for courses and educational tours. We also share documents, information and procedures freely with the public, and the Earthsong website (www.earthsong.org.nz) is a mine of information for those interested. All of this aims to support wider knowledge and implementation of more sustainable practices in housing developments.

COHOUSING

Earthsong is a cohousing neighbourhood. Cohousing is a specific model of resident-led cooperative housing; a proven, viable and fully rounded system backed up by decades of experience.[1] Like standard housing, cohousing offers the autonomy and privacy we expect in the twenty-first century. People own their own fully self-contained homes with all the usual facilities – kitchen, dining and living rooms, bedrooms, bathroom and private outdoor space.

However, cohousing offers so much more than this. It adds another layer of 'home' between the single house and public space. In cohousing there are individual homes and gardens, and also the common house and shared gardens of the cohousing neighbourhood. Residents have access to many shared facilities, and to the support, belonging and neighbourliness of a defined community.

Cohousing doesn't substitute community for privacy; on the contrary, it seeks to provide *both* community *and* privacy, *both* autonomy *and* cooperation. It increases our choices, rather than diminishing them. The needs and rights of the individual are balanced with the needs and rights of the collective, so that both can flourish. This is incorporated into all aspects of the neighbourhood, from house and site design to ownership structure and decision making. Individual ownership, autonomy and privacy live alongside shared ownership, shared decision making, cooperation and community.

Residents run their own lives and finances, while at the same time enjoying considerable economies through cooperation. With any shared management system there is inevitably a time cost, as we meet to collectively work out the systems we want. This is part of 'the community tax' (McCamant and Durett, 2011, p. 19) – that is, the effort required and the little annoyances that sometimes come with cooperating with neighbours to achieve all the benefits of cohousing.

Six common characteristics (McCamant and Durett, 2011, p. 25) define the co-housing model:

- **Participatory process**
  Future residents work together to organise and drive the development, planning and design, with professional support as required.
- **Designs that facilitate community**
  The physical layout and design are carefully planned to encourage a strong sense of community, while maintaining individual privacy.
- **Extensive common facilities**
  Shared facilities such as a common house, gardens, open space, and children's play areas supplement the individual homes and are part of the shared 'home'.
- **Complete resident management**
  Ongoing management of common spaces and other shared agreements is by the residents themselves, generating a strong sense of ownership and participation.
- **Non-hierarchical structure**
  Consensus decision-making structures allow all adult residents to participate in and share responsibility for decisions of common concern.
- **Separate income sources**
  Residents run their own lives and household finances. Households pay annual fees to cover the costs of shared facilities.

Most cohousing neighbourhoods value intergenerational living with a diversity of ages. The cohousing model can also be applied very successfully to self-managed housing for older people, and senior cohousing is one of the fastest growing categories in the USA.[2]

While cohousing neighbourhoods can vary hugely in form, character and circumstance, there are both large and subtle design elements that facilitate a healthy sense of community, described in Chapter 7. These can be applied to a wide range of locations, densities, and architectural styles: urban, suburban or rural; separate dwelling, attached townhouses or high-rise apartments; new-build or infill; commercial or industrial retrofit.

There are other ways to create cohousing: by gradually buying up a group of houses in an area, pulling down the fences and establishing common space in one of the buildings; or the lot-development model, where the overall site is designed for cohousing but residents buy their own lot and design and build their own house within the community.

There are brilliant examples of each of these around the world. What they have in common are the six characteristics mentioned, and a wish to build intentional good neighbourliness together. Cohousing is about valuing the strength, belonging and resilience of connected community, and being willing to give up some of your separateness for a greater sense of interdependence and richer relationships with your neighbours. Cohousing is not a prescriptive lifestyle, but a high-functioning neighbourhood.

> The value of the cohousing model in regard to social *and* environmental sustainability is its recognition of, and attempt to address, some of the failings of the late 20th century society: the breakdown of community, alienation of the individual, and the neglect of disadvantaged groups such as single parents, the elderly and the young. It addresses these issues via the hardware of site layout, building design and shared resources as well as, and perhaps more importantly, the software of participatory process, shared decision-making and an interactive social agenda. MELTZER (2002, P. 136)

• • •

How did a group of ordinary, extraordinary people develop a thirty-two-home eco-neighbourhood from a compelling idea, and what were the challenges and satisfactions along the way? What can we learn from their efforts that will make it easier for others to do the same? This book is the story of the initiating energy, the planning and development, the challenges and the successful completion of the construction of Earthsong and of the group who were involved, told from one person's perspective. The story chapters that follow tell the story of this heroic journey.

The interleaved theme chapters are a distillation of what we learned along the way. They explore key themes and describe the elements, structures and tools that were critical to our success, allowing a group of diverse individuals with ordinary lives and skills to work together over many years to create a large innovative housing development. The story and theme chapters complement and illuminate each other by looking at cohousing and Earthsong through two different lenses.

Earthsong Eco-Neighbourhood is a thriving community of diverse people. The reality reflects the vision carried for so long, and this vision of cooperation with and respect for one another and for the planet continues to unfold as attention is paid to ongoing systems.

Communities such as Earthsong add another layer of belonging into the standard suburban model, a layer of community relationships and governance that doesn't reduce our personal autonomy in our own homes but adds the enormous richness of a cohesive neighbourhood within the more impersonal wider suburb and city.

SEARCHING FOR COMMUNITY

2

STORY

I was born in the Southern Hemisphere at five minutes to midday, two days before summer solstice, a fire-sign Sagittarius, setting a trajectory to my life of orientation towards the sun. From early adulthood I felt strongly that awareness of latitude and climate was a key to living sustainably; that knowing where we are located on our planet and how to work with our primary source of energy, the sun, is crucial. Not that the sun was always my friend; one of the reliable indicators of summer was my pale redhead's skin burning to a painful bright red, followed inevitably by large blisters and subsequent peeling and itching.

I was the second child of my homemaker mother Jeanette and my architect father David. My elder brother Everard was always ahead of me as a child, more competent and allowed more freedom. My sister Lesley was behind me, a 'mini-me', younger and generally biddable. I was a slightly anxious child, with a frown of concentration often on my face; 'always trying to work things out', said Mum.

Perhaps being the middle child led me to explore the meeting place or edge between two worlds; sometimes considered one of the older children with my brother, but more usually lumped in with my younger sister, the two girls. At least

**Pixie in the middle:
Lesley, Robin and
Everard Allison**

I became comfortable and curious about the middle, feeling that all the possibilities along a continuum were much more interesting than the extreme positions at each end.

Until my teenage years we lived in a small, shabby house in a breathtaking location. Our home used to be my grandparents' bach, on a clifftop overlooking the Tamaki estuary as it emerged between Glendowie and Bucklands Beach, wove past the Tāhuna Tōrea sandspit directly in front of us, and out towards the sea. It was a dynamic and beautiful view, always changing with tide and light, and with the constant female shape of Rangitoto Island, my maunga, sitting in the centre of the horizon.

Bucklands Beach in the 1950s and '60s was an unpretentious small-town beach community, separated by farmland from the city of Auckland. Dad was benign but distant, driving our single car into work in Auckland every day and returning late. Mum was home with the kids, doing her best to be a good '50s' housewife and mother, involved in the local Playcentre and tennis club, and yearning for more in her life.

It was hard for my mum, but a wonderful place to grow up. Our garden sloped down towards the clifftop and sea. From there a steep wooden staircase zig-zagged down the cliff to the rock pools below, and many happy hours of my childhood were spent searching for cat's eyes (shellfish) and gently poking my finger into anemones in the rock pools. One of my regular routes home from school was to walk along the beach, around the rocks, and up the steep cliff stairs to my home at the top. We knew all the kids in the neighbourhood and hung out together for hours at a time on the street and spare sections around our homes.

As well as my mum, dad and we three kids, my grandma and uncle were very much part of our family, babysitting often and joining us for family occasions and camping holidays. My mother's mother Gladys was a strong and characterful presence in my childhood years, and I like to think I was her favourite. She had taken the unusual path in her own life of training to be a doctor, meeting my grandfather

Our back yard at Bucklands Beach

Everard at medical school in Dunedin before the First World War. My grandfather had died a few years before I was born, after his already delicate health had been compromised while serving in the Medical Corp in the First World War. The other adult in my life was my Uncle Oswald, my mother's brother, a grumpy shadow to Grandma's large and commanding presence.

We weren't a family who talked about how we felt or asked for help, so I learned to be self-sufficient. I remember one day, when I was thirteen years old and my mum was late to pick me up from school one day, surprising even myself with my reticence to accept an offered lift home from a neighbour, anxious not to misinterpret the offer or put anyone to any trouble. I can see I was hard to help, even at that age.

Dad, being a good husband and father in the 1950s and '60s, devoted most of his time and energy to his architectural practice. Though he didn't talk about his work with us children, I had a familiarity with the architectural world throughout my childhood. I would sometimes go with him to his office when he worked on a Saturday, playing with tracing paper, pens and other office supplies that spawned my abiding love of stationery. Wherever we went on holiday, he would stop to look around new buildings of interest despite our protests. With Grandma as a role model and with Dad's encouragement, I felt I 'could do anything', even being allowed onto the roof to 'help' him paint it at quite a young age.

For architects, designing their own home brings together their personal and professional lives and is often one of the most meaningful projects in their careers. In the late 1960s Dad designed his home for us on a steep site in Remuera. It was simple, elegant and airy, with exposed timber beams, concrete block walls and huge sliding glass doors opening onto the intimate patio and garden. We left the sleepy idyllic backwater of Bucklands Beach for the city, and for me the more pressured world of Epsom Girls Grammar School.

I can remember the moment, at age sixteen, when I was first awakened to the impact that humans were having on the world. A teacher, Celia Stemson, relieving for our usual teacher, took the opportunity to tell us riveting stories of her travels in South-East Asia. We also got talking about nuclear energy, and she told us about the growing problem of nuclear waste from power plants, which would remain lethal for hundreds of thousands of years. I was shocked and deeply concerned. As I listened and then read more, I imagined that the scale of the problem meant that the world was unlikely to last more than another few years. Although my life carried on as normal, it affected me deeply inside, and I couldn't see that I was going to live past the age of twenty-five.

I moved into Maths and Science subjects and did well academically at Epsom Girls, but found life there stifling at times. As I grew into my mid-teens, I was more interested in having adventures with my two best friends and pushing the boundaries of parental guidance. In the final couple of years of secondary school, I was encouraged to consider any and all of the professions as a future career path and felt most drawn to architecture. But when my elder brother chose that field it no longer seemed an option for me, needing as I did to assert my individuality and independence. In any case I was ready to leave home by the end of my school years and decided to attend the University of Otago in Dunedin in 1973 to become a doctor like my beloved grandmother.

Life in Dunedin was a revelation. I loved the freedom to find myself and run my own life. I soon changed my course of study away from medicine to what I considered the much more interesting subjects of anthropology and psychology. A couple of friends and I found an unoccupied semi-derelict house on the Otago Peninsula and squatted there for the next year, had parties, smoked dope, talked philosophy; and I even passed my papers. In the following year I dropped out of university altogether to expand my horizons and experience life for myself. After working as a truck driver around Dunedin and then in shearing sheds in the heart of Southland, with my then boyfriend I bought a small rotting house and 2.5 acres (1 hectare) of land for $6500 in Waitati, a small town 19 km north of Dunedin.

Waitati was a small village where many other 'alternative lifestylers' had bought homes, and the relationships that developed over time between neighbours provided fertile ground for a number of cooperative activities. We set up a food co-op in a little shop, and a community garden in an empty section. The Waitati Spring Festival of 1975 was held on my back paddock. The self-sufficiency magazine *Mushroom* was produced from Waitati and I helped, alongside my neighbours, to put together the first few issues. Some of us bought the old railway station building from a neighbouring town for a few dollars and spent a couple of weekends chain-sawing it into sections. We brought them back to Waitati on trailers and propped them against my back hedge, intending to put them back together as a community house. I left Waitati shortly afterwards and can only presume the motivation died away as they rotted into the ground.

We milked cows, had chooks and gardens, and sat together on our verandahs in the long summer evenings discussing the state of the world. It was anarchic and sometimes chaotic, but there was a real sense of camaraderie, belonging and

The hippie life at Waitati

possibility that came with living close to others on a daily basis and building ongoing relationships. Although I was only in Waitati for one-and-a-half years, it was a formative time and my first experience of living with others in community, albeit a fairly ad hoc version.

After moving back to Auckland for a year and working as the groundskeeper at the Teachers' College hostel in Epsom, I left New Zealand in 1977 to see the world. I met my future mate Max in Melbourne just one month before leaving to travel in South America with two women friends, with Max joining me six months later. While the larger cities were just as developed and cosmopolitan as many European cities, in the rural areas we often felt as if we were stepping back centuries. In some hill towns in Bolivia, the only public toilet was the earth floor in a ruined house. Seeing the poverty and hardship and sometimes this lack of even the most basic services opened my eyes to my own affluence. So much of what I was used to having was not necessary for a happy life, but at the same time, some basic necessities like sanitation and clean water should have been possible for everyone – why was it that in some places there was not the will or the knowledge to provide these things? How did societies get so rundown that they no longer had functioning services?

Arriving in London after a year amongst this level of simplicity and deprivation, I found going to a supermarket and seeing the rows and rows of shiny packaged products shouting to be bought a truly surreal experience.

With my truck-driving background, I found a job as a driver and caregiver at a hostel for physically disabled adults in Islington, London. This hostel aimed to be resident-led rather than organisation-led, a very progressive attitude for the time. Our job as caregivers was to be available to the residents when they required help, assisting them to organise their own lives as much as possible. I drove the wheelchair ambulance and was available to drive residents at their request around London to visit their families, go to the movies and generally participate in life. I became aware for the first time of the unnecessary obstacles placed in the way of anyone who relies on wheels for mobility, through lack of thought or poor design.

While travelling around the UK during that year I lived in London, two places made a particular impression on me and helped to seed ideas about what I wanted to get involved with. One was the Centre for Alternative Technology (CAT) in Machynlleth, Wales. CAT was a demonstration centre in an old quarry, set up to trial, demonstrate and disseminate information on various forms of renewable energy and sustainable systems. There was an array of different types of solar hot water heaters, with information sheets describing them and their relative attributes, and in some cases with instructions so that you could build them yourself. There were wind and water turbines for generating electricity, organic gardens and composting demonstrations, aquaculture and biogas production. I found it incredibly inspiring and wondered if I could set up something similar in New Zealand someday.

The other place was Findhorn community near Forres in Scotland, then famous for its garden divas and the size of its cabbages. Max and I were bicycling around parts of Scotland and dropped in for an afternoon to this inspirational community we had heard about. We talked with a man working on the rock wall foundation for their new Universal Hall and heard a little of how the community worked. While not impressed with the windswept feel of the ex-air force base and the shabby caravan accommodation, something of the energy of Findhorn stayed with me and fed my musings over the years.

After a little over a year in London, I began to get restless. I was coming up to that twenty-five-year-old mark, and the world hadn't ended; but I had seen enough to know that humans were causing huge problems for ourselves and the planet, and I knew we could do better. I'd been travelling for two-and-a-half years, looking at other people getting on with their lives, and not really being in place in my own. I realised I could either continue to live my life as if my actions and choices were of no consequence to the continued survival of the planet; or I could learn a skill with which I could contribute to a more just and sustainable world.

Architecture was the field that still drew me and seemed to best match my interests and skills: both practical and creative, both technical and people-oriented, incorporating solar design, renewable energy and the natural world. I had put enough distance between myself and my family to feel it was my independent decision, rather than just following the family line. I applied to the School of Architecture at The University of Auckland and we packed up our life in London.

On our way back to New Zealand, Max and I spent the summer in Melbourne near his family, and his Christmas present to me that year was the book *Permaculture One* (1978) by Bill Mollison and David Holmgren, which had recently been published. Permaculture recognises the beauty and intelligence of nature, identifies the elements which help to create a healthy natural ecosystem, and applies that knowledge to create sustainable human environments. Everything in that book made sense to me and I felt both huge excitement and a sense of 'of course!'. Another thread had found its way into my fabric.

Architecture school was intense and highly stimulating, full of good people, ideas and challenge. I was disappointed, however, to find that climate-responsive and low-energy design principles were not considered essential elements of good design, but an optional extra. When I asked for a studio design exercise on passive solar design, the response was 'we did that last year'. Only one lecturer, Graham Stevens, was passionate about solar energy and included the theory in his lectures. Despite this I learned what I could and won a national competition in my second year, designing a passive solar retrofit to an existing house.

Max and I bought an old house in an inner suburb of Auckland. After two years of intense study I needed time to rebalance my life and was keen to have a child. I took a year off from study to work on renovations to our home while pregnant with our baby. Our son, Willow, was born at home in September 1982, and I fell in love with him from the first moment I looked into his eyes. Growing a baby within my body was a profound physical experience of the connectedness of life. Giving birth created new connections between my mind and emotions and opened up my love in a whole new way.

I was determined to become an architect and completed the last two full-time years of study over four busy part-time years. The topics I found most interesting and which helped to shape my thinking were often on less-mainstream topics, such as Community Architecture with Russell Withers, Vernacular Architecture with Tony Watkins, and Sarah Treadwell's Women in Architecture. I wrote a research paper on the 'Environmental Implications of Building Materials', in which I proposed a frame-work for assessing building materials according to their impact both on workers and on the environment in terms of their extraction, manufacture, transport, installation and use. This information is still not easily available to architects!

I was always rushing from university to crèche or Playcentre to university, trying to be both a student and the mother of a toddler. It was exhausting. There wasn't enough time to do either properly, and I lost a lot of confidence both as a mother and as a designer. I increasingly felt like an outsider at the architecture school, with different values to my classmates and lecturers. I let go my focus on sustainability and tried to produce the kind of work that was expected and rewarded at the architecture school, but my heart wasn't in it. I got through my degree, but it was a struggle, and I lost my focus in the process.

Until the last year, that is, most of which was spent writing my sub-thesis, a precious opportunity to explore all the directions I cared about. I was interested in how physical form influenced, and was influenced by, our world-view and our behaviour. I explored the concept of 'edge', the place where two states meet and interact, and the complexity and fertility that resides there. I realised that the desirability of edge applied not only to architectural edge-places between inside and outside such as window seats, verandahs and sheltered courtyards – often the most desirable locations in a building – but also to so many other aspects of life more usually seen as separate and opposite.

Researching and writing my sub-thesis for my architecture degree was a formative experience. It essentially became my manifesto of life, weaving elements of permaculture, feminism, community, and spirituality into a theory of edge as a place of connection rather than separation, a world-view that recognised that having

a deep sense of connection with Gaia was intrinsic to sustainability and life. I conceived my second son, Erin, during that year. I handed in my thesis not long before he was born and marched up Queen Street in May 1987 to be capped in my graduation gown with my new baby strapped to my chest, as proud of one achievement as I was of the other!

Having started my architecture studies 'late' at the age of twenty-five and having had two children along the way, I found it very hard to get started in my career once I graduated at the age of thirty-two. Most architecture students gained basic experience during their studies doing summer work in architectural offices. I hadn't done that because once the university year finished, I longed to spend the summer with my child. When my second baby was six months old, in late 1987, I felt ready to take on a paid architectural job, just at the time when a significant financial crash pushed the building industry into recession. Architectural jobs evaporated, especially any opportunities for an inexperienced older female graduate needing flexible part-time work to combine with mothering.

Over the next two years I managed to get several

Graduation day, and the kids have had enough – Robin, Max, Erin and Willow

short-term contracts working for architects on specific jobs, and some private jobs designing renovations to old houses. I slowly gained confidence, only to have it slip away again when each job finished. I loved my kids but felt consumed by the day-to-day reality of caring for them. My relationship with my husband was comfortable and he was always supportive in co-parenting and household tasks, but we had lost our deeper connection. I had ongoing headaches and illness. I was generally rundown, and very disappointed.

I had gained a skill to be more effective in the world and was trying to integrate that with loving and nurturing children. I was trying to be everything; not losing myself in my kids, like Mum, or in my work, like Dad – but losing myself anyway. My commitment to renewable energies and sustainable technology, my key motivations for studying architecture, had been shelved due to lack of support at the architecture school and the struggle of finishing my degree with a small child. I'd worked so hard for my qualification, but felt my career slipping away.

I reached a level of despair that forced a reassessment of my life and my relationship with architecture. I realised I was still excited by community and sustainability, designing living environments for people that fitted within what the earth could support. I wanted to use my hard-won training in service to what I felt mattered most: healthy connected people on a healthy flourishing planet. Once I recommitted to my original values and intentions, doors started to open.

Graham Stevens had retired, and a new lecturer, Graeme Robertson, had picked up the baton of solar architecture at the Auckland School of Architecture. I didn't know him personally but worked up my courage and gave him a call. His friendliness, enthusiasm and support brought me in from the cold. With Graeme's help and encouragement, I got some tutoring work on a studio programme at the architecture school, found some design work with a passive solar architect, and became involved in Solar Action.

Solar Action was the New Zealand branch of the Australian and New Zealand Solar Energy Society, promoting solar and other renewable energies, and there I met others who were aware of and concerned about the enormous cost to the planet of fossil-fuel use and were doing something about it. Our work included organising talks, seminars and displays; writing submissions; and commenting in the media. At the end of 1990 I became the chairperson for two years and found I was very good at organisational thinking and running effective meetings. I gained enormous experience and confidence; but over time also started feeling the weight of carrying the organisation. This is another theme in my life: how to be competent and willing, with energy and ideas, and encourage others to also contribute in their own way.

In early 1990 I applied for a full-time job as a graduate architect with the government social housing provider the Housing Corporation and was overjoyed when successful. Max by then was running his own computer programming business and was willing to work part-time while being the hands-on parent, so I could have my turn at building my career. On my first day I was given a project well beyond my experience and had an acute crisis of confidence, but I quickly found my feet and started to thrive with the challenge and stimulation. So long as the houses I designed met the spatial and cost criteria required by the state, I was given a lot of freedom and responsibility, and for me that meant designing climate-responsive houses. I became very practised at designing innovative low-cost passive solar houses for state rental, and on several occasions, I also worked with individual tenants to design accessible houses for their specific mobility requirements.

This was a highly productive, challenging and very satisfying time, but with two little children, a distant husband and a stressful more-than-full-time job, I felt quite isolated in my family life. I yearned for a more cooperative living situation and met with others a few times to talk about creating community. I was browsing in The Women's Bookshop one day and came across a book called *Cohousing*[1] and was completely taken with every aspect of the concept. It was so inspiring to see described the kind of community I yearned for but hadn't yet been able to articulate. There was a big 'YES!!!' inside me: yes, I want to live this way, I want my children to grow up in this kind of community. Now I had a compelling and inspiring picture, but still didn't know how to make it happen.

The year 1992 was a pivotal one. It started badly with all the stress of my triple life catching up with me: trying to be a devoted parent, to hold down a challenging job and to lead an activist organisation. I spent two weeks over Christmas/New Year in bed at home and then in hospital with pneumonia. While reluctant to give anything up, I was able to reduce my work hours to four days a week, and slowly recovered my energy over the next few months.

I came across a flyer for a gathering in July called 'Heart Politics', which intrigued me. Devised by local activists Vivian Hutchinson, Elaine Dyer and Rex McCann, the gathering would be a space to explore social activism with heart, a politics of connection rather than conflict and opposition. The name was borrowed from a book by the American comedienne Fran Peavey,[2] describing her work around the world as an 'American willing to listen', asking long-lever questions[3] to help local people recognise and solve their own environmental and social issues. The flyer invited people of heart to gather for four days at the Tauhara Centre in Taupō in the central North Island, to share stories of their work in the world and explore together how to work more effectively for positive social change. I knew I had to be there.

I attended the gathering in Taupō that winter, and it felt like coming home. I found a diverse group of people working in a wide variety of different fields but with similar values to mine. It was such a relief to find people who cared about things outside their own immediate lives, who recognised that our individual actions and choices were significant and 'political' and were committed to learning to be more effective in championing their values. The gathering was a time to step back from our lives, to reflect, go deep and share the successes and challenges we each faced. By the end of the four days I knew I had found my tribe.

Fran Peavey herself attended the gathering, and she had many powerful and humorous stories of her work in the world. At one point, to illustrate something she was saying, she pointed at the large piece of carpet in the centre of the room. 'That piece of carpet is heavy and awkward and almost impossible for one person to shift on their own. But with enough people working together and each one lifting just the edge of the carpet closest to them, it is possible to move it easily.' 'Lifting my piece of the carpet' became powerful shorthand for remembering that none of us needs to solve everything; what is important is doing the work that it is possible for each of us to do, alongside others doing their own piece of the collective work.

Another memorable Fran-ism was a reassuring but rueful chant: 'The people, united, will sometimes win and sometimes lose!' Not as rallying as the original chant but much more realistic.

Heart Politics has been enormously significant in my life ever since. I attended once or twice a year for more than twenty years, was active in organising many of the gatherings and eventually became a Heart Politics trustee. It has been a community of peers, each engaged in our own journeys and fields of endeavour, but willing to share our failures and successes, our questions and dilemmas. I also learned the power of ritual at these gatherings, calling on the wider and deeper context of Gaia rather than just our individual lives, of setting intention and following through. I believe without any doubt that I would never have sustained my commitment to Earthsong without the friendships, community, support and challenge that Heart Politics was for me through those years. In the words of Margaret Mead:

Never doubt that a small group of thoughtful, committed citizens can change the world; indeed, it's the only thing that ever has.[4]

Also in the winter of 1992 I started attending meetings in Auckland to explore the idea of building an ecovillage. This was another 'homecoming' for me – finding a group of people who wanted more community in their lives, who were exploring and researching the wide range of issues involved and working to create a more sustainable living environment.

Meetings were held once a fortnight, each with a theme such as legal structures, eco-design or decision making. It was a rather loose and changing group, and after a few months a core group of six, including me, were elected to consolidate some of the ideas and make more effective progress. The core group brainstormed and wordsmithed a Mission Statement for what we wanted to achieve:

To establish an Ecovillage, based on the principles of permaculture, that will serve as a model of a socially and environmentally sustainable community.

We set up a mailing list called the 'Friends of Ecovillage' and established the Ecovillage Seeding Fund. We explored environmental issues, consensus models and group dynamics, legal issues, financial structures, planning, land and eco-design. We started the *Ecovillage* newsletter, full of discussion pieces about what we were learning and thinking about sustainability and community.

After a few months the core group realised that we were the only ones doing any work and everyone else was waiting for us to sort it out. We were making progress, but at the expense of developing a larger committed, cohesive group who were all involved in evolving our project. The core group disbanded back into the wider group again, and we started having full weekend meetings every six weeks at a rural property in Mangawhai. Camping together and sharing good food gave a wonderful sense of community, and time to explore, again, the range of issues: different models of how to make decisions, sustainable design, ethics and legal structures. Task groups started working on specific areas such as finances, land, energy systems, process and education.

Although some wanted a more remote location, there was a significant group who pictured establishing the ecovillage on semi-rural land within one hour's drive of Auckland City. This group found a large rural property on Te Henga Road in August

Ecovillage group and representatives of WCC visit a site

1993 and visited the site with three key people from Waitakere City Council (WCC): Councillor Helen Haslam, General Manager of Strategy and Development Ann Magee, and Chair of the Waitakere Community Board Penny Hulse. Although this property eventually became part of the Centennial Park, this first personal contact with Helen, Ann and Penny, at the time establishing the eco-city policy for Waitakere City Council, was the start of a supportive relationship with Council which later led to WENT (Waitakere Eco-Neighbourhood Trust, as Earthsong was first known) deciding to seek land in Waitakere City.

Through 1993, having achieved my registration as an architect based on my work experience at the Housing Corporation, I was establishing my own architectural practice and learning to more publicly express my approach to architecture. I had been part of a women architects' group for several years and contributed to a national display of the work of women architects. I was invited to speak for the affirmative at an architectural debate with the title: 'Sustainability is Not Just Another Form of Male Mastery'; a fairly jokey affair but at least bringing sustainability onto the table. I developed a whakataukī to contribute to the New Zealand Institute of Architects conference later that year; another opportunity to dig deep into my values and express them in a meaningful way.

I was also teaching the Thermal Environment paper to second-year students at the Auckland School of Architecture. Thanks to Graeme Robertson's influence, energy-efficient and passive solar design had become a core part of the curriculum,

Respect for people and place

Robin Allison   Aotearoa   New Zealand

Whakataukī

and I covered the range of design issues and technical information to encourage students to include climate-responsive design principles in their work. I felt a growing confidence in my architecture and what I stood for.

Although initially interested in the ecovillage idea and sometimes attending the weekend meetings, my husband Max was undergoing his own life reassessment, and our life together started to unravel. I was clear that eco-community was my future; he was exploring his own directions through the men's movement, finding himself and his feelings in a way he hadn't before. For a time I felt he was opening up, beginning to meet me emotionally in a way I had craved for years, and becoming my best friend again. But he swept past me with the profound changes on his new path and left me behind. This came to a head in August 1993 and we separated after fifteen years together. Willow was ten and Erin was six.

I felt as though someone had chopped through my anchor rope and I was drifting, lurching through storms and doldrums. There were no major rocks in sight, but my position felt really insecure. I needed to get my sails up and take control; I was starting to sort them out on the deck, but I didn't know how to get them up the mast. The only thing that kept my spirits up was the faraway island of ecovillage, sometimes clear, sometimes obscured and distant.

The next year was a very painful, confusing and deeply unhappy time, helped only by my two fledgling whānau of Heart Politics friends and ecovillage community. Max moved out but stayed close enough that he could continue to co-parent the kids. Our two boys bounced back and forth between us on a daily basis – one of us would pick them up from school and take them home for the night, before dropping them off at school the next morning. That afternoon the other one would do the same. We would alternate weekends, although they always spent Sunday night at my place to consolidate and prepare for the week ahead. This worked really well for several years and meant that we each had daily contact with our two beloved boys; though having two homes was perhaps a little unsettling for them.

The Ecovillage group was enormously useful for exploring ideas, learning about group dynamics and developing skills and experience to move the concept towards reality, but there were also frustrations. There was a continual turnover of people who attended meetings, with no certainty as to their levels of commitment. The same issues came up again and again as new people wanted to talk about issues that some of us had been through several times. We shared our visions and ideas and struggled with how to progress towards the reality of an ecovillage while still allowing enough time for interpersonal relationships and the building of community within the group. A few people did most of the work, thinking and organising and putting out the newsletters, and others felt like passengers. Progress and momentum began to stall.

In response to this, a small process group formed within the larger group at the end of 1993. This group of eight people became known as the 'Hedgehogs' and was committed to building deeper personal relationships and a shared vision from which the ecovillage could grow. We met weekly at one another's houses, spent a whole weekend telling one another our life stories and went camping together over New Year. We asked each other key questions, such as: What is my primary motivation? How ready am I to commit to it? What is essential for me in the shared vision?

The wider Ecovillage group also continued to meet sporadically, with site visits to existing eco-hamlets and occasional public meetings with a speaker. It became clear that, rather than resulting in one village, the Ecovillage group was an umbrella group that provided the opportunity to explore ideas. It contributed to the development of several rural ecovillage or eco-subdivision projects in New Zealand as people within the group branched off into their own projects.

At Easter 1994 my two sons and I went camping at one of our favourite spots, Hot Water Beach on the Coromandel Peninsula. At low tide one evening we wandered along the beach with our spades to the place where the hot water seeps up through the sand and dug ourselves a pool with appropriate hot- and cold-water inlets for a comfortable soak. We reclined together in the steaming water, watching the sun go down and the stars come out. That evening we were treated to a display of shooting stars that continued for an hour. It was wondrous and very healing, and I knew we'd be all right. It felt from that moment that my two sons and I had reformed as a family of three.

Life was busy and productive. In addition to running my small architectural practice, being a mum and meeting with the Hedgehogs, I did some facilitation training and a two-week Permaculture Design certificate course, learning essential skills for creating the eco-community I craved.

That year I and several others felt called to organise a gathering for women, with similar values and culture to Heart Politics but a different emphasis: a place to value our differences, challenge our thinking, learn from one another and support and be supported. It would be a space to review our beliefs and values and take courage to envision and try the new as we grew and thrived as women. We created a four-day gathering for women called 'Coming Into our Own' which was held at the Tauhara Centre in Taupō in September. It was a life-changing event for many women, and the beginning of twenty years of annual Women's Gatherings at Tauhara.

By the middle of 1994 differences began appearing between members of the Hedgehogs. One weekend was spent together in an old lodge at Huia on the Manukau Harbour. We worked on a conceptual plan of a village, talked about the process for inducting new people and discussed our respective non-negotiables. After dinner on Saturday we broached a delicate topic that we felt needed to be talked about if we were to live in community: our attitudes to sexuality. This was an important issue to address, because the most high-profile community in New Zealand at that time, Centrepoint, was known as the place where the 'guru' and six other male leaders had recently been convicted of sexual assault and rape of minors. Whenever 'community' was mentioned in almost any context, Centrepoint was the first association in people's minds.

Most of us at the Hedgehogs weekend were in accord that while children certainly needed to be protected, sexuality between adults was a matter of personal choice and responsibility, and we had no intention of writing rules about such issues as multiple partners or homosexuality. If different individual approaches caused conflict or upset, then we would deal with that as we would with any other conflict.

For the first time I found myself saying in a group that there was just as much chance of my forming an intimate relationship with a woman as with a man at that time. I felt strong and proud, and a bit vulnerable. Most of the Hedgehogs were comfortable with my sharing, but it was challenging to one couple, the discussion became too upsetting, and the two withdrew. The weekend came to a grinding halt. The strong feelings raised by the topic were too big for us to handle, and we couldn't do further work with any sense of togetherness as a group until the issues were resolved. The Hedgehogs never really picked up steam again after that. Gradually people withdrew, and by the end of 1994 the Ecovillage group, including the Hedgehogs, had effectively ceased to exist.

The Ecovillage group was dissolving, but I wasn't ready to leave the ideas behind. I was in transition in my personal life, still trying to re-establish myself as an independent adult after fifteen years of partnership and marriage, with the help and support of a psychotherapist. My practice as an architect entered a new phase as I moved my office out of the spare room at home and into an office space shared with friends. I felt part of a strong network of Heart Politics friends, and the Women's Gathering was opening another, deeper door into who I was and wanted to become.

After another reassessment of my life and priorities I found the clarity I needed. It all came together one afternoon in November 1994, when I came out of my yoga class to a glorious late spring evening and drove to Pt Chevalier beach to watch the sun go down. I was elated; I laughed and whooped at the colours playing on the clouds, as the sun sank in a blaze of glory behind the vivid blue Waitakere Ranges.

Across the harbour and in front of the ranges was Te Atatū Peninsula, with a large area of undeveloped land looking east towards the central city. It was owned by WCC and they were planning a subdivision called 'Harbour View Estate'. I realised that night, walking along the beach in the sunset, that I wanted to build an urban eco-community based on the cohousing model. And I wanted to build it there, on the Harbour View land, with the blessing and support of WCC, by then identified as an eco-city.

Things had crystallised at last into a form that felt right. Exploring sustainable ways of living in cities felt more important than leaving the city behind to populate rural land. I enjoyed being a city dweller, and I knew it was going to be important to my children as they grew into teenagers. Cohousing was the concept that encapsulated for me all the elements that made up the community life I wanted. I wanted to live in cohousing, and Harbour View was where I wanted to build it. I felt a great surge of energy and clarity. My friend Vivian had said to me: 'You have to be a bit arrogant, believe in yourself and what you're doing; stick your neck out, and expect flak sometimes.' And I felt a huge 'Yes!' inside. I have the background, the skills, the values and ethics, the passion to make it happen. This is what I want to do. It was a defining moment.

I had maintained my links with WCC, and shortly after that afternoon in November, Council granted me $500 to attend a regional ecovillage conference at Crystal Waters community in Australia. This was an enormous vote of confidence and it felt fantastic that things were falling into place. 'That's because you've chosen the path with heart,' said my good friend Rosie.

Another pivotal event was my fortieth birthday celebration at the end of 1994. The last year-and-a-half had been a time of enormous pain, change and growth. After many years of a settled, happy life with one constant companion, I had been thrown into intense turmoil and felt at times quite powerless. I felt several layers of skin had rubbed off, which left me both more alive and more vulnerable. I needed a rite of passage.

Surely at forty I could ask for what I wanted. I wanted to claim my ability to act according to my values, which I framed as 'stepping into my power'. I invited close friends to witness my intention, to support me and hold me accountable into the future. It was certainly several steps outside my comfort zone into visibility, asking people I respected to focus their time and energy on me for an evening.

The preparation beforehand, the intention, the enactment and the support and gifts of those who came, were highly significant. We sat in a circle under the huge oak tree in my garden. I shared with my friends where I was in my life and how I hoped to grow. They offered symbolic gifts and wisdom to support me in that intention – a tiny warrior-woman figure, a candle to light the dark times, a beautiful kauri snail shell with the inner core gradually opening to the light. At the end I gave a small gift to each person as an offering to them of that powerful energy. I had also placed a pair of soft leather ankle boots in the middle of the circle, and for years afterwards, whenever I was going into a situation where I especially needed to stand strong, I would wear my 'power boots'. This event changed my life and formed a key step in my developing the confidence and self-belief to imagine I could create a place like Earthsong.

The last year had been a time for looking inward, for grieving, healing, and finding myself, culminating in my birthday and claiming my power. This helped me turn outward in 1995, to focus on my dream of building urban eco-cohousing.

VISION AND ACTION

3

Oh you who follow your dreams and visions,
with love in your heart and courage,
Oh you who follow your dreams and visions,
I join you now at last.

KATE AND INI[1]

If you have ever despaired at the state of the world, ever felt frustrated or angry because something could be better than it is, then you have some sense of what 'better' might be. One of the wonders of being human is the ability to imagine or envision a situation that is different from our present reality. And if we can imagine it, in most cases we have some ability or opportunity to do things a little 'better'.

If you would like to work towards a more desirable future, engage your imagination and envision the kind of world you would like to live in. The clearer you are about what this looks and feels like, the more effective your actions will be in moving towards it. It can be much more rewarding to put energy towards the life you want, rather than feeling distressed by how things are.

It took me years to clarify my own vision and life purpose, years of getting to know myself and the world, to believe enough in my values, my skills and the opportunities available to me. At one point, in despair at the state of the world, I considered running away from my responsibilities and joining a Greenpeace boat to protest the destruction of our environment. I felt that nothing else mattered if our planet was in jeopardy. But ... I was afraid of deep water! I realised that, while I supported and valued the work that Greenpeace activists were doing, my path was different. I had useful and hard-won skills in architecture, and that was the path through which I could contribute towards my desired future.

Even as an architecture student I was trying to excel in the way that others excelled, trying to design the kinds of projects that were rewarded by the tutors – and achieving mediocre results because my heart wasn't in it. I was seeing designs for buildings that stood there alone and proud; often beautiful objects in their own way, but with little relationship with their context or even with the people who might inhabit them. I gradually lost focus and direction while a student at architectural school.

Writing the sub-thesis for my architecture degree was a powerful antidote to the pressure I had felt to conform to what others saw as important, and a major step in recognising and reaffirming my own values. It gave me permission to explore ideas that mattered to me, to weave them together and express them in a document that others would read. It empowered me to put my energies into the kind of architecture that excited me: low-impact, respectful buildings that responded to their users, location and circumstances.

Later, at both Heart Politics and the Ecovillage group, I met others who believed in taking actions to create something different. With this stimulus and encouragement, I started to articulate and write down my own 'best reality'.

What do I want from an ecovillage? I want a place where the guiding principle is to care for the earth, to recognise the interdependence of all things and our responsibility to maintain or create anew the intricate balance that keeps earth healthy. I would like to know that my presence on the land was beneficial, was healthy and nourishing to the earth. I want to live with other people in such a way that my privacy and autonomy don't feel compromised, but the opportunities for interaction and community are frequent and easy. I'd like to live near people of varying ages and cultures. The community must be socially sustainable for teenagers as well as adults, old people and children.[2]

I kept evolving and writing my vision for what I wanted to work towards, from the general qualities to a more specific sense of how it would feel, and the values on which it would be based.

THE POWER OF A CLEAR VISION

Whatever the situation or project you want to bring into being, clearly imagining its successful manifestation makes it more likely you will arrive there. Researching, imagining, clarifying, articulating and – when you are ready – writing down a concise statement that captures the essence of what you want to work towards, whether as an individual or as a group, are invaluable for setting your intention and guiding your movements towards it. Having a clearly articulated vision gives direction and purpose to your efforts. It is not a map, and it doesn't tell you how to get there. But it reminds you where you want to go and helps you to navigate the terrain as you move towards it.

Envisioning a preferred physical reality is not just about the visual; it requires all our senses, a bodily experience of being there – what does it smell like, sound like, taste like? How do you feel? Who else is there, and what are you all doing? What is your movement through space?

If you can envision or imagine something, it already exists on some level, and the actions bring what already exists into being. There is the story of Michelangelo, who believed the sculpture existed in the stone and his work was to reveal what was already there.

I learned a similar thing from my yoga teacher Margaritha in 1992. After the warm-up, she guided us into a quite challenging physical posture, which we each managed to some extent. After unfurling, we sat quietly as she led us in a guided visualisation, imaging ourselves going further into that posture with grace and ease. We then repeated the physical posture and found ourselves bending much further than before. I learned the power of visualisation, that being able to *imagine* my body doing something made the actual movement much more possible.

Science backs this up. Margaret Wheatley says,

Brains can change without us doing any physical effort; they can change because of what we think. The motor cortex also grows in people who never sit down at a piano but who spend time consciously imagining that they are playing the piano ... athletes can prepare successfully for races by visualising each part of the course in great detail. WHEATLEY (2012, PP. 44-45)

I was once being driven at night through the German countryside by a friend, who was terrified of driving at night because of the lights of the cars and trucks coming towards her. I realised she was focusing on the lights, and I suggested she not look at the lights she was trying to avoid, but at the road ahead, the direction she wanted to travel. She said this helped her enormously. This is true also when going through a small gap – it is best not to look at the narrow sides of the gap, the obstacles, but at the space in between; keeping the obstacles in your peripheral vision while focusing on the path you want to follow. We tend to move towards what we focus on. What we pay attention to is what we tend to get.

At some point, when you've been thinking about what really matters to you and what you want to put your energies into, it is helpful to write this down, to articulate it as clearly as you can in words or images – or both. When you can articulate or draw an idea, it becomes more available to you to consider and refine. It also helps to explain it to others who can then interact with those ideas and help develop and progress them. It can be surprising to realise how much you are clear about, and the action of externalising this in a form that both you and others can understand is a powerful step in bringing it into reality.

In my case, I realised that there were several aspects that were fundamental to the project I wanted to bring into being. Eco-building and permaculture design were non-negotiables for me. I wanted to stay within the city in a suburban context. Cohousing described perfectly the kind of community I craved. And all of this had a wider context than just creating a wonderful neighbourhood for myself and my neighbours; it is part of the story of this time, of people striving to learn how to be good neighbours to other species and the wider ecosystem, and sharing what we learn to contribute to that. Crafting these ideas into a concise yet powerful statement was a key step in beginning to take effective action towards it.

COLLECTIVELY HELD VISION

In my experience, visioning starts with the individual, even when the vision is of a community project. Even mass movements or political change start with individuals who stand up, question the way things are, and propose how it could be different. In Fay Weldon's words, 'Change comes about through individual acts of courage.'[3]

But how do you get from a vision held by an individual to one embraced by a group? When your vision includes being part of a cooperative group, this can feel like a paradox; but any group has both individual and collective elements. It is important for people to get clear about their individual values and what they hold dear; and for a group endeavour, the individual values and visions need to be sufficiently aligned that you choose to work together towards an agreed common vision. By articulating and sharing with others your growing clarity about the world you want, you are more likely to find people with compatible visions for the future – people who are attracted by the world you describe and join you to help bring it about.

Community projects require people to be inspired by and signed up to a shared vision. A written statement of your vision is helpful for one person; for a group it is essential. A 'Vision Statement' is a powerful, succinct statement that expresses the essence of what you collectively want to achieve. Ideally it is articulated and agreed by the founding members of a group, is agreed to as a condition by all subsequent members and guides the development of the group endeavour at every level. (See Appendix 2: Developing a Vision Statement as a Group.)

The Auckland Ecovillage group's Mission Statement arose from a brainstorm in 1992. After several months of research and meetings, the small core group of six people sat together in my living room and brainstormed the key themes of our project, and what was important to each of us. Brief points from each person were written on a large sheet of paper and then clumped into similar categories. Two of us took the ideas and wordsmithed them into a concise statement that captured the essence of the collective ideas.

Ecovillage Mission Statement 1992

To establish a village, based on the principles of permaculture, that will serve as a model of a socially and environmentally sustainable community.

After the Ecovillage group ceased meeting, I refined my direction towards creating an urban cohousing neighbourhood, rather than the semi-rural ecovillage we had been planning. I adapted the Mission Statement accordingly, and Earthsong's Vision Statement (see p. 16) was born.

I had been actively thinking, researching and planning for three years, and was now clear about my own direction. However, I needed companions on the journey, and I didn't know how to find them. Before I would find others to join me, they needed to know there was something to join, to hear what I envisaged so they could consider and evolve ideas of what a sustainable community might look like. Hearing a clearly stated vision that matches your underlying values and beliefs can be inspiring and energising. We all build on the ideas of others. We can respond to others' ideas by doing our own individual visioning process, and then see if our visions are compatible. We can then decide if there is value in joining together to create our shared vision.

Earthsong's Vision Statement has proved very stable and continues to be aspirational. It is clear about values and direction, without saying *how* that might be achieved. It names two very powerful and well-developed systems of organisation: cohousing and permaculture. It has three equally important commitments: to environmental sustainability, to social sustainability and to education. It packs a lot into a short statement and is the shining star that has guided our efforts and decisions for more than twenty years.

A clear, agreed vision and shared values or group culture allows the group to be looser about how to implement that vision. It allows action that is aligned with the agreed vision, and more space for individuals to bring their own energy, creativity and diversity. A strong, agreed intention allows more flexible implementation (Wheatley, 2006, p. 129).

One of the keys to intentional community is having a shared vision which unites diverse individuals and encapsulates the highest values and aspirations of the group. When we can articulate a clear vision of the best, most flourishing human settlement that we can imagine, we can take steps towards it. One thing that has shone through again and again during the development of Earthsong is the value of having a committed group aligned with an inspirational vision. The vision is both the goal, and the nourishment that sustains the effort.

TAKING ACTION TOWARDS YOUR VISION

Creating a powerful, inspirational vision is a great start, but vision by itself won't achieve a project. We need to engage both imagination and will. Clarifying your vision is the precursor to *action*, to doing what it takes to bring your vision into reality. Identify what needs to happen to bring your vision into being. Be prepared to give it all you've got for as long as it takes. Remember the old homily that says any creative endeavour is 10% inspiration and 90% perspiration.

My therapist once gave me a small card on which she had written:

Robin Allison had a vision of an eco-neighbourhood. And then she worked. **Hard**.

Belief and persistence are both required. Belief that it's important, and persistence to make it happen. A combination of vision, self-reflection and perseverance can achieve great things.

Hope is important but it's not enough. Hope to me means there is some doubt about it. I have hope for the future of the planet (but I also have doubts about the future). Earthsong wouldn't have happened just with hope. Earthsong needed **belief**. I **knew** that this was possible, was the right thing to be doing, was worth doing for its own sake, was going to happen. I put in the requisite energy at every step.[4]

Keep going back to your vision, assessing what you are doing; is this action taking me closer or further away? Ask yourself strategic questions (see Appendix 1): Which is my piece of the carpet? What are the actions I can take, what are the roles I can play in moving towards this vision? What else needs to happen? Whom do I need to enrol?

My friend Wolfgang tells a story:

There lived a tribe who had experienced a long drought. Every now and then they would do their special rain dance, but it never seemed to work. They heard of a neighbouring village that had much better success, and so they sent a delegation to that village. The people in the second village confirmed that, yes, every time they did their dance, it rained.

The people from the first village were anxious to learn how to do the successful rain dance, but as they watched the villagers dance, it looked pretty similar to theirs. They danced, they sang, they beat the drum. So they asked the dancers what their secret was. And the dancers said: we dance and dance, and keep dancing until it rains.[5]

When you are doing something different from the way things have been done before, there are times when you must step ahead of what you know. We did this many times at Earthsong, but not blindly and recklessly. We did solid research and carefully considered each action, and then, when we needed to, we moved forward before all the i's were dotted and the t's crossed. We had a strong and inspirational vision, and a belief that we could pull this off. And time and time again things fell into place *after* our decision to proceed. In William Murray's words, often attributed to Goethe,

> Until one is committed, there is hesitancy, the chance to draw back, always ineffectiveness. Concerning all acts of initiative and creation, there is one elementary truth, the ignorance of which kills countless ideas and splendid plans: that the moment one definitely commits oneself, then providence moves too.
>
> All sorts of things occur to help one that would never otherwise have occurred. A whole stream of events issues from the decision, raising in one's favour all manner of unforeseen incidents, meetings and material assistance which no man could have dreamed would have come his way.
>
> Whatever you can do or dream you can, begin it. Boldness has genius, power and magic in it. Begin it now.[6]

KEY VISION LEARNINGS

- Consider what you are most concerned or passionate about and have the will to change.
- Give more energy to your positive vision of how life could be, than to what is wrong with now. Keep the obstacles in your peripheral vision while focusing on the path you want to follow.
- Don't be put off by the voices that dismiss your dreams as unrealistic, an unattainable Utopia.
- Always make new mistakes. Don't wait until you know everything before you take action. Move into the dance.
- Remember to notice and appreciate how working towards a positive vision for the future enlivens your life now. Try not to sacrifice the present for the future.

- Take leadership in your vision. Don't wait until others join you before starting, because how do they know what they are joining until it is articulated clearly? Stating your vision clearly allows others to catch a glimpse of something new, and empowers them to imagine their own desired future.
- A crucial task for the founding members of every new collective endeavour is to articulate and agree a clear, concise and inspirational Vision Statement that encapsulates the essence and values of your project. This will remain a key aspect of what all subsequent members agree to on joining your project.
- Working with others towards a shared vision is exhilarating and difficult.
- Any bold vision requires commitment and perseverance. It's not easy. But the satisfaction of following your own unique path; being true to your own values and purpose; and living your life in the best, most useful way you know, is incalculable.

See Appendices 1 and 2 for practices and processes for visioning.

URBAN COHOUSING

STORY

It takes a village to raise a child, and it takes a group to build a village. I'd clarified my own vision of an urban cohousing eco-neighbourhood, but I needed to find others who would help to create this dream. At the Heart Politics gathering in January 1995 I held a workshop about starting a sustainable community, and a good number of people attended. I held back my own ideas so that others could share their visions of community and we could co-create something together. But most people hadn't yet given it much thought, and the discussion wandered off down trails that left them confused and me frustrated.

After the workshop, two experienced social activists, Warwick Pudney and Katrina Shields, sat me down. They said, 'You don't have to wait until there's a group of people who want to do it too. You are clear about what you want to do. Start writing it down and putting it out.' They supported me to write a short proposal to Waitakere City Council (WCC).

The Harbour View land was at that time being prepared for development by Waitakere Properties, the property arm of Council. After discussions with supportive councillors and staff, I chose a likely site on this land, designed a concept layout for thirty houses and common facilities and put together a 'Preliminary Proposal for an Eco-Neighbourhood on Harbour View'. It was politely received by the City Development Committee meeting in February 1995.

Momentum was boosted in March with the visit to Auckland of Dr Robert Gilman,[1] founder of *In Context* magazine and co-author of the seminal report *Eco-Villages and Sustainable Communities* (1991). Robert lived at that time in Winslow Cohousing in Seattle. Through contacts in the Ecovillage group, I became his host and organised his public talk and seminar in Auckland and another at WCC. As well as giving his perspectives on sustainability, economics and society, he described the layout and workings of his cohousing community including their use of the coloured card consensus system. Robert was a major theoretical thinker in the global ecovillage movement, who lived in cohousing, and was telling us that it really *works*. His inspiring visit helped to prepare the ground at Council to be responsive to our project.

A one-page newspaper article about Dr Robert Gilman included my name as the local contact, and several people got in touch. One of these was Mary Rose, who had her own dream of creating a women's house and could see it fitting in with the idea of cohousing. We met with two others a couple of times and decided to hold a public meeting to explain the project and attract more people. We distributed flyers, invited friends and I produced a last issue of the *Ecovillage* newsletter outlining the ideas. The public meeting was held on 14 June 1995 at a church hall in Te Atatū, and the Waitakere Eco-Neighbourhood Project was launched.

Using a slideshow by Kathryn McCamant and Charles Durett, the authors of the *Cohousing* book, I described the cohousing model and talked about my plan to build cohousing on a site at Harbour View Estate. With Warwick and Katrina's coaching, I was clear that this project would be urban, sustainable and based on the cohousing model, because that was the culmination for me of three years of study, discussion and thinking. If people were drawn to that vision, they were very welcome to be part of developing the project from that time forward.

The meeting generated a high level of excitement and interest, especially from Cathy Angell and John Hammond, for whom the meeting was an 'Aha!' experience. They had lived in communities in the past which hadn't endured for a variety of reasons and were currently living in suburbia. They hadn't known they were looking for something more, but they immediately knew in their bones that they had found it. They sat up in bed the next morning and each wrote their own vision for the community life they wanted. Cathy turned up on my doorstep at work soon after that to show me how completely compatible their visions were with mine. They immediately got involved and have been an integral part of the project ever since.

Cathy, John, Mary, another man Simon and I met weekly as a core group over the next few months. Early meetings discussed basic meeting procedure and agreements and adopted the coloured card system of decision making (see Chapter 5) which Robert Gilman had described. We confirmed our Vision Statement and added three further statements on environment, interpersonal relationships and education. Monthly Sunday pot-luck lunches were started as a way of reaching out to interested people and drawing them into the group.

That winter I also started meeting with a group of women to acknowledge the eight seasonal points in the year that mark the turning of the earth relative to the sun: summer and winter solstice, spring and autumn equinox, and the midpoints between these. This group has been a regular touchstone in my life ever since. Taking time to pause at these regular times keeps me connected with the rhythms of the seasons and how they interconnect with the rhythms of my life, often allowing profound insights, and providing space and support to set intentions for the future.

Troubles simmered in the core group, however, with one person very much wanting to get on with tasks and uncomfortable talking about process issues, and another unwilling or unable to work on tasks when relationships felt unclear to her. With the help of an outside facilitator we worked through this and wrote our interpersonal relationship and communication guidelines, still in place today. We also invented the black card as part of our decision-making system to signify interpersonal issues that needed addressing. While these processes felt extremely useful, the two involved felt bruised by the conflict and withdrew from the group soon afterwards. This left Cathy, John and me to carry the project forward.

In late 1995 Max and I decided to sell our family home. An old Victorian villa, it had been our family nest for fourteen years. Both our children had been born in that home, their whenua were buried in the garden, and it had held much love, laughter and – more recently – trouble and grief. It felt time to complete that part of our lives and move on.

A few days before the auction, my boys and I said our farewell and blessings to the house. We moved from room to room, telling each other stories of our life in that house. We wrote blessings and hopes on little pieces of paper, folding them up small and tucking them into cracks and crevices around the house and garden, some perhaps to be found and many not. My children had lived under the spreading arms of a huge oak tree in the back garden all their lives. Willow put together a little basket of gemstones and tucked it into a cleft in the trunk, with a poem saying, 'you may take these jewels, but please leave the tree'. It was a beautiful way of thanking the land and home that had sheltered us for so long and releasing it to the next guardians.

Within two weeks of selling our old home I had found the perfect next stopping point for my boys and me: a brand new, clean, white house full of light in Pt Chevalier, with a gate though the fence into a small local park, and no history held in its bones. It was a blank sheet. I knew it was a temporary haven, the perfect setting within which I could work towards my dream of community.

A typical agenda – with embellishments

Cathy, John and I had all been fairly shaken by the process/task conflict, so we made a conscious decision not to attract other people into the group until we had foundation agreements in place. We three met once a week at my house, sometimes more, for most of 1996. Cathy was enthusiastic and attentive to detail, and John was quieter, thoughtful and a little hesitant. My kids were often around the edges of those early meetings, sometimes being mischievous and illustrating our agenda on the whiteboard with animals, figures and smart comments. A tradition evolved: John would bring a packet of chocolate biscuits in his briefcase, and Willow would devise a range of tricks to distract our attention while Erin raided the biscuits.

The first task of the year was writing detailed submissions to the *Waitakere City Council Proposed District Plan*. In line with its policy of increasing the density of housing around public transport nodes, Council introduced the Medium Density Housing criteria. These allowed a much more flexible housing layout than standard subdivision rules, while safeguarding such aspects as privacy and sunlight, and were very in tune with what we were proposing. Some of our suggestions were adopted, including a change to the definition of medium-density housing to include the possibility of shared spaces that ultimately enabled our subsequent design.

We worked on core internal organising agreements and produced a handbook that outlined our project in enough detail that it would be clear to future members what they were joining. Many meetings also went into drafting a trust deed for Waitakere Eco-Neighbourhood Trust, although in the end we didn't proceed with a trust structure.

These were much happier times for me, full of purpose and satisfaction. I was getting interesting architectural jobs which extended my knowledge, skills and confidence, including earth-brick houses, house renovations for accessibility and working with people in organisations to design workspaces that met their collective needs. I became a BRANZ (Building Research Association of New Zealand) Green Home Assessor. I loved my new house and all the new possibilities that it represented. I was motivated and energised by doing solid work towards the cohousing project, along with two allies, Cathy and John. Willow (aged thirteen) and Erin (aged nine) were happier and we were enjoying life.

Max and I were co-parenting in a steady rhythm, and it seemed to work well. We had had the usual amount of anger, bitterness and blame between us in our separating, but I like to think we spared the kids the worst of that. One day, a few weeks before we were due to get divorced, Max showed me something he had been working on. He had carried a passport photo of me, taken when we met, in his wallet throughout the time we were together. What he showed me now was a small portrait he had painted, of me, from this photo. I was amazed and very moved. Max had never shown any interest or talent in art before, and in our interactions together over the last three years he had been distant at best and occasionally hostile. And yet he had taken a painting class and chosen to paint me at the time when we fell in love, and it was beautiful.

And then we did a very good thing, for ourselves and our children. Two evenings before our divorce, we went out for dinner – Max, me and our children. We arranged to have the upstairs room in a small restaurant, where we would get fed but not be disturbed by anyone else, and spent that evening telling each other the story of our lives together. We started with that magic month in Melbourne in 1977 when we had first met and fell in love, telling the story lovingly and joyfully. Then stories from our time in South America and London, coming back to Auckland so I could start university, buying our house together. First Willow, then Erin joining our family. As we got to times that the kids remembered they each contributed their own stories. We progressed over the course of the evening, remembering and acknowledging the times we had shared together. When we got up to the last year or so before we separated, I felt that Max took over the telling, not leaving much space for me, and I started to feel annoyed. 'Hey this is my story too!' So we arrived at the end in disarray, as might be expected.

I knew Max was planning to give me his painting, and in return I had printed and framed a beautiful black-and-white photo I had taken of him, in that first magic month, with love shining from his eyes. We exchanged these images of the people we had fallen in love with, and it felt like a profound acknowledgement of the love we had once shared, and a giving back of each of us to ourselves. Two days later we met again in the government office to sign the divorce papers and headed our separate ways. It was a good completion.

Cathy, John and I were a tight, efficient working team, but by then we were feeling the strain of carrying the project between the three of us and were looking at how we could include more people. The Sunday lunches had continued intermittently with generally small attendance. An enrolment meeting was held in July, and there was a good level of interest and much affirmation of what we'd done, but very little tangible support came out of it. A walk over the Harbour View site was organised for August and again there was a lot of interest but little follow-up. In order to encourage interest and involvement we invited people to sign a letter of intent to purchase a house in the eco-neighbourhood. Only a few people signed up.

We realised that we'd reached a crossroads and needed to explore the physical aspects of the project so that both potential residents and council contacts could more fully understand what we proposed. In November we established a Design Group with a $100 non-refundable joining fee, to meet fortnightly and work on design and planning. We chose a theoretical site at Harbour View and started working on concept plans in order to help clarify what we wanted as a group and to boost our enthusiasm.

We also realised that the project would progress a lot faster if one of us could put in serious time. I had my own practice as an eco-architect and was a half-time solo parent of two boys. I was putting more and more time into the project but finding that hard to sustain financially. We looked at how to fund a paid project coordinator, but quickly realised that applying for grants for that purpose would completely divert our energy from actually advancing the project. Some members pledged loans

Early Design Group with John Hammond, Cathy Angell and Robin Allison

to pay for a coordinator, but this never eventuated. I continued putting many hours per week into the planning, researching, thinking and writing that were required at that time, giving these equal priority with my paid architectural work. I started saying I was working on a PhD in Cohousing, partly in jest but also to justify to myself the time I was spending on the project.

Ongoing negotiations with Waitakere Properties had continued all year over the possible purchase of a site within the Harbour View Estate large enough for what we needed. They were polite but made no attempt to incorporate a large site within the subdivision of single-home sections that they were planning. The reality was that we didn't have the financial capacity at that point to buy land, but we hoped that Council would recognise it was worth supporting us, even for a couple of years while we set the project up.

I realise now we should also have been working on the political level, informing and working with elected councillors, some of whom were right behind us. Waitakere Properties had the job of returning the biggest profit to Council from this land, and

Stall at the Environmental Building Field Day, 1997

as the year progressed the prices firmed up and moved further and further out of our reach. In December we made the decision to let go of that part of the dream and to look around for other suitable sites in Waitakere City, primarily around town centres and transport nodes in line with eco-city and urban sustainability values.

The first part of 1997 saw more meetings with various council officers, developers and others, and several sites were investigated. The Design Group developed a set of criteria for site selection. A display of our project at the Environmental Building Field Day in March generated plenty of interest and some new supporters, one of whom, Cathy Sheehan, worked for the government agency EECA (Energy Efficiency and Conservation Authority). Cathy set up a website for us and wrote an excellent article about cohousing in general and our project in particular for the EECA magazine *EnergyWise News*, which was seen by a surprising number of people. A camp at Pataua South near Whangārei Heads over Easter was much enjoyed by the nineteen adults and children who attended, providing a glimpse of community life and much needed rejuvenation.

I'd felt for some years that my parents and siblings weren't interested or didn't understand my energy for our cohousing project. Increasingly Mum accused me of wasting my life – 'such a waste of talent and promise'. What they saw was my marriage break-up and part-time architecture practice; what they didn't seem interested in was what I was truly passionate about. Thinking, planning and working towards the cohousing project had been my major focus for five years, and we'd hardly ever discussed it. I wanted them to be interested, to take it seriously and offer ideas and occasional support. I made a date with my parents, asked my sister along for moral support, and told them how important this project was to me. They didn't have to agree or value the same things, but I wanted them to understand I was using my skills in the most important way I could imagine, as well as doing the best I could for my children. From that time, though the concept of community remained foreign to them, they made the effort to take more interest.

There was something else I wanted them to accept about my life, and I chose that time to reveal it; that over the last two years I'd done a lot of thinking and re-evaluating of who I was, and I now identified as a lesbian. I was in my first relationship with a woman at that time, and though it had been increasingly stormy and difficult, being with a woman felt 'right'. My parents had always taught me to think for myself, though they probably hoped that my choices would be similar to theirs. I wasn't used to revealing intimate things about myself to them, and they didn't agree with the course I was taking, but it was a calm, rational and caring conversation. It was a relief to be honest with them, and another step in becoming my own self.

In April 1.5 acres (0.6 hectares) of land with a well-designed house near Henderson came on the market and met many of our recently agreed criteria. This precipitated an enormous flurry of research and meetings with Council, lawyer, bank manager, developers and members, but after three weeks of intense effort we decided there wasn't enough support to put an offer in to buy it. A strong sense of both disappointment and relief was felt by many; at the very least it had been useful as a trial run.

The effort, along with other family and personal crises, took its toll. My relationship was going through an intense and difficult break-up; an important friend had recently died; I was trying to run an architectural practice and look after my kids. I felt mentally and emotionally burnt out. By July the Design Group had dropped back down to John, Cathy and me, plus one new member, Rowan Bell. At one meeting I found myself crying, feeling so low and drained. Cathy was also feeling exhausted. It was so hard to put the project down and wonder whether it would die, but I couldn't continue without a break. We decided to go into recess for a month or so, although John and Rowan would keep the project ticking over and planned to hold an information meeting to enrol new energy.

During that time, we were approached by David Steemson of Radio New Zealand who wanted to interview us for National Radio. He came with us to a site we'd looked at, asked us about cohousing and what we were planning, and then came to one of our Sunday meetings to interview others in the wider group. This was the first of several interviews with him over the years as we got closer to our goal, which helped to spread the word, and also gave us confidence that we were doing something of wider importance than just building our own homes.

I took my kids to Bali for two weeks in October 1997 as part of my time out, and when I got back Peter Scott and Geraldine Hughes (former members of the Hedgehogs) and Robin Lightfoot had joined, and the group had restarted with new vigour. We had kept the group small in order to build the foundations, but the time had come when it was ready to expand. Peter and Geraldine had been knocking on our door for some time, writing letters full of questions that they needed answers to before they felt able to join, which to the three of us had just felt like more work when we had enough to do. They realised that they needed to get involved if they wanted to be part of forming the neighbourhood the way they wanted it.

From this point on Cathy, John and I ceased to meet separately, and the Design Group became the core group. Another promising site near Henderson prompted a lot of research and discussion, and at one very enjoyable meeting we arranged scaled house blocks on a site plan to get a feel as a group for how our cohousing village might look. Much thinking went into legal and financial issues, subdivision development costs, land purchase logistics, membership structure and meeting agreements.

With the increased numbers, we divided the tasks into three task groups: Legal and Finance, Membership and Promotion, and Site and Design. Each member became involved in one or two of the specific task groups and we only met as a full group every second week. None of these groups had a 'leader', but people stepped into leadership. Cathy focused on the legal side, Geraldine took leadership on membership issues and I was the key driver on site and design. Peter, his long ponytail and languid demeanour belying his sharp mind and determined personality, increasingly stepped up on specific aspects of feasibility, and Peter, Cathy and I were all engaged in thinking about the development and financial issues at this point.

An additional boost came when we heard that another group in Auckland at that time, led by Jill Whitmore, had organised for Kathryn (Katie) McCamant and Charles (Chuck) Durrett – the authors of the *Cohousing* book – to come to New Zealand for a public meeting and to run workshops with their group. This generated a flurry of activity. Katie agreed to run a one-day workshop for our group while she and Chuck were here. We agreed on a new name, 'Waitakere Eco-Neighbourhood Cohousing Project' (WENCP) just in time to print the new handbook and flyers for the public talk in February 1998.

The public talk and Katie's workshop with our group were pivotal and inspiring events. Katie showed slides of many different projects in the USA and Denmark to illustrate aspects of community design and gave us clear guidance on many other issues we were grappling with, such as membership process, development and finance.

With the media coverage of Katie and Chuck's visit, WENCP attracted new members and moved into higher gear. We worked on a detailed Information Booklet and a Members' Resource File, including short biographies of members. We talked with lawyers, got tax advice, and did a Financial Questionnaire of members. We talked with developers and visited many sites in West Auckland. Geraldine and Peter separated at this time, but both remained active within the group.

We developed our membership process along the lines that Katie suggested, and drafted a one-page document that we called the 'Initial Organising Agreement' (IOA), outlining our vision and agreements about membership, decision making and financial contributions, with a $100 fee to become a member. The IOA also established a Full Member category with a contribution of $2000 to the project as seed money to begin paying for consultants. In May 1998 we acknowledged a major milestone as fifteen people signed the IOA in the order that they had joined the project. Fifteen members, all committed to the vision and agreeing to actively participate in the tasks to bring it about.

Matters proceeded apace, with all task groups working hard. We started promoting the project more widely with articles and advertisements in the local paper and magazines, a stall at a local market and monthly orientation meetings for possible new members. Our systems developed and refined as numbers increased. Group dynamics were becoming more complex as the group became larger, so we established the Process Task Group to keep a focus on our internal relationships and processes.

In July 1998 we held another significant hui, creating a development timeline for our increasingly complex project by playing the Timeline Game.[2] This planning tool was developed to help cohousing groups understand the many tasks involved in developing cohousing, their sequence and their relationships to each other. I had found it online and facilitated the process over the course of a day as we grappled with all the tasks required and how they fitted together. As well as being a great team-building exercise, this process was enormously useful in understanding the steps and creating a map to help us get to the beginning of construction.

We engaged a lawyer and accountant and began work on our major legal and financial document, the Cohousing Agreement, to define how we put money into the project. Alongside that went extensive research into legal ownership structures and development entities, and we eventually chose to use a unit title ownership structure. We refined our requirements with questionnaires to members on financial issues, housing and site location. I formulated a site rating system and site feasibility checklist, and we visited and considered many sites over that year.

Some members visited a rammed-earth café and fell in love with the solidity of that material, so we began to consider rammed-earth construction. I had started a correspondence course in Building Biology and Ecology[3] and was expanding my knowledge of building materials and systems that better suited the wider ecology of the planet. We talked with various developers, learning about development budgets and looking for potential joint-venture partners willing to work alongside us. There was a building sense of energy and momentum, but with three or four meetings a week, the beginnings again of exhaustion.

In September 1998 we heard of a property about to come onto the market. The 4 acre (1.6 hectare) orchard, right next to the Ranui shops, had been owned by the Prideaux family for sixty years. The last member of that family, Brian Prideaux, had been a vintage car enthusiast and clock repairer, and Rowan's wife Linda had befriended him after taking a clock for repair. When he died, she felt this property might suit our needs.

Ranui was an unassuming suburb on the western edge of the Auckland suburban area, largely developed in the 1960s as low-cost housing with little physical charm. Although much further out of central Auckland than many of us wanted, the area had other advantages, being on the western train line and close to the magnificent west coast beaches.

Some of us visited the site and liked it; it 'felt right'. As well as the rows of gnarled apple and pear trees and overgrown shelter trees around the edges, there were two small existing houses made of home-made concrete blocks, a row of old concrete garages and two large derelict packing sheds. Organically managed for many years, the land fulfilled our criteria better than any other site we'd seen, including proximity to the local neighbourhood shops and railway station, and was

Peter and Cathy at the front of 457 Swanson Road, Ranui

in an ethnically diverse township where some of us felt our project could be a real catalyst for positive change.

The property officially came on the market in early December. I obtained the existing plans from Council and sketched out a site plan that worked for twenty-four houses. We corresponded with the vendors' solicitor and did some soul searching within our group. We put in an expression of interest to buy the land and engaged an experienced property developer to advise us on how to put in a formal offer. More people visited the site, and the feeling grew that this was the place for us.

As part of strategising about how to proceed once we had secured land, I'd been thinking hard for most of the year about where my skills could be of most use to the project. As a student in 1983 I had written an assignment for the Community Architecture paper where I put the case that the most appropriate position from which to design for a community was as a member of that community. I believed that the best architecture arose out of a creative collaboration between the architect and the clients and felt that my being both would be a huge asset. By being embedded in the community, as architect I could be the channel through which the design arose directly from the group, without requiring translation to and interpretation

The old house in the orchard

by an outside person with his/her own agendas and understandings. I didn't assume I would be the architect, but it felt like the natural progression and ultimate culmination of my work, values and effort to that date.

I was also exhausted; money-stressed and lonely; a solo mother with kids to look after and an architectural practice to run; a woman in the very male world of design and construction; and questioning if I had the emotional, family and financial support to be the architect and deal with all the rivalries and power issues that would inevitably turn up. Even acknowledging those doubts, I believed that bringing this project into being was my life purpose and that I could be of most service to the project as the architect.

In reaching that conclusion, I looked around for a partner and approached an architect colleague Rick Lambourne. The project was too big and complex for a sole practitioner, and I felt the combined skills and perspectives of Rick and me would be a great combination. It would allow me to continue being a group member and managing other aspects of the project as well as the architecture, while Rick concentrated on the design.

In the Site and Design Task Group, we had discussed our criteria for suitable architects for our project, including knowledge of sustainable and passive solar design, experience in multi-unit residential projects and a track record of projects being on time and on budget. But there was resistance by some to take the next step and consider whether someone from our group could or should play that role. I wanted the Full Group to know that I was considering putting my name forward as a possible architect, so we could all start thinking and talking about implications, fears and strategies for making it work. A special Full Group meeting was held in early February 1999 to talk about it. I made it clear at the meeting that the most important thing for me was finding the best place for my skills to be useful to the project, and that we needed to hear from one another so we could decide together what my role would be. Some spoke of their worries and concerns, and many others expressed huge trust and support for me. It was a good meeting, but only the beginning of the discussion that was needed.

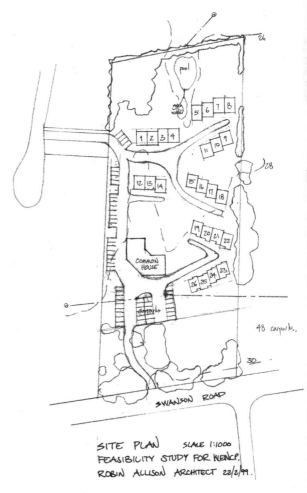

The very next day, the developer advised me that we should do a feasibility study for buying the Ranui land by hiring an architect to do a quick house and site sketch plan, get it costed by a Quantity Surveyor (QS), get a valuation on the site and then refine our development budget to determine a reasonable price to pay for the land. We had a deadline of one week to make a realistic offer on the site. I relayed this to the Full Group, who agreed to pay me a small fee to do these indicative sketch plans within a timeframe of two working days. I had already started drafting some ideas, so I was able to produce a site plan for twenty-six houses (very similar to the site plan we have ended up with), a workable house plan, elevations and sections, and a materials schedule.

It was not a real house design, just a diagram of a layout that worked, of the approximate size and likely materials; close enough to get an indicative cost-to-build from the QS of the type of house we wanted. I didn't want to leap ahead of the group design process. I was really looking forward to going deeply with the group into our collective mind and soul and midwifing a form that arose out of the energy of the group. Being part of the group was essential to that process.

The atmosphere was quite tense when I presented my sketches to Site and Design. I was so wired up, had pumped out the plans in such a short time frame and knew it wasn't *the* house design, just a diagram for the purposes of the Feasibility Study. I was very aware of keeping costs within reason, and perhaps I was too impatient when I defended some of my design decisions – all of which had been unilateral, given the time frame. We just didn't have the luxury of time for this part of the process, and it didn't need to be perfect anyway. I'm not sure how much the members of Site and Design understood this or assumed that this feasibility concept would be the design I would stick with if I was the architect.

The work was accepted by the group and we put our feasibility together. Investigations, negotiations and many late-night group meetings followed. We decided to form our own company, Cohousing New Zealand Ltd (CNZL), as the development entity for the project. We talked with our lawyers, corresponded with the vendors' solicitor, and did much soul searching within our group.

At one pivotal late-night meeting in February, we considered all the information from the Feasibility Study and debated whether to go ahead. Ranui was a low socio-economic and ethnically diverse suburb, and not everyone felt they could live there. The site valuation of $660,000 was more than we had bargained for, but the numbers stacked up to confirm that the houses would be worth more than the total costs. We asked for a declaration of who intended to buy a unit in this project on this land, and of the fifteen members in the room that night, most were in favour, with only a couple reluctant.

I committed to sell my house in Pt Chevalier and pay for over a third of the price of the land. Others pledged significant amounts. Eventually, at 1.30 a.m. five members or couples put up our hands to be the 'front group', putting in equal amounts of money to pay the deposit on the land and becoming the first shareholders of CNZL, on the expectation and trust that many others would contribute funds further down the track once the Cohousing Agreement was finalised. We made an offer on the orchard in Ranui.

Two weeks of negotiations, setting up the company, raising funds, meetings, uncertainty and strain followed, knowing we wanted this land so much. The five

Cathy and Robin signing the AGSAP for the orchard

parties of the 'front group' were joined by two other couples in signing a Deed of Indemnity, pledging funds to cover the entire purchase price between us. The beneficiaries of Brian Prideaux's estate seemed to favour our buying it, but the lawyer involved was not particularly helpful. We were told there was a slightly higher offer (but with conditions) from a large residential developer, but also that Brian Prideaux would have hated 'ticky-tacky boxes' on his land. After several meetings with the beneficiaries and lawyer, increasing our offer and providing security – including a letter from my parents guaranteeing to pay $200,000 at settlement if I had not sold my house by then – on 15 March 1999 they finally signed the Agreement for Sale and Purchase (AGSAP) of the property for $660,000.

My journal entry of 15 March 1999 reads:

They've signed. Yahooooo!!!

I can hardly believe it. So exhausted there isn't much bounce and joy in me, but little bubbles of excitement come through sometimes. We've bought some land. After all this time, all this effort. Wow. We've got some land! This is really going to happen! We have a home!

Mind racing, thinking ahead, all the things to be done. Soil tests, LIM [Land Information Memorandum] report. Mortgage from my bank for my part of the deposit. Set up a company. Get a surveyor to do a topo. Choose an architect. Talk to Rick about how we'd work together. Have a party! Put the word out, tell everyone.

We've got land and it's beautiful!!! Ranui here we come …

After all those years and all that effort, it was mind-blowing to realise we'd finally bought some land. It felt as though we'd scaled a massive mountain, and there was huge exhilaration and sense of achievement. But we were also aware of the range of mountains in front of us, rising higher than the one we were on, also unexplored and with who knows what crevasses and slippery slopes to challenge us.

In a project of this sort, what you can see once it has been completed is merely the tip of a pyramid buried deeply in the ground. All the years of preparation and planning, though invisible to those who come after, were in many ways the hardest part, relying on vision, persistence and belief that something that didn't exist yet would happen, and this built a very solid and stable foundation for the whole project. Once we'd bought land and were engaged in the design process, it became much more tangible and credible to people, and this was reflected in the influx of people into the group after we committed to buying our site in Ranui.

COMMUNITY GOVERNANCE AND GROUP DECISION MAKING

5

THEME

If you want to go fast, go alone.
If you want to go far, go together.

AFRICAN PROVERB

How did a self-selected group of opinionated individuals from different backgrounds make decisions over many years to plan, finance and develop an innovative thirty-two-home sustainable housing development? By consensus, of course!

In most organisations, a few people make decisions on behalf of all. Some attempts at inclusive governance allow input and opinions from those affected ... but true community governance, where decisions are made collectively, is rare, and all too often effective action gets bogged down in long frustrating meetings or one or two people blocking progress.

It doesn't have to be that way. Though it is not always easy, it is possible for a diverse group of people to think and work constructively together and find ways forward that all are willing to support. Good community governance happens within clear structures and group agreements, with appropriate tools and processes that support effective decision making.

At Earthsong, all decisions of any importance have been made by consensus of the Full Group of members. From the beginning, prospective residents have worked together, with appropriate support from consultants, to create the legal structures

Decision making at Earthsong

required, design the site and buildings and fund the construction. Residents are now managing the ongoing life of the neighbourhood. When you consider that Earthsong is a $15-million project of thirty-two houses and common facilities, using non-standard design, materials and systems and self-developed by the group, you can see that consensus can and does work.

THE LIMITATIONS OF BINARY THINKING

'Democracy' is defined as government by all the people, direct or representative.[1] But even with a range of political parties and proportional representation, two main parties or party groupings usually dominate. One becomes the 'Government' and the other is known as the 'Opposition', as if that defines their purpose: to oppose the Government. Imagine what could be achieved if all parties identified the values they shared and worked together to agree on the actions required – holding their individual principles and values strongly *and* being willing to collaborate.

Many groups and organisations make decisions by voting. Voting turns a decision into a choice between two alternatives, one of which will be chosen and one rejected – this idea or that idea, this person or that person, yes or no. When voting is based on achieving a simple majority, it is possible that up to half the citizens are overruled, resenting the decision imposed on them and perhaps ignoring or undermining it.

Rarely is an issue solved with a binary question.
MCCAMANT AND DURETT (2011, P. 23)

'Consensus' is a group decision-making process in which group members develop, and agree to support, a decision in the best interest of the whole. Consensus implies a willingness to find agreement. This doesn't mean that a decision is every person's first choice, but rather that everyone is willing to consent and move forward together, and occasionally to yield for the benefit of the group. Part of being in a group is accepting that at times things will go in a different direction than any individual might want. The value of consensus is that the attention is on what we can agree about, on finding a way forward together, not on positions that are inherently divisive and often incompatible. Consensus embraces complexity and creativity.

In some cases, even when consensus is the goal, the possible solutions can seem incompatible. A step out of binary thinking is to compromise: to see the continuum between two positions and find the place on that continuum that satisfies, enough, the proponents of each so that all are willing to agree. Though better than the win/lose of binary voting, compromise does mean each party gives up something in order to meet others somewhere in the middle.

Earthsong's cat policy is an example of compromise. Some members strongly opposed having any pet cats in our neighbourhood, because cats are predators of native birds and other wildlife. Other members had a deeply felt need for a cat companion for themselves or for their children and argued that, even if we had no resident cats, they would still come in from the wider neighbourhood. The solution finally agreed was somewhere in the middle, allowing an upper limit of eight cats at Earthsong, with protocols including that the cats would wear a collar and bell and would be shut in at night to give the birds a better chance.

The real magic of consensus happens when the group doesn't settle for compromise but looks for a creative solution, a leap out of binary thinking into three dimensions, a new solution that arises out of the chemistry of the group. It requires space for all the ideas to be shared within the group and the willingness to hear and understand the perspectives of others. The solution often satisfies underlying needs rather than the more obvious problem and is different from any individual solution. It takes time, and the excitement of feeling that 'Yes!' from the whole group when the creative solution is verbalised is incredibly rewarding.[2]

BENEFITS AND CHALLENGES OF CONSENSUS

Being part of a well-functioning group considering issues together and collectively agreeing on a course of action can be a rewarding and empowering experience. It fulfils two primal needs of being human – the sense of belonging to a group, and the sense of agency in our lives, that our perspective matters, that we have some influence on our wider context. Consensus doesn't mean we all think the same or we all have the same skills. Consensus still requires leadership (not one leader but acts of leadership).[3]

A useful analogy is to imagine yourself playing a musical instrument with other musicians. It's a jam session; there is no written score to follow, but there are a few ground rules understood between you such as beat and tempo. Good music requires you to be very present both to the music you yourself are playing, and also to the music you are creating together. Both listening and contributing are crucial, a balance of individual expression and harmony with the whole, lightly holding both the individual and the group presence.[4]

Enormous creativity is possible when people think together. We each come with our own perspectives, skills, background and experience. Harvesting the best ideas of the group leads to informed decisions that are generally stronger from the input of the group mind. Hearing the perspectives of others widens our own understandings, and issues that we may have thought were simple and obvious can encompass a range of issues that we hadn't considered. It can get complicated! Embracing that complexity for long enough to understand what will work for different people leads to more robust decisions.

The shadow of this is 'groupthink', which occurs when individuals suppress or ignore their own judgement in order to 'belong' to the group. The key is to maintain your own integrity, values and judgement, while also respecting the shared purpose of the group. Both/and again: *both* keeping our own moral compass *and* looking for the creative solution that all can agree to.

Consensus is not appropriate for all situations. For example, there needs to be a relationship between risk and control. It is important that those included in consensus have 'skin in the game' – they have something to lose if the decision leads to undesirable outcomes, or if no decision is made at all. This is the incentive that keeps members working to find a solution, and without it, other forms such as representation or hierarchy may be more appropriate.

The experience most likely to cause frustration, anger and disillusionment has been called the 'tyranny of the dissenter' – when an individual or small number of people can veto a course of action indefinitely, with no agreed procedure for coming to agreement and moving forward. This is a common complaint about consensus, but it doesn't have to be. Various ways to address this are outlined later in this chapter.

At Earthsong we have all, at some time or other, had to let go of things that we dearly wanted, in order for the project to move forward. The overall goal is more important than any one decision. Keep your eye on the vision, learn to trust the wisdom of the group and be willing to let go some of the details.

COMMUNITY GOVERNANCE STRUCTURES

There are several key conditions that, in my experience, are the foundation for effective community governance.

1. A strongly held *shared vision* or purpose.
2. Defined *membership process.*
3. Agreed ground rules for *effective communication.*
4. Defined *decision-making structure and procedures.*
5. Access to *information* for all those involved in decision making.

1. Shared vision (see Chapter 3)

The importance of a clearly worded and agreed Vision Statement to a group making decisions on a project cannot be overstated. A common vision or purpose guides the decision making and helps to differentiate individual needs and wants from what would work best for the group. Members' investment in achieving the overall vision becomes more important than getting their preferred option every time. We all know why we are there and what our goal is, even as we work out how to achieve that vision together.

2. Membership process

In consensus decision making, the group of members needs to become an entity, a whole that is more than the sum of its parts. Having clarity around membership of that entity is an important aspect of the social infrastructure. It is crucial, especially during the establishment phase of a project, to know that those participating in the decision making are aligned with the vision, have agreed to make decisions by consensus and are committed to the project's success.

At Earthsong we don't select members; an individual, not the group, decides for her/himself whether to become a member or not. Part of sustainability is learning to live with a wide variety of people. We don't get to choose most of our family members, so how can we pass judgement on strangers? We have, instead, concentrated on building a robust culture and processes that encompass a diversity of people and world-views.

Our membership process is designed to ensure that an individual fully understands the vision and agreements of the group before choosing to become a member. The process includes being assigned a 'buddy' to walk alongside them as they get to know the community and to answer their many questions. They must attend two or more Full Group meetings as an observer, read key documents and understand Earthsong culture and agreements. They are encouraged to attend social events, working bees and common dinners to meet other members.

Once these prerequisites have been fulfilled, the defining step is to pay the $100 membership fee and sign our one-page membership document. During development this was called the Initial Organising Agreement (IOA). A succinct, clear and easily understood legal document, the IOA defined the key elements of membership of the group, including the group's purpose, membership rights and responsibilities, and basic agreements about money and decision making. This is essentially a social contract. The fee is small but important and signing one's name to a contract usually

WAITAKERE ECO-NEIGHBOURHOOD
COHOUSING PROJECT

INITIAL ORGANISING AGREEMENT

We the undersigned members
agree to work together on the following basis:

PREAMBLE

0.1 This document covers the development period of the project, and may be built on by other agreements.

0.2 'Project' hereinafter means Waitakere Eco-Neighbourhood Cohousing Project.

0.3 '*Cohousing* book' refers to McCamant and Durrett (1994), *Cohousing—A Contemporary Approach to Housing Ourselves* (2nd edition).

0.4 'Information booklet' refers to the Project's Information booklet.

0.5 'Member' means, unless otherwise stated, a person who has paid an associate membership fee and whose name currently appears on the membership list over.

PURPOSE

1.1 The group's purpose is to bring about the development of an urban cohousing neighbourhood, to be probably located in West Auckland.

1.2 This will be based upon the concept of cohousing, as described in the *Cohousing* book, as well as the project Vision Statement and other material laid out in our Information Booklet.

MEMBERSHIP

2.1 As members it is our intention to purchase and/or reside in a unit of the completed project.

2.2 We also actively participate in the tasks toward bringing about our vision.

2.3 We have read and agree with the principles laid out in the Cohousing book and in our Information Booklet.

2.4 We have read summaries of past minutes and understand that decisions made to date may only be reopened by the processes laid out in 4.5

2.5 We honour and adhere to our Communication Agreements, as set out in the Information Booklet.

2.6 We also understand that households will have choice of units based upon the order of full membership fee payment.

2.7 Members wishing to withdraw from the project temporarily or permanently, will advise this intention in writing.

2.8 Otherwise, a member who is absent from more than three consecutive meetings and deemed by the consensus of the meeting to have ceased being involved, shall be contacted prior to being deleted from the membership list over.

MONEY

3.1 On becoming an Associate member a fee of $100 is paid per person. This is non-refundable in the event of withdrawal at any stage.

3.2 Full member households are those that have invested in the project a minimum of $2000. Upon withdrawal, funds beyond the associate membership fee, will be refunded when all units are sold or sooner if cash flow allows.

3.3 All money contributed is credited to personal unit purchase accounts. Such money will accrue an agreed upon interest factor, which will be credited at the time of unit purchase.

3.4 Members will be collectively responsible for raising sufficient funds in order that financial institutions will provide the balance of finance for the project.

3.5 Each member will provide such personal financial information as is needed for the project. This information is to remain confidential to members and finance professionals as required.

3.6 All project expenditure must be authorised in terms of current spending policy.

MEETINGS

4.1 Meeting procedure is as laid out in the Project's Resource File and in the Information booklet.

4.2 Decision-making is by the consensus of members. All decisions must be passed using the coloured cards and recorded in the minutes.

4.3 If consensus is not reached after two meetings, or if the meeting considers that time constraints require and notice is given to all members, then a decision may be taken at a subsequent meeting by a 75% majority vote. Such vote shall be on the basis of one vote per full membership fee, to a maximum of one vote per person.

4.4 A quorum of 25% of members is required to make decisions. Apologies will be given to the facilitator if unable to attend a meeting.

4.5 A member absent from a meeting may request to revisit a decision made at that meeting, at the next meeting only. Otherwise decisions may only be reopened with the prior agreement of 50% of members.

DISSOLUTION

5.1 We acknowledge that while we are working toward the project's success, in the event of the project not proceeding we can't guarantee that all moneys contributed will be refunded.

5.2 Any funds remaining will be distributed to the members on a pro rata basis.

indicates that the person signing is serious about coming on board. Once they have 'stepped over the threshold' into commitment to the group and the vision, the new member becomes a full and equal participant in consensus decision making at Earthsong.

During the development phase, when we were needing future buyers and renters, membership was open to anyone who fulfilled the steps and chose to become a member. Owners and renters at Earthsong have always been equal in terms of membership and therefore also equal in decision making. We did, however, have two levels of membership. Associate Membership, just described, gave the member all the rights of membership including participation in decision making.

We also wanted to encourage a higher level of commitment and needed seed funding to enable early work to happen. Paying a further $2000 achieved what we called 'Full Membership', which was a prerequisite to buying a house, and had two other benefits and incentives: the order of becoming a Full Member determined a member's place in the 'picking order' to choose their house, and in the rare case when consensus was not reached in important and urgent decisions, Full Members got voting rights in the 75% voting process described further on.

Only one person in each household was required to be a member, and some partners or tenants lived at Earthsong for many years without fully joining in. More recently the IOA has been superseded by an updated Membership Agreement, which requires all adults except short-term residents to become members. Expecting a similar level of commitment to the whole, with all residents having the same rights and responsibilities, encourages the sense of belonging and agency that builds a strong community.

3.   Effective communication

One of the most useful founding agreements for any group is an agreed set of guidelines around communication. Consensus decision making requires effective, respectful communication that builds trust and confidence and allows each to have a voice. Earthsong's Communication Agreements are aspirational; we don't all get it right all the time, but we have agreed what is important and we can remind one another that this is the culture we value and aspire to.

Earthsong's Communication Agreements

1. I will use 'I' statements, and speak for myself, not others.

2. I will speak succinctly (short and to the point).

3. I will take responsibility for owning and naming my own feelings.

4. I will respect others' rights to speak without interruption.

5. I undertake to respect others' privacy by not discussing outside the group other people's personal issues which may arise within the group process.

6. I undertake to value and respect different contributions and perspectives of all individuals.

7. I undertake to keep relationships clear within the group by dealing with any problematic issues directly with the persons concerned.

8. I recognise that we work best together when we remember to have fun!

4. Decision-making structure and procedures

The central decision-making body at Earthsong is the Full Group of all members of Earthsong Eco-Neighbourhood. All decisions of importance are brought to the monthly Full Group meeting for discussion and decision making by all members.

We also have a range of Focus Groups which meet fortnightly or monthly depending on the urgency of the issues and workload of the group. The Focus Groups manage specific areas of Earthsong life: they research and collate information, discuss issues, formulate proposals to the Full Group and carry out tasks once agreement has been reached. Participation in each Focus Group is voluntary and open to all members. Meeting times, agendas and minutes are sent to all members, so that everyone who has an interest in an issue can attend or comment if they wish.

The Focus Groups can make decisions on minor issues or those within a previously agreed policy. However, any issue considered of sufficient importance or potentially contentious is brought as a proposal to the Full Group meeting.

The Focus Groups have changed over time with the needs and stage of the project. During the construction phase, the key areas of concern were covered by the Development Team, Site and Design, Legal and Finance, and Membership and Promotion. Once construction had been completed, Focus Groups were organised around the ongoing management of common facilities such as the common house, water systems and gardens; resident issues such as membership and community life, and education. The structure we developed post-construction is illustrated in the 'Brainstormygramme' diagram.

Brainstormygramme
Tasks and groups
2008

**ABC
(Admin Body Corp)**
- Body Corp (BC) Secretary and Treasurer
- Insurance and valuations
- GST, tax, levies, service charges
- S36 and other legal docs
- BC budget process
- Financial policy proposals to FG (e.g. investment of funds, deferments)
- Legal issues
- AGM
- Register for emergencies
- Car parking levies

**CHuM
(Common House
Management Team)**
- Common house functions
- Equipment
- Internal maintenance
- Members' bookings
- Kitchenettes (cooking rosters)
- Key muster

Permaculture
- Planting gardens
- Composting
- Garden maintenance and equipment
- Harvesting policy proposals

Site management
- Maintenance of common property (tanks, solar, downpipes and gutters, workshop building, electrical shed, pond)
- Monitoring projects (MOU)
- Rubbish
- Parking

**E.C. Trust
(Earthsong Centre Trust)**
- External interface
- Legal and financial obligations of Trust

**Earthsong
Full Group
(FG)**

Design
- Review of design proposals of members and FG

Education/Outreach
- Tours
- Education and workshop programme
- Liaison with Trust
- External bookings
- External interface
- Promotion of Earthsong
- Liaising with WCC re. MOU
- Checking messages on phone/email

IT
- Intranet
- Website
- Email addresses
- Educate
- Server and other hardware/ infrastructure

Membership/Community life
- Organising FG meetings
- New members and enquiries
- Facilitating on-sales
- Vege co-op
- Green $
- Members' issues
- Membership fee
- Families
- Events calendar
- Decision log and minute archive

Workshop
- Building common stuff
- Managing the workshop facilities and equipment

The following meeting procedure and decision-making process are key parts of the structure within which we collectively govern our community.

Meeting procedure

It is a privilege to sit with a large group of diverse neighbours, each willing to spend several hours of their time listening to each other and seeking to understand and agree on a course of action. Clear and effective procedures help to make this experience rewarding and useful.

The physical arrangement of space is important. Chairs are placed in a circle so that everyone can see everyone else. One of our members creates a beautiful centre-piece for every Full Group meeting, with a candle and seasonal flowers, leaves and fruit. Our eyes rest on this centrepiece at times throughout the meeting, a reminder of our wider and deeper purpose.

Full Group meetings have a facilitator and also a co-facilitator, who can take over if the facilitator wants to participate more fully in any item. They are drawn from the pool of member facilitators, who support and mentor one another as peers by

Centre table at a Full Group meeting

gathering after each meeting to review the process. A minute taker has volunteered before the meeting, and a timekeeper and card counter are sought from those present.

Sufficient members must be present to satisfy the agreed quorum (25% of Earthsong members) before any decisions are made. Proxies, when someone unable to attend a meeting asks another to exercise their vote, are not compatible with consensus. Consensus requires people to be present, to listen to the concerns of the others and to be willing to change their minds and accept a solution that meets the needs of the group.

A vital part of all our meetings at Earthsong is the way we begin, by each member having space to 'check in' on a personal level, sharing some aspect of our life that we want our community to know, or something we would like to name and let go in order to be fully present. We make better decisions in the business part of the meeting when we understand and feel more connected to one another as people. Speaking in the check-in also makes it easier for those less confident to speak again.

Decision-making process

At Earthsong we use a powerful but simple tool of coloured cards for facilitating discussion and making decisions at our Full Group meetings.[5] The cards are also useful in the smaller Focus Groups when numbers get larger than six or seven participants. This system is used successfully by many cohousing groups worldwide, and we have added some refinements of our own.

Every member has a set of six coloured cards which are used in meetings in two different ways, as set out following.

DISCUSSION MODE

An issue will be presented by a Focus Group, who have researched, discussed and formulated a carefully worded proposal to the Full Group. This proposal is written up or projected so that all participants at the meeting can see it. At the meeting, each member indicates their wish to speak by raising a card of the appropriate colour (as set out following) at any time during the discussion. The facilitator calls on people to speak according to the following priority:

Black	I have an interpersonal difficulty that is preventing my full participation.
Red	I have a process observation.
Orange	I wish to acknowledge someone or something.
Yellow	I have a question, or need clarification.
Green	I can provide information or clarification to that question.
Blue	I have a comment or opinion.

The black card has first priority and can be an important safety valve. When a black card goes up, the facilitator asks the holder to state their difficulty and how they would like the matter dealt with. For example, 'I'm offended by what you have just said because ...'. If someone finds themselves very upset in a meeting and there is no opportunity to acknowledge this, that person might behave in unhelpful ways, perhaps by storming out of the meeting, or staying and undermining the process. Allowing them to voice their concern and feel heard is often all that is needed for that person to reintegrate into the group. The key is that the *group*, via the facilitator, decides whether this is a group issue that needs time within the meeting or suggests that the individuals work it out between themselves outside the meeting.

The red card has the next priority and is used to point out a process issue such as a breach of procedure, discussion going off-topic or over-time, or to make a group observation (e.g. 'it's getting heated in here, can we have a break?'). Next, people holding up orange cards are called upon to deliver their acknowledgement(s). Orange cards are an easy way to say, 'well said', 'I agree', or 'thanks for your work on this'.

After a question has been asked about the proposal using a yellow card, people raise green cards to provide clarification or information to help answer that question. Only after all questions have been answered does the facilitator call on those holding blue cards to state their comments and opinions. At times a lot of information comes out in the meeting through questions and answers before the blue cards are called, allowing people to quietly shift their position before stating their opinions and then perhaps feeling the need to defend them.

DECISION-MAKING MODE

After a period of discussion, the facilitator will check with the group whether people feel ready to decide. The proposal is then read by the minute taker, and each person chooses a card to indicate their level of support for the proposal as follows:

Green	I agree with the proposal as written.
Blue	I am neutral or basically for it, with some slight reservation.
Yellow	I have a question to be answered before I can make a decision.
Orange	I have a serious reservation, but I am not willing to block consensus.
Red	I will block consensus and I am willing to help find a collective solution.

If a yellow card is shown at this point it is dealt with by the discussion mode process outlined earlier, before all members are asked to show cards again. If orange or red cards are raised, people holding those cards are asked to briefly restate their concerns. Small amendments or clarifications may be made to the proposal to address concerns. A second show of cards then follows. On the second carding a proposal is passed unless one or more red cards are still being raised. The card counts of both cardings are noted in the minutes.

If consensus is not reached on the first or second carding, the proposal is sent back to the appropriate Focus Group for more work. The Focus Group will consider the opinions and any new information that has arisen in the Full Group meeting and may alter their proposal and bring it back to the Full Group.

In some cases, the Focus Group may still support the original proposal and choose to present it again with little or no change. In this case, if consensus is still not reached at a subsequent Full Group meeting, and the proposal is considered both important and urgent, we can decide to go to a vote. A third meeting is called, and all members notified of the impending vote. At this meeting the decision can be made by a 75% majority vote of people eligible to take part in the decision making. During the development phase of Earthsong, votes were by Full Members and in proportion to shareholding. This was important as some had a lot more financial risk than others, and there needs to be some relationship between risk and control.

We have voted only twice in more than twenty years of decision making at Earthsong. Both were at crucial times during development when the consequences of having the decision stopped or delayed would have been serious and potentially fatal to the project. The voting backstop has been important so that progress couldn't be stopped by a veto of one or two people, but our commitment has always been to work issues through to reach consensus if at all possible.

There are only two ways in which, once made, a decision may be revisited. Any member who is absent from a meeting has until the next meeting to request to revisit a decision made at that meeting. Otherwise a decision may be reopened only with agreement from at least 50% of members. This provision honours a member's right to have a say in issues they feel strongly about even when they were not able to be present at that meeting, but avoids the situation where decisions could be continually reopened unless it is clear that there is broad support from others to have another look at a particular issue.

We have found the coloured card system to be extremely useful in encouraging every member in the room to participate in discussion and decision making. Dominant personalities find it harder to push their ideas through at the expense of less vocal members, and less confident members find it helpful to be given a space to talk, rather than having to find their own gap in a robust discussion. The shades of meaning in the decision-making mode allow members to voice reservations while still allowing the proposal to proceed.

5. Information

Those who are involved in decision making need access to information in order to make informed decisions. The key is that all the information is available, not that everyone will read everything. In this information-rich world we are all learning to manage the overload and make individual choices about what to read and what to leave. To paraphrase Margaret Wheatley:

> The free flow of information is nourishment to a self-organising group.
>
> WHEATLEY (2006, P. 101)

Agendas for all Focus Group and Full Group meetings at Earthsong are emailed out to all members a day or two before the meeting, so everyone knows what is likely to be discussed and can attend if they choose. Key information is also sent out before the meeting, and background documents are available to all members on request. Full minutes of every meeting are emailed to all members after the meeting and stored on our intranet. In this way all the information is in the group domain and everyone makes their own choice about how much they read.

Over the years we have made many thousands of decisions. Creating a searchable decision log and keeping it up to date is extremely important. Every Focus Group should keep a log of policy decisions in their area, easily searched by all members of the community. We all need reminding at times, and it is uncomfortable for a new member to trip over an invisible policy decision made years before.

CONFLICT AND DISSENT

We value diversity, but working as a group of diverse and strong-minded people can be challenging. It is hard enough sometimes getting along with your own family members, let alone with thirty-one other households. Conflict and difference are part of the fabric of being in relationship and will always arrive in community. Conflict can be seen as the growing edge of relationships, and it's not comfortable. Part of the work of community is to acknowledge and attend to conflict and be willing to work it through rather than walk away firing shots from a distance. There are many social tools available to help with this. As Laird Schaub has said,

> One of the key challenges of cooperative living is learning how to work through issues where the stakes are high and people disagree, and doing that in a way that enhances relationships rather than degrades them.[6]

We all bring our histories, experience and beliefs with us, and unconscious dynamics can get enacted in the group. Our previous experience of groups is commonly in our family of origin, our schooling or our workplaces, and working as a group may bring up family dynamics, attitudes to power, authority and control, voice-lessness, anxiety or fears of which we aren't even conscious. Community can be a mirror, forcing us all to look more closely at our own behaviour patterns.

At Earthsong we don't have one agreed conflict-resolution process; rather we have a kete (basket) of possible processes to move issues forward. Commitment to the shared vision helps to keep things in perspective and knowing that you are neighbours and unlikely to be able to avoid each other for long is a good incentive to sort things out. The Communication Agreements and Decision-Making Processes provide stable ground to the relationships between neighbours and help to keep things clear.

Residents who find themselves in conflict are encouraged to sort it out between them, perhaps by asking a neighbour to sit with them while they talk it through to help create a safe environment for both. Sometimes the conflict presents as an individual or interpersonal issue but has wider implications for the group. As a group we have sometimes paid for an outside mediator to work with two or three people who held crucial roles in the development, and who got into conflict because of those roles.

In a well-functioning group, individual members pay attention to and care about the collective entity as well as individuals within it. Splitting off into subgroups can happen especially as the group gets larger, which fragments the energy and can become oppositional. Attention is needed to the whole-group dynamics.

> Don't hide your perspective, but also don't dominate with it; you have only one piece of the truth, and it takes all pieces to make the whole. Give away your ideas to the group, don't 'lobby' them. SANDELIN (1998, P. 11)

Blocks and vetoes

In our society, dissenting voices are often given more attention and more power than positive voices. In a meeting, even when several people speak passionately and articulately for a certain proposal, one person speaking passionately against the proposal can sometimes disproportionately affect the decision. It is often harder to start than to stop something, and we need to pay attention to this dynamic.

In the coloured card system, a red card is a 'no' card, but it is important to clarify exactly what kind of 'no' it is. The exact wording is important, and so is the underlying cultural understanding within the group. Saying 'no' to a proposal, after there has been full exploration and discussion working towards consensus of the group, is a significant act. Many users of the coloured card system believe that each person should use the red card only two or three times in their lifetime, for issues that are life-threatening to the project.

During Earthsong's development and construction, the wording on the red card was 'I am entirely *against the proposal and will block consensus*'. Because the goal of the group was to complete the project, there was an implicit expectation that people who use a red card would keep working to find a way forward. There was also an unwritten understanding that the red card meant, 'I believe this is not in the best interests of the project'.

There has been a gradual shift over the years towards some members using the red card to say, 'I personally don't want this', and not being willing to keep working to find a way forward. It is important to respect the 'no' and give space to that opinion; they might hold a piece of the truth that others haven't seen yet. It is also important to respect the 'yes's', and for anyone who blocks to put effort into finding a way forward. We have been trialling the wording: *'I will block consensus and I am willing to help find a collective solution'*, but this has been resisted by some and we are still working towards a resolution.

Red-carding a decision and not being willing to help find a solution is essentially a veto, which is not compatible with consensus. In my opinion it is not appropriate that one or two members hold more power in the community than others by saying 'no' without proposing other viable solutions to meet the needs of all. If an issue is important enough for someone to red-card a decision that others in the group agree with, then that person or people must prioritise time and energy to work it through. If they are not willing to do that, it is respectful of the whole group to step aside and agree not to impede implementation.

N Street Cohousing in Sacramento, USA has used the following method successfully for twenty-five years, and other cohousing groups have adopted it:

> If no one blocks, the proposal passes.
>
> If one or more people block the proposal, they must meet with small groups of other members, including some of those who supported the proposal, in a series of solution-oriented, consensus-building meetings. Their job is to think through the issues and mutually agree on a new proposal that addresses the same problem as the blocked proposal. The person(s) blocking are responsible for organising the meetings. If a new mutually agreed proposal is created, it goes back to the whole group for approval. If the meetings don't happen, or those at the meetings can't come up with a mutually-agreed-on new proposal within up to 6 meetings in up to 3 months, the original proposal goes back to the Full Group, and can be passed with a 75% majority of those present.
>
> In practise this method has been effective partly because people think hard about whether the issue is worth all the extra work of opposing it. In the few cases when proposals have been blocked, the issues were resolved informally with a 'let's-try-it' approach, or took a maximum of 2 meetings to come up with a new proposal that all could support. This method respects both the supporters and the opposers of a proposal, within the overriding goal of finding agreement that all can live with. It balances power with responsibility to the group.[7]

ONGOING GOVERNANCE

Consciously created, high-functioning neighborhoods ... cannot be reproduced today in a haphazard fashion. It has to be forged, crafted really, and then maintained.   MCCAMANT AND DURETT (2011, P. 57)

Over the years since the development of Earthsong was completed, many residents have moved on and new people have arrived. People move to Earthsong because they see it as a desirable place to live, not necessarily because they share a vision of working together for social and environmental sustainability. There are now only a handful of people still living at Earthsong who were involved in the visioning, planning and construction phases. How do we maintain and grow the sense of connection, belonging and agency, as residents change? How does a community keep inclusive governance functioning well, within the dominant wider culture that favours separation and individuality? This is a common issue for communities as the generations change.

Just as the earth can be understood as a complex living organism or Gaia, we can see a community as a living entity. Have the conversations: who is this collective being that we are all part of, and who do we want to be? Maintain that deep sense of belonging to and caring about the wellbeing of the whole group. Relationships within the community need to be built and maintained, or decision making will revert to being simply a management system for shared resources and facilities.

Being in community is the willingness to be in relationship with others, to support and be accountable. It is not Utopia – community isn't easy! The sense of community and the cohesion of the group cannot be taken for granted but require ongoing attention and effort; much like a garden. The soil needs to be nurtured with nourishing relationships and satisfying group endeavours. New ideas need to be planted, and the fruit of previous effort harvested and appreciated. Weeds will surely grow and must be attended to and cleared sufficiently to allow the desired plants to thrive.

Ongoing management of shared facilities does require time and effort to understand one another and reach agreement, and as with any group of people, there are occasional interpersonal challenges that have to be worked through. While this can be uncomfortable and time-consuming, it is part of learning to interact with and respect one another. Learning to work together and make decisions for the common good is both challenging and hugely valuable in helping us rebuild interdependence in our individualistic world. The processes we have developed at Earthsong for working together over twenty years and more have been fundamental to the success of our development and continue to enrich our ongoing community life.

KEY GOVERNANCE LEARNINGS

- Effective community governance sits on a stable foundation of relationship agreements, is supported by a clear structure of procedures and thrives within the context of an agreed vision.
- Careful and thorough 'buddying' of new members is crucial through the development stage. It remains crucial into the future as houses change hands because the underlying values and agreements become less visible over time unless care is taken to keep them current.
- Maintain a library of relevant policy documents, easily searchable by all members.
- Some strategies for moving forward on an issue if consensus is difficult:
  - Work to get agreement on the overall intent before attempting the specifics, e.g. agreement that we want more shade on the common green, before proposing where or what.
  - Break the decision down into smaller pieces and build up agreement on the areas that you can.
  - Build in a sunset clause to try something out, e.g. 'we agree to try this for one year and will then review it'.
  - Convene meetings of those who feel strongly about the issue from different points of view, tasked with finding a way forward. If they can do it, it is likely that the rest of the group will agree.
  - If an issue seems to be stuck, there are often underlying issues that need to be resolved before agreement can be reached. Anything that we can each do to more fully understand our own motivations and assumptions will help the group process.
  - An individual or the group may need skilled help from outside.
  - It just might mean more time is needed for all to be heard. See Appendix 3 for other processes that can help to move an issue forward.

IT'S ALL ON! BECOMING DEVELOPERS

6

STORY

We'd thought we'd been busy before, but now the project went into overdrive. With five individuals or couples having invested significant money to pay the deposit, we were straight into serious planning and time pressure. We had eight months to settle the purchase of the land, and in that time we planned to do our design process, apply for Resource Consent and finish the construction drawings so we could begin construction in March 2000.

The selection and hiring of the architect was the first priority. I was committed to the group choosing our architect on merit, though I expected them to recognise and value the unique opportunity that designing from within the group would give us. I suggested the process we should use: invite architects to a briefing meeting, ask for written offers of services, shortlist the most likely firms, interview them, visit some of their buildings and have presentations to the group. I named all the architects I felt would be most suitable (and my strongest competitors) and brought to the group's attention various articles from the cohousing world that addressed the advantages and disadvantages of in-group professionals. I wanted to make the selection as fair as possible for the other architects, and to give space to the group to make the decision.

I had expected to be excluded from the final discussions and decision making. But as the only architect, and indeed the only member of the group with any building-industry experience, I had expected to be involved at least in the shortlisting. If another architect was chosen, I knew it was likely to be I who would interact most intensively with him/her, and it was crucial that I felt able to work with the person selected.

The group decided this was not the way they wanted it. There was discomfort from some members that I was one of the contenders, particularly in the Site and Design Task Group, and particularly from Peter who played a leadership role in the architect selection process. It emerged later, as part of the group processing of this time that we called 'The Long Story', that several members of Site and Design had decided, even before we started the selection process, that they didn't want to employ anyone from within the group.

> I personally had made a stand seeing in-group professionals as too hard, thinking that neither I nor the group had the resources emotionally to deal with it.

> My gut feeling was that we would be opening a nest full of vipers if we went with in-group professionals, so I personally made up my mind early in the piece.
>
> TWO COMMENTS FROM 'THE LONG STORY'

It was clear that Site and Design wanted to exclude me completely from the architect selection process, and while not feeling personally that such secrecy was necessary to conduct a fair and respectful process, I accepted the group's wish. In effect I was excluded and isolated from the whole group for the three-week period of this process, unable to participate in any other decisions around the project at that crucial time.

> I did clearly say it was OK to exclude me at this point. I see now I was trying so hard to make it comfortable for everyone else I didn't look after myself and state clearly what would work best for me. I was surprised to be excluded from so much. It was very lonely, but I trusted the group.   ROBIN, IN 'THE LONG STORY'

I can see now that it was too hard for me to disengage completely and become just one of several possible candidates. I didn't have that relationship with the project.

I'd carried the vision for so long in my heart and soul, I couldn't just put it down and step away. So, because we hadn't worked out any other way of doing it, the group felt they had to shut me out, in order to carry out an 'arm's length', 'objective' process.

Rick and I sorted out our background agreements and put our application together. Members of Site and Design assessed the applications and shortlisted four architects or partnerships, including Rick and me. They interviewed us and visited examples of our work, wrote information summaries and scheduled our presentations to the whole group. Rick and I were scheduled as the first presenters, with the other three shortlisted architects to follow on succeeding evenings.

I spent the weekend before our presentation at a retreat centre at Piha, a wild, black-sand, west coast beach near Auckland, grounding myself, facing into my fears and reconnecting with the source of my passion for the project – my intense love for and connection with this planet. I enacted a profound private ritual where I placed myself in the hands of Gaia.

> I release this project into your loving hands, mother Gaia.
> Nurture and sustain our community.
> I dedicate my life to you.
> Direct me and sustain me in ways that will serve you best.[1]

Rick and I gave our presentation to the group on Monday night, 26 April 1999. I wore a bowler hat as my 'architect's hat'. At the end I took the hat off and spoke as a group member, saying that my top priority was what was in the best interests of the project. The vision, shape and values of the project to date intrinsically described my agenda as an architect. I spoke about my belief in the synergy of the client–architect collaboration and compared my possible role as both a group member and an architect to the permaculture notion of 'edge', the fertile place most conducive to abundance and creativity than either state on its own.

I knew some members might see it as a breach of boundaries to step out of the role of 'architect pitching for a job' into speaking as a group member. I felt it was important to acknowledge that I *was* a group member so we could talk about it, rather than ignoring that reality and pushing it underground. I'd put a lot of thought into the more difficult issues we might face if I was the architect and gave the group a paper I had written on ideas to manage the situation.

Our session went well, but I was starting to feel very anxious. I was in a very different situation to the other architects – to them it was a job and they would walk away if they didn't get it; but whatever the outcome, I would continue in the group and if another architect were chosen, would very likely be the one who would liaise with him/her. After our presentation I realised how helpful it would be for me to hear the others, so that if another was chosen, I would have a better understanding of what they offered and why they were chosen. With encouragement from a friend, I sent an email to the group that night requesting that I be allowed to sit at the back and listen to the other presentations, without interacting or asking questions. Having already given my presentation, I didn't feel this could possibly advantage me.

What I had thought was an innocent request caused a furore in the group, taking the lid off the unexpressed resistance from some to my applying for the role. One member phoned and accused me of being dishonourable and breaking agreements; but as I'd been excluded from all meetings and minutes of meetings, I hadn't known that Site and Design had specifically decided against this. It obviously wasn't general knowledge in the wider group either, as other members understood my reasons for asking and felt it was a reasonable request.

It was my worst nightmare – that previously undeclared strong feelings in the group were suddenly erupting in the middle of the selection process, and that it would taint the whole process. It was excruciatingly painful to be silenced and out of communication at that time. I felt completely disempowered and isolated from the project that had been my soul child for so many years. It was one of the most terrible times of my life.

I was in agony that week. I knew there was huge conflict going on in the group and that a lot of it was concerning me, but I wasn't being included in the discussion or the emails to know what was being said, and therefore was unable to respond. And all of this was happening directly before a huge momentous decision by the group, *huge* for the project, and *huge* for me personally.

One of the reasons I've worked so hard on this project is that I really want and need community in my life. I found myself excluded from my community at a time when it was going through probably the most significant time in its history; and not only that, but I felt I was the subject/recipient of a lot of anger and bad feeling from the group. This was my community that meant so much to me, and I was alone again and feeling devastated. I don't think I've ever felt so lonely.   ROBIN, IN 'THE LONG STORY'

Conflict, accusations and hurt bounced around in the group for the rest of the week. Site and Design came under fire for withholding information from the Full Group and felt betrayed because they were working so hard to keep the boundaries clear. One member urged others to 'impute good intent', a phrase that has been in our lexicon ever since. Some people realised a little of how isolated I'd become and sent me loving emails. But now that I was temporarily out of the group, there was a power struggle going on.

I was picking up some strong energy from the Site Task Group – which I **now** hear Peter explaining as the Task Group taking on very seriously the 'job' to hold the boundaries between Robin as Architect and the rest of the group – increased – as Peter explains it – because he saw that Robin wasn't doing her part of that job. I picked up the 'tight holding' energy – didn't know what the Task Group was rightly holding onto, and read it like 'Trust us, we'll do it **our** way!'

The transition of power within the Site and Design Task Group had both positive and negative effects. It seems that when Robin left, the ball landed in their court, they grabbed it and ran with it – brilliantly; and gave the whole group the best week's theatre we've seen all year. The negative was the total exclusion of Robin. Was this necessary? Could the group have been even more brilliant than they were if Robin had been included? We will never know. Maybe it was Robin's gift to the group to be excluded in order that others may shine.

TWO COMMENTS FROM 'THE LONG STORY'

I feel the group pushed the boundaries so far out for their own comfort that it really disempowered me. There was such an emphasis on not advantaging me in any way that I ended up being disadvantaged. The fact that I was a group member was seen as a major threat to the selection process. However, any acknowledgement that I was a group member, allowing me access to information that wouldn't have advantaged me but would have kept me a little more connected, was withheld. Instead of being both architect and group member, I was neither.

During this three-week process I was acutely aware that the group was making a decision that would determine the direction of my life, at least for the next few years. It felt like having my baby forcibly put up for adoption. I'd gestated and birthed this baby and been a devoted mother for four years. I knew I loved this child deeply and fiercely, but I'd given my soul baby into the hands of others to decide if there was a parent better qualified to care for it than I was.

The Full Group meeting to choose the architect was held ten days after Rick's and my presentation. I heard later that this was a very emotionally charged meeting. Site and Design had devised an Evaluation Chart to objectively assess each of the shortlisted architects for a range of attributes. Peter, who had previously declared strong reservations about employing in-house professionals, held the pen that recorded the responses of the group. One of these attributes, called 'Professional Boundaries', became a lightning rod for all the unexpressed feelings about both in-group professionals and me in that role, and conflict erupted in the group.

At the end of this process an indicative carding showed that architect Bill Algie had more support than others and a proposal was put to the group to appoint Bill as the architect. This was red-carded by one member who was distressed at the attacks, accusations and unnamed strong feelings. Another meeting was held on Saturday night two days later with a sharing process that allowed space for the expression of strong emotions, after which the group passed the proposal to appoint Bill.

There was a small delegation of members at my door on Sunday morning. I took one look at their glum faces and turned away inside, shocked. This wasn't possible. Even with all the doubt and fear and waiting, on some level I'd still believed the group would recognise that I was the natural choice for architect. Shock, disbelief, then grief, then anger rocked through my body. I created this job, from nothing!! I'd lived and breathed this project for years to get to this point, the juicy, creative, design stage. The fire in my belly all those years was because I *was* an architect, it's what I loved doing, my skills and training, and I'd put all my fire and passion into creating this job. How could they give that to someone else?

The members stayed for an hour or two, trying to be caring, but I just wanted them gone. My parents came over and sat on my couch, knowing how badly disappointed I felt but at a loss themselves. My architect dad said, 'They have no idea what is involved in designing and developing such a project, they just think it's a grand adventure.' I felt the group had no idea of the depth of the emotional holding required, let alone the tasks of the architect.

I spent a couple of days on Waiheke Island near Auckland being looked after by two friends, who held me while I cried, cooked me lovely food, were outraged on my behalf. We went for a long walk on Onetangi Beach on a warm still day. I submerged myself in the calm clear waters of Gaia and felt a little replenished.

A huge gulf had opened between the group and me. They had all been on an enormous journey together and had grown and changed through that process. I'd been on my own huge painful journey, but I'd been alone. That was what hurt the most, that I'd been shut out of the group, my community that I'd worked so hard to nurture. I didn't know where I stood with many of the group; I didn't know where my place was any more.

I wrote a long letter to the group, angry that they were still withholding all information about the process. The climate of secrecy and withholding was so alien to what I had thought was our group culture. I desperately needed access to the other architects' presentation material, to the notes, minutes, charts and emails that had been withheld from me for those few weeks, to walk in their footsteps so I could come to some understanding of what had happened and why Bill had been chosen.

I went to the Full Group meeting five days later feeling even angrier. The lack of access to records or information continued to isolate and exclude me. Every day of delay was painful. For them it was over, they'd got a result and were exhausted. They didn't realise how badly I needed to know WHY? This was not just a job I didn't get. This was my life.

> To still be denied information about the selection process, the other architects, and Bill in particular, for five more days felt like callous torture, and demonstrated to me the degree to which the group had lost sight of my humanity.
>
> ROBIN, IN 'THE LONG STORY'

It was six days after the decision before I got access to some of this information. There are some things that I've never seen, such as the applications and presentation material of the other architects. I asked people to tell me their perspective of what happened, and very few did.

When I did see the information sheet on Rick and myself collated by Site and Design, it contained some confusing comments: on the one hand I was seen as 'too rigid about solar access', and on the other as 'too willing to compromise'. It appeared that the group saw the feasibility concept I had done earlier as an indication of what I would design as the architect. I had stressed at the time that it was a diagram, not a design, based on very preliminary group thinking about site layout and house requirements, and done in an impossibly short time frame.

The Evaluation Chart written up by the group in the final selection process seemed to me deeply flawed. Several aspects listed in our criteria for architects, such as experience of designing lower cost buildings or a track record of projects on time and on budget, were missing from this chart. Despite the facts that Rick and I both had track records as green architects and both had taught environmental design to architecture students, we didn't get any 'green circle' recognition for environmental design. Our fee estimate was very similar to Bill's, but he got a green circle and we did not. His buildings, while beautiful, were not low cost. And we had been clear at the start of the process that our very large and complex project was too big for a sole practitioner.

But despite the 'objective' Evaluation Chart, my impression was that the decision was made on gut feel. One member said that Bill felt to him like a benign father figure. Another member who had joined the group only weeks earlier said that the quality of light in one of his buildings had made her cry. I believe that, in the end, most decisions – even if there is a rational evaluation process – are made on intuition and emotions, and I don't disagree with that. More honesty about that would have made it easier for me.

The biggest disconnection between my experience and the group's experience was that I put myself forward as the architect because I was ready to give everything I had to make our project happen. It was the logical progression from envisioning and guiding the project to that stage, and my contribution to a more sustainable planet.

For the group, the process of choosing the architect deliberately separated them from that awareness. They discounted that commitment, assessed my skills as though I were just another architect pitching for the job, and then overlaid the assessment with doubts and anxiety about power struggles and how difficult it might be. They struggled with the issues and tried to be rational and objective, when the driving energy of our project was so much more about heart and spirit.

In retrospect I feel that if the group members had been willing to really talk with one another and with me, we may together have reached a similar conclusion: that given the composition of the group and the complexity of the project, the most useful role I could play was to be the coordinator, driver and champion of the vision, working together with an outside architect. And there may have been other creative possibilities, various levels of collaboration that might have emerged if I had been included in thinking it through. A challenging and difficult task perhaps, but this was a challenging project, and we needed to use *all* our skills and goodwill to navigate it. They grabbed it off me rather than being willing to work it out together.

We had a few clearings, a facilitated Full Group meeting, another clearing at a Site and Design meeting. Over the next couple of months some of us met several times to talk about what happened and record our insights on a long roll of paper we called 'The Long Story'. A level of understanding was reached, but I had a huge rock in my belly. My beliefs in my place in the world were shaken to the core. Did I make such a big mistake, thinking this was my life path? Where was my path now?

The pace of development moved into high gear immediately after the architect decision, as we felt intense pressure to meet our development programme. I went through the motions of participating, trying to find my place again, though conflict continued to play out in the group over the next year. Some members were surprised that I remained in the group and saw the courage that took; but this was my soul child, I couldn't just walk away. I did feel love and support from many people. What a relief, that they saw my good-heartedness, and weren't misinterpreting my motives!

Site and Design, largely led by Peter and me, moved immediately into leading the process to formulate and agree on the Design Brief so the architect could start work. We scheduled four full weekend hui every second weekend through June and July to brainstorm, discuss and prioritise our site, common-house and private-house design criteria. Cathy and another member were leading the parallel process of refining our legal agreements for the Cohousing Agreement.

The Design Brief coming together

Within a couple of weeks, the group realised that because we now had an architect from outside the group, we needed someone from inside the group to be the key contact and liaison person with him and all our other outside professionals. The developer, who had advised us on the feasibility process to assess the site before we bought the land, gave strong advice that a project of this size needed a full-time driver, someone with skills in the building industry who lived and breathed the project, and lay awake at night thinking and planning. He had been in the development business for twenty years, and he told us he worked full-time seven days a week with two or three others when doing a project of the scale of ours.

Both he and the architect strongly advised, for a project of our size and complexity, that we have one project coordinator from within the group working full-time to keep the overview, from now to the end of construction. The developer had confidence that we could manage this on our own, be our own development company, and buy in any of the skills we couldn't cover ourselves. He strongly endorsed my skills as being ideal for the role of project coordinator.

I was able and willing to take on the role, and no less determined to do what I could to make the project happen. Meetings were held to discuss the employment of in-house professionals. Many could see the value and necessity for this, providing that clear parameters were agreed, but some remained opposed to any group member being paid to do work for the project. The group eventually agreed, in June 1999, to take me on as Development Coordinator (DC) for up to twenty hours per week at $30 per hour. Though this was less than half my charge-out rate as an architect at that time, I wound down my private architectural practice so I could concentrate on the task.

The Development Team (DT) was set up to work with me, with representatives from each of the other task groups. I felt under siege from Peter for several months in DT meetings as he had not supported my being paid. He eventually realised he could only support me in my role if he were also paid, so he presented the group with a suggested job description and pay rate for himself as my deputy.

After some reassessment of what was needed to get the project moving through this phase, the paid positions were expanded and divided among three people. Cathy, who had previously worked as a legal executive and was now a landscape gardener, became the Legal and Landscaping Coordinator at 6 hours per week. Peter, at that time a Planning student at university, became Planning Coordinator at 3¾ hours per week to lead us through the Resource Consent process. My role as Development Coordinator was reduced to 15¼ hours per week, with responsibility for the overall coordination of development and specifically design and budgets. An Employment Team was established to oversee the contracts and employment of paid members.

One of the conditions stipulated by the group was that we three put in detailed timesheets every two weeks to justify our pay. For the first few months our timesheets were studied in detail by some members and sometimes challenged, but as time went on and people saw the amount of work, skill and dedication we brought to our roles, a higher level of trust was achieved. With this structure in place, things settled down between us and we worked well as a team for the next couple of years.

My work as DC rapidly gained speed until I was doing sixty-hour weeks (paid and unpaid) through the second half of 1999. I developed the project timeline; liaised with our architect Bill Algie over the initial design of the site layout, common house, and unit types; researched and interviewed project managers. We established a Green Team of members to research eco-building materials and to work with Bill on eco-design. The Full Group started meeting every two weeks in the Avondale Church hall, our meeting home for the next couple of years. Weekend hui were held at the tertiary institution Unitec, thanks to Cathy's contacts in the Landscape department.

We'd been advised that banks would lend us money for construction only if we had professional project managers involved, so after research and deliberation, in August DT proposed to the Full Group that we engage Promanco Kenman (Auckland) Limited (PKA) as our project managers. Our newest member at the time thought this was a bad idea, and, without participating in the discussion or proposing a

Site planning with architect Bill Algie

viable alternative beforehand, red-carded the proposal. There was a lot of anger and frustration by other members who saw him as abusing the consensus process and effectively trying to veto. With the huge pressure to maintain progress, this proposal was eventually passed by a vote at a later meeting, the first of only two occasions to date when the group has resorted to voting rather than consensus to make a decision. Soon after this we decided to halt new memberships for the rest of the year, so that a stable group could coalesce for this critical design phase leading to applying for Resource Consent.

By September we were well into sketch design; were finalising contracts with town planners, water engineers, project managers, and the structural engineer; and were on target to apply for Resource Consent by 21 December. An enormous amount of work from the three coordinators was going into research and decisions around building design, materials, on-site services and costs, continuing legal complexities, and finances. Pressure was building and, in addition to the work being done by us three in our working weeks, all members including us attended many evening meetings and the day-long hui every second weekend that we scheduled to the end of the year.

The development budget was of increasing concern to group members, and anxiety about this added to other ongoing disagreements, in particular about unit types and numbers. As the site planning evolved, house numbers rose from the twenty-six we originally envisaged, to thirty and, finally, to thirty-two. Adding more units helped with the overall development budget, allowed more diversity in unit sizes, and still created the balance we wanted between private and common space.

Another conflict arose over the existence of 'ley lines', lines of electromagnetic energy or geopathic stress, considered by some as important and by others as 'pseudoscience'. We had engaged an expert in diagnosing ley lines who identified that they crossed our land in several places. Some members were adamant that they wanted the placement of buildings to avoid these lines, while others were truly upset that they could be taken seriously. As it turned out, it was possible to adjust the position of all buildings to miss these lines without compromising the site plan, so this was what we did.

In September I sold my house so I could contribute the money to settling the land purchase. I used some of it to fund a trip to the USA to attend the biennial cohousing conference near Boston. It was a wonderful three weeks mixing with other people passionate about cohousing, visiting many cohousing neighbourhoods, eating in

Weekend hui to consider the design

their common houses, and replenishing my belief that this really was a good idea and worth all the effort and pain to get there.

I returned in time to be part of the signing of the Cohousing Agreement, our major legal document, on 18 October 1999. Twenty-eight members signed, committing to lend various amounts of money to our company Cohousing New Zealand Ltd (CNZL) in order to complete the purchase of the land, pay for the upfront development costs and contribute enough equity to CNZL that we could later obtain a bank loan for construction. This agreement signified major emotional and financial commitments to the project and ensured that we could proceed together with confidence.

By late October the site planning was firming up, and the architect Bill had introduced the central planning theme of a figure-of-8 path, which met with immediate acceptance. He arranged the houses around this path so that all front doors opened off it, giving an intense feeling of community connection but with many houses joined on their north sides to their neighbours, compromising solar gain and giving awkward private outdoor spaces. Determined that we could have *both* north orientation for passive solar design *and* good community-scale clusters,

I redrew the site plan with secondary paths off the main figure-of-8 path to make this possible. Site and Design accepted this plan with enthusiasm; it was passed on to Bill and became our basic site layout.

This process happened several times with both the site and house planning. Because I was part of the group and immersed in cohousing, I became a channel for expressing what we wanted on paper to give to Bill. My skills were particularly in the layout and planning, while Bill brought a lovely feel for shape, materials and detailing, so together it became a good collaboration. Throughout the design process, however, for my own safety after the trauma of the selection process, I was very careful to minimise the visibility of my input, ensuring that Site and Design took full ownership for any instructions I passed on to the architect.

The bruising pace continued in November. We were lining up all the money from individual members for settlement, getting ready to take over the site, finalising concept plans for Resource Consent, planning, strategising, liaising, finalising budgets, attending many meetings and hui. We had commissioned a water report from engineers to propose an on-site wastewater treatment system for our site. This was presented to the regional water body Watercare, which informed us it would oppose our plan. With the extreme time pressure we were under, we decided not to pursue that part of our sustainable design at that time, but made sure we built in the possibility of doing it later.

I was packing up my home ready to move into the old house on our land. We had begun calling it 'Tūī House', after the art deco tūī (indigenous songbird) design sandblasted on the glass front door. I had been studying for the Building Biology and Ecology[2] diploma for the previous eighteen months and had my final exam in November, presenting my research project for the diploma, which was of course Waitakere Eco-Neighbourhood Cohousing Project.

On 26 November 1999 we settled the site purchase and the land finally became ours. We had a party in the concrete garage, with a cake made by new member Chris Free in the shape of the land, with all the buildings and fruit trees showing in their proper places. We danced a bit and talked about how it would be; we were exhilarated but exhausted.

I left my clean, white house in Pt Chevalier and moved into shabby and mouldy Tūī House. Another member, Robin L, moved into the smaller Bee Cottage, so named by us because of the wild bees that lived in a hive in the kitchen cupboard and out under the eaves. Three weeks later I packed up the architectural office I still had in

Site settlement party

Grey Lynn and moved that, too, into Tūī House. I was seriously overstressed, verging on undernourished, and desperately exhausted. I was working sixty-hour weeks for Earthsong (paid and unpaid), and trying to spend some time with my kids (then aged twelve and seventeen), with no other adult at home to keep things going, make the dinners, talk things through or lean on when things were tough.

There was support from some members. Bruce painted inside Tūī House to cover the shabbiness before I moved in. Geraldine helped me pack, and Mary helped me clean my Pt Chevalier house. Cathy was working hard on the details of the settlement. Rose, who had moved into a neighbouring house in Ranui, began bringing dinner once or twice a week for my boys and me, a truly wonderful act of support.

After ongoing conflict for most of the year, we finally agreed on the house types and numbers for the site plan and lodged the Resource Consent application just before Christmas. Several members set up tents amongst the trees after Christmas, spending more gentle time with one another and starting to learn the land. One member, Bryan Pulham, mowed the route of the main figure-of-8 path through the trees, and from that moment the land carried both shapes, the old shape of the orchard and the coming shape of the village. We established a fire pit on the future common green with large rocks from the local quarry, and spent evenings talking, yarning and laughing. Together we saw in the new millennium.

COMMUNITY DESIGN

The buildings are the picture frame, the people and the life between the buildings are the picture

CHARLES DURETT, 2019, PERSONAL EMAIL

Picture a common scenario: you need to buy some groceries. You get into your car within your private dwelling or yard and drive to a supermarket or shopping mall. You see few people you recognise, and even if you do, there is little opportunity to interact with them, and no control of the environment beyond your front door or gate.

Picture another scenario: you step out of your private dwelling and walk through gardens, play areas and open space that you share with your closest neighbours, whom you know well. You walk to the nearby shops, encountering other local residents on the way. There are wide footpaths and areas of seating, places to rest and watch the world go by, to be people rather than just consumers.

For most of us, buildings and urban space are just the background to our lives, and we have little influence on the shape of the buildings or towns within which we live. Yet our built environment fundamentally shapes our lives as individuals and as a society.

Most architecture and urban planning assumes households are completely unrelated to their neighbours except by proximity. While it serves the consumer culture to separate households from each other and from shops, schools and

Outdoor seating by Ranui Library

workplaces, it doesn't serve us socially or work well environmentally. Each household operates as an independent unit, leaving many people living without the support they really need, including single people, young families, older people and others less able to be 'independent' for whatever reason. Isolation and loss of community encourage consumerism and consumption, and excessive consumption is a root cause of environmental degradation.

Those who have explored parts of the world where villages and towns evolved over centuries before the private car have experienced the very different shape and layout between the houses, and the different quality of life and relationships between people that this allows.

We live in a time of enormous change, and there is growing awareness that the world is finite and the environmental cost of how we live is too great. Socially things are changing too. In many countries there is a rise in single-person and single-parent households, an ageing population, and much greater diversity of lifestyles and ethnic backgrounds than ever before.

It's time to rethink the shapes of flourishing human settlement. Let's envision and build other forms of housing and neighbourhood that more closely match the lives we want.

DESIGNS THAT FACILITATE COMMUNITY

Architecture cannot create or destroy community; but it can provide a context within which community can flourish, or it can seriously hinder community interconnectedness among neighbours.

When cohousing groups design their own neighbourhoods, the buildings and site layouts arise from the social structures and values they aspire to. The architecture of cohousing focuses on the relationships between a group of homes, supporting and generating life between them, and adding another layer of home between the individual household and the public realm.

There are many design elements that affect our relationships with one another, affect how easy it is to interact or be separate, and whether we feel powerless or in control of our home environment. The design elements that, in my experience, facilitate and contribute to a healthy community life are described here. Some are obvious, such as shared facilities or shared open space. Many are more subtle – aspects of size, distance, shape and layers. Interestingly, many of these design elements have both community and environmental benefits.

I mostly refer to 'dwellings' or 'homes'; sometimes 'houses', 'units' or 'apartments'. While each of these names evokes a different type of habitation, most of these design elements can be applied to the full range of dwelling types from separate houses to high-rise apartments and high-density living.

People-oriented design

Cars are very useful tools, but should we prioritise the needs of cars when we design our living environments? If we place a higher value on our relationships with each other than on our relationships with our cars, the layout of a neighbourhood can look very different.

Carparks placed near the entrance to the neighbourhood, close enough to dwellings for convenience and security but not amongst the houses, ensure that people walk through community space to their individual homes.

Pedestrian pathways from the carparks to the homes become key connectors and social space for interaction with neighbours. The car-free environment allows safe play in almost all areas of the neighbourhood. The occasional inconvenience of rain or having goods to carry

Carparks near the entrance

The main thoroughfare at Earthsong

between home and car is, in our experience at Earthsong, more than offset by the benefits every day of having a peaceful, safe and attractive living space around the houses. Natural sounds, the smells of foliage and flowers, picking fruit on your way home, the beauty of trees and gardens, reduction in stress ... every aspect of our sensory environment is enhanced when cars are kept away from our homes.

Wheelchair-accessible pathways with a hard, even surface and gentle gradient make moving around the neighbourhood easy for both pedestrians and wheeled devices. Everyone uses wheels for mobility in many ways over their lifetimes, whether in a baby buggy, on a bike or skateboard, with a walking frame or in a wheelchair; not to mention the many types of wheeled trolleys and carts that make shifting anything easy, including a piano or heavy furniture.

Shared facilities

A common house with a large community kitchen, dining area and gathering space forms the heart of cohousing communities. It is a space large enough for the community to gather for meetings and celebrations, and to eat together on a regular basis. Other shared facilities often included are a laundry, children's playroom, guest room/s for occasional visitors, gym or office space.

The key to weaving the common house into daily life is to place it at the focal point or the movement hub of the site, where people pass by or through on their way home. Include reasons for residents to use the common house daily, such as checking their mail or using the laundry, to provide many opportunities for spontaneous interactions. The common house is 'home' to all residents and complements the individual homes, and all residents get access to a range of facilities that no single household needs to provide for itself.

Formal and informal gathering spaces around the neighbourhood, such as gardens, open space and children's play areas, give multiple opportunities for casual inter-action with neighbours, all of which builds community cohesion.

Other shared facilities such as a well-stocked wood-working workshop, a pool or sauna, can be much more achievable when their cost and management are spread among a group of households.

Dwellings within community

Clusters of dwellings accessed from smaller nodes of common space within the larger neighbourhood encourage a sense of belonging and identity with the closest neighbours.

Compact self-contained dwellings can be smaller than normal because of the shared facilities, but still have a full kitchen, bathroom, bedrooms, living space – everything a household needs for a comfortable private life.

A range of dwelling types and sizes accommodates diverse household needs, including units that are fully accessible for older people or those on wheels. While supporting diversity, this also allows households to move between units to up-size or down-size as required, while still remaining part of the same neighbourhood. At Earthsong we built seven ground-level dwellings of one or two bedrooms and designed even two-storey houses with wheelchair-accessible front door thresholds, so that all homes can be visited by everyone.

Fronts and backs. Every house has a community side, with entrance off the path and kitchen overlooking the path, and a more private side with living space opening to a private garden or terrace. Residents can choose how much interaction or privacy they want at any time.

Individuality within overall coherence. Standardisation of materials and design reduces costs and gives overall coherence to the neighbourhood, with the palette of materials and shapes used in different ways to give variety. Households can express their own individuality over time.

Individuality within coherence

Human scale

This includes both physical scale (size and distance) and emotional scale (numbers of people).

Height of buildings. Consider the human experience of height, both for those inside a building and for those on the ground. For most able-bodied people, two or three flights of stairs are still comfortable; any higher gets increasingly difficult. For older or less able people, ground-floor homes or mechanical lifts to upper-level apartments are often required. Up to the second or third storey, a parent inside can still observe their children playing outside; it is even possible to lean out of the window to have a conversation with a neighbour on the path.

Beyond the third floor it becomes much harder to interact with people or the environment outside. For those on the ground, depending how close the building is and how engaging or rebutting the architecture, any more than three or four storeys can feel oppressive and overwhelming.

Space between houses. Notice what feels comfortable when looking towards another's home or being inside with others moving past outside. The space between homes, and between the home and a thoroughfare, strongly affects both privacy and engagement. Individual free-standing houses with windows looking sideways into the neighbouring house need more space around them for privacy than do attached houses. So long as there is good acoustic insulation in the party wall, attached houses can feel much more private than free-standing houses, because all windows look front and back rather than sideways. Privacy is directional, as well as affected by distance and screening.

This applies also to the distance between front doors of houses facing each other across the path. Paradoxically, closer can be more visually private than further away, because those walking down the path between the houses have less opportunity in a narrower space to glance sideways into units. At Earthsong this distance is typically twelve to fifteen metres, and this feels very comfortable.

People who move into cohousing communities often find they are happier living closer to their neighbours than they expected to be, because attention has been paid to both privacy and interaction.

Distance. If cars are left in a carpark, the distance to home needs to feel comfortable, and common facilities need to be close enough to home to encourage daily use. Think of a one-minute commute. At Earthsong, a distance of up to seventy metres works well between home and common house, or home and carpark, particularly with carts and trolleys to carry the groceries. Older or less able people may need to be closer to their vehicles, and accessible units can be located near to the carparks.

Shape. Imagine you are at a banquet, sitting at a long table piled with food and lined with chairs. There is a hubbub of voices, laughter and music, and you would like to interact with the people around you. At best, you may manage a conversation with your neighbour on either side, and perhaps the person or two across the table. It is unlikely you'll be able to have a meaningful conversation with anyone else due to distance and noise levels.

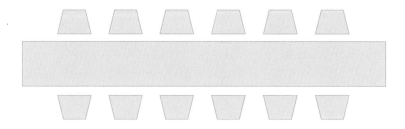

The constraints of this shape are similar if we consider a suburban road, where rows of houses sit side by side facing the street. We may know or at least recognise the neighbour to either side, and perhaps one or two across the street, depending on how wide and busy it is. Beyond that we are unlikely to see our neighbours often enough to get to know them, or sometimes to even recognise who they are.

Now consider that same banquet, but seating diners at separate tables of six or eight people. With this arrangement you are sitting closer to more people and it is possible to have a conversation with almost every other person at the table. More importantly, it becomes possible to have a whole-table conversation, with everyone able to hear and participate.

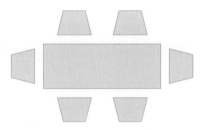

Applying this shape to a housing arrangement, we can see that a cul-de-sac or clusters of six to eight houses around a path can also give more opportunities for interaction between households, either one-on-one or as a whole.[1]

Number of households. Experience from many community sources suggests that communities of between about fifteen and thirty households, or around fifty adults maximum, have the best chance of creating and maintaining a cohesive community. Having at least fifteen households allows a good diversity of age, household type and circumstances, and the complementary skills that together make up a rich community. Between them, this number of households can usually support a good range of common facilities. Smaller communities usually have more limited common facilities, and individual personalities have a greater effect. It matters more if any one person is out of step with the group or doesn't contribute positively to the community for whatever reason.

As a neighbourhood gets larger than thirty households, it becomes harder to know and care about everyone else. The number of relationships that we can manage in our lives at any time is different for each of us, but if the group gets too big it can become overwhelming. The tendency is to split off into smaller groups of like-minded people whom you can know well; but this can lead to factions within the community and make it harder to work together as a cohesive group.[2]

Zones

One of the key structural elements of permaculture is the concept of 'zones'. Zone planning in permaculture means placing items and systems according to how much we use them or how often we need to service them. Zone 0 is the house and Zone 1 the home garden, visited daily. Zone 2 is still intensively maintained, but outside the immediate surrounds of the home. Zone 3 (orchards, water systems and animal areas) and Zone 4 (semi-wild) are progressively further from the home and require less intensive management and fewer visits.

Applying this thinking to cohousing, and even suburbs and cities, gives some useful insights. Zone 0 is the individual home and Zone 1 the home garden, together constituting a fully functioning household managed by the householders.

Zone 2 could be seen as a cluster of six to eight houses, like the table for six to eight diners. These are the immediate neighbours, people one might see coming and going most days, and these neighbours can cooperate in creating and maintaining a small area of shared open space, with trees and a garden table and chairs, or a children's play area.

Zone 3 is the cohousing neighbourhood of fifteen to thirty homes, made up of several Zone 2s. The community is of a size that it can support a common house, open space, gardens and other common facilities. Governance is by the whole group of intentional neighbours, who come together for meetings, common dinners and other events, and together build a neighbourhood culture.

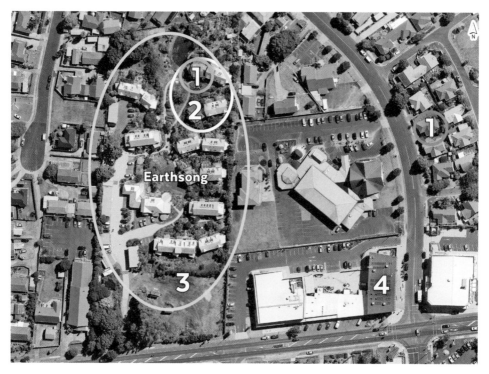

Zones

The public streets and the wider town or suburb are Zone 4. This zone has the population to support larger facilities such as shops, a library and other community facilities, and is usually run by a local government of citizen representatives.

Each of these zones allows some shared space and facilities appropriate to the scale, and governance of those shared facilities. Each zone allows a different level of belonging, of personality, of control.

In a standard urban or rural layout there are many individual homes, Zone 0s and Zone 1s. These usually front directly onto public space, Zone 4. There are no zones in between, no semi-private but shared space. A resident steps out of their individual home straight into public space, a relatively anonymous citizen amongst many others, with limited influence even on the environment directly outside their home.

Learning from a healthy natural ecosystem, of organisms within guilds within local habitats within bioregion, gives us a concept of what a healthy city might look like: households within a cluster, clusters within a neighbourhood, neighbourhoods within a suburb, suburbs within a city. Paying attention to these zones and designing well for the life, relationships and governance of each zone, from individual household to city, could help restore our sense of belonging and agency in a well-functioning society.

Layers and transitions

Maintaining privacy while also fostering community may seem like a paradox, but safeguarding the privacy of individual homes while also designing to facilitate community interaction is essential. The key is to design a wider range of edges or transition places between private and community spaces that allow people to choose the level of solitude or interaction that feels comfortable and appropriate at any time.

At the basic level, a design where each house has both a community side and a more private side allows interaction or withdrawal as needed. Front doors that open from the community pathways, with kitchens overlooking common space, give easy connection with the surrounding neighbourhood. Living areas on the private side of the house opening onto individual outdoor space allows privacy and solitude when needed.

There are other layers that can be built into the continuum within the community; a hierarchy of spaces and subtle transitions that enrich the possibilities. A front porch, verandah or patio outside the front door for sitting out on the community side allows one to be a little more available to conversations with neighbours going past, while still being in one's own space. A small gathering node within a cluster of houses becomes a 'front yard' that is shared with the closest neighbours.

Larger areas of shared open space can accommodate active play, gardens and a range of other activities that give many opportunities for socialising or working together with neighbours. The most social community space is the common house and outside terraces. Having these common spaces visible from many houses increases the likelihood that residents will be drawn from their own homes to join a gathering in common space.

If I'm working from home and stop for a cup of tea, there are many options for where to sit, depending how much I want to remain in my own thoughts or whether I want to have a chat with someone else. Having many opportunities for 'loitering with intent', or unplanned, spontaneous but welcomed interactions with known neighbours, builds community cohesion and helps to prevent the isolation so endemic in our Western culture.

PARTICIPATORY DESIGN – DESIGN BY COMMUNITY

It is possible for a group of people to design their own small-scale neighbourhood to reflect their values, world-view and the relationships they would like to grow between them. Participatory community design can be exhilarating, challenging, and intensely rewarding. Real commitment and generosity are required between people in the group. The buildings are the framework within which the life of the community can flourish. The real goal is community health and empowerment, rather than getting the house you've always wanted.

> Community isn't something you get once the project is done, it's a treasure you build, each step along the way. The way you work together during design and planning will set the course for how you live together later.   SANDELIN (1998, P. 11)

As a group of future residents of Earthsong designing and developing housing for ourselves, we were willing to make design decisions on aspects, important to us, that a developer might consider too risky for speculative housing. One example is our car-free neighbourhood; a standard developer might well assume that the market wasn't ready for this. But in eighteen years of living at Earthsong, I have only once heard any of my neighbours complaining that they can't drive their cars up to their houses. Even in wet weather, with a hungry child or heavy groceries to get from the carpark to their home, people accept the slight inconvenience because we all experience the huge benefits of having a car-free environment around our homes – a peaceful attractive pedestrian environment, with more space for gardens and people.

An individual or couple planning their own home will have their own processes to decide what they want to build and where; some of it rational, much of it intuitive. When a group of many individuals is involved, the process needs to be more intentional and explicit; drawing out and making visible all the individual preferences so the group can examine them together, build a sense of the whole, and make collective decisions guided by their shared Vision Statement. Some suggestions to help guide a group of people to design their own neighbourhood follow.

Clarifying key site criteria

Unless the site of your future neighbourhood is already a given, the very first design task of your group is to clarify and agree on the goals and criteria for an appropriate site that will fit your vision. Before falling in love with a particular piece of land or an existing building that could be repurposed – which may turn out to be unsuitable for a variety of reasons that you forgot to take into account at the time – it is important for the group to agree on the most important characteristics you are looking for. (See Appendix 4.)

This then becomes an important measure against which each site can be evaluated. The site you choose may not have every attribute, but it is helpful to be reminded of what you have agreed is important, so you can move more quickly and be more confident that the site in question is suitable and will meet your vision.

**Criteria for Land for Waitakere Eco-Neighbourhood,
as agreed 19 June 1997**

- Available now or soon
- Affordable price
- Large enough for 15–30 households
- Unobstructed exposure to north
- Sheltered from strong winds
- Sense of openness and space
- Near bush, water, or open space
- Enough land for growing food
- At least one-third of the land available as open space
- Ability to manage stormwater and grey water on site
- Large tree
- Minimal toxic spraying or extra-ordinary pollution
- Good earth energies
- Cleared with local iwi
- Quiet neighbourhood
- Walkable to regular public transport
- Near community facilities
- Supportive and encouraging council and neighbourhood
- Benevolent and patient vendor

Compiling design ideas

There are many ways to learn about the preferences and ideas of your future neigh-bours and begin to be inspired together. One is to create a shared place where members can collate images, ideas and suggestions for the design of your neighbour-hood. This could be a design scrapbook or folder, to which members add photos, writing or magazine images, or it could be an online space using an appropriate app. Ask members to include their name and some commentary about what they like about the images or ideas they have contributed.

Encourage members to be curious about spatial layout and design everywhere they go, to visit open homes, to notice spaces, distances and 'feel'. It is useful to learn to pace out distance by measuring and, if possible, adjusting your pace to around one metre, so you can better understand what, for example, a five-metre distance actually feels and looks like. Take a tape measure in your pocket wherever you go to check out sizes and distances.

Organise visits as a group to other neighbourhoods that have some elements of what you imagine; perhaps some older parts of town, or a retirement village, or a new apartment development. Assess the places you visit together – how does it feel in terms of size and proximity of the dwellings? What works, and what doesn't work, for what you envisage? Pace out the distance between houses across a narrow street. Does this feel about right?

A housing questionnaire at key times can be useful to build a collective picture of what might suit your members.

Early Earthsong Housing Questionnaire

- Are you planning to rent or buy?
- What is your preferred house size and type, e.g. single- or two-storey; number of bedrooms and bathrooms; small or large living spaces?
- What price are you willing to pay?
- Any special requirements? E.g. mobility, ground floor, carport or shed, etc.

There is no undertaking to fulfil any person's wishes; it is simply another way to collate individual ideas in order to build a picture of what would work for you collectively, by making the answers available to the group and learning a little more about what your group members may require. The key is to keep your attention on what will work best for the whole and avoid bending too far to accommodate any one person. There are plenty of other contexts for someone with very specific or non-negotiable needs to get their own bespoke home; what you are doing is the hard but rewarding task of working together on a collective vision to design a neighbourhood.

Writing the Design Brief [3]

After securing the site, and prior to beginning the actual design, the single most important input from the group in the design process is to develop the Design Brief. Ideally the architect would be involved; however, she/he may have little experience of working with a diverse, passionate, committed consensus group to the extent that cohousing requires and expects, and you may need to organise and facilitate the design-brief process yourselves or with other assistance.

However you do it, don't skip or minimise this process. The Design Brief is the key foundational document that sets out what you want as a group. The process of working this out together builds a strong foundation to help you through the challenges ahead. Having an agreed document to measure design decisions against, both for the group and for your design professionals, will keep the design on track and will help to avoid delays when the pressure is on.

The Design Brief establishes the goals and criteria for the site, the common house, and the private houses. It moves from general to specific, starting with the project Vision Statement, outlining the broad goals, then moving to activities, spaces and attributes. It is performance oriented, not prescriptive – i.e. it is 'what the group wants'

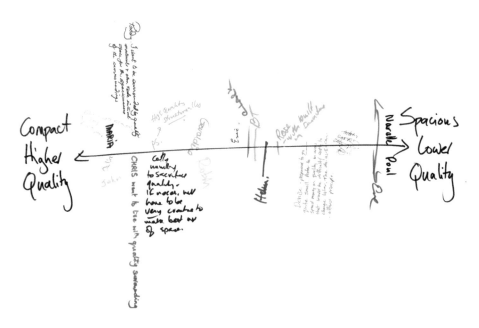

Recording a continuum for the design-brief process

not 'how to achieve it'. For example, it would say, 'a dining room to accommodate *x* number of diners and these other functions' rather than 'a dining room *x* by *x* metres'.

It is good to have as many committed future households as possible involved in the design-brief process, because it is an intense but rewarding bonding experience for your fledgling community, and the group will be more representative of your final neighbourhood. It may be useful, though, not to integrate any new members during this time. At Earthsong we halted new memberships for the two-month period of developing the Design Brief, so the existing group could focus on this pivotal and foundational work.

In the Earthsong process we met as a Full Group for two full days every second weekend for two months to develop our Design Brief. These four weekend hui covered, in turn, site layout, common house, private houses and final issues. Full notes and records were taken of all the processes and of what emerged. After each weekend hui, I and another member took the raw results of the brainstorms, prioritisations and other processes, summarised the ideas, and wrote them up in an easily understood format. These were circulated back to the group within a week, to be reviewed, fine-tuned if necessary and agreed at the next hui. Any issues that didn't reach agreement were noted for further work.

(See Appendix 5: Group Site Assessment and Mapping and Appendix 6: Processes for Participatory Design.)

Working with the architect

The Design Brief describes in words what the group wants to create. The architect's skill comes in translating these words into the shapes of space and the structure of building fabric, through the language of architectural plans.

In our experience at Earthsong, the design phase was a very iterative process. This meant the architect worked to translate the brief into a design for our site. He met regularly with the group (one morning every two weeks during the initial site-planning phase) and explained his concept as it was evolving. The group discussed the plans and provided feedback to the architect. Both architect and group learned more about what was required and what would work.

The architect worked up the ideas based on the feedback and returned with a more evolved design two weeks later. During this time, other work also occurred which informed the whole process more – the design was costed at various points, group members researched materials, more work was done on other aspects of the project such as finance, legal issues and membership. It is a spiral, and you will go around it many times, each time more informed and in finer detail.

At each stage the designs are evaluated against the goals in the brief, to keep it all on track. This includes what you want in the buildings, how the evolving design meets your overall vision, how it is tracking cost-wise and whether it meets your membership ideals.

Most people are not fluent in reading architectural plans, so it is important to use different ways of explaining and understanding the design to keep including all members. Verbal explanation and discussion help. Computer 3D modelling is a powerful way of experiencing and understanding the spaces and is a quick way of manipulating individual aspects of the design to test their implications.

Physical models have advantages too. Cardboard models of individual houses can be made with sufficient detail to help people really understand what they will look like, and these can be placed in the sun to check the implications of different orientations on sunlight and shading. Site-plan models give a bird's-eye view and are a useful group design tool to understand the overall layout and try out different options by physically moving the buildings.

At various times other ways can be used to help all members understand what the plans are saying. Larger quick models can be set up with chalk and tape on a concrete driveway or garage floor, large enough almost to be able to walk through the village. Full-size house layouts can be mocked-up in a garden, using real furniture and with string marking out the walls, to imagine how that living room might feel. Physical models are important tools that allow all group members to understand and feel ownership of the design.

Site plan on the garage floor

- **Establish a design group** of members to work more intensively with the architect. The design group can research unusual materials, propose detailed design layouts (e.g. for the common-house kitchen), research and approve door hardware, bathroom fittings, etc. There are hundreds of individual decisions required through the design process, and a dedicated design group, while always answerable to the Full Group, can achieve results more quickly than would be the case if the whole group needed to approve every detail.

- **Maximum input of the group at earlier stages of design.** A group that is integrally involved in putting together the Design Brief and working with the architect on the site layout and the initial house and common-house designs, will feel a real ownership of the project. However, as the design progresses it is wise to leave more and more of the detail to the professionals. What you are building is a cohesive neighbourhood, not any one member's dream house, so trust the architect to bring his or her skills, experience and creativity to designing the best houses possible within your brief and budget.

- **Design the common elements first,** before designing the individual homes. This builds the group culture of focusing on the best outcome for the whole neighbourhood. It also informs the individual house design. If you have already designed comfortable, attractive common rooms, perhaps with children's space, a common laundry and guest rooms in the common house, individuals will be more willing to let go of the need for these in their own homes. If people can see there will be a shared workshop and garden areas close by, they will better understand how they can live with smaller individual yards while still having access to more resources than they've had before.

- **Design for universal accessibility.** Houses that are accessible to those on wheels will also work well for children, older people and moving anything else on wheels. We are not all fit, healthy adults, and even fit, healthy adults age or can have unexpected changes in circumstances.

- **Standardise the house designs.** Choose a small number of unit types that suit the household types you want to attract and can be replicated several times within the neighbourhood. There is a big difference in build cost between standard design and custom design.

- **Build well-designed but simple houses,** and if cost is an issue, consider leaving out any non-essential items, such as built-in wardrobes or even some internal walls. This also gives owners a way of fine-tuning their own homes once they have taken possession.
- **Delay the house-choosing time.** Design the entire neighbourhood before individuals choose their units, so everyone is working for the maximum benefit of the whole, not focusing on their own place. No unit a lemon!
- **Resist customisation during design or construction.** Resist pressure from individuals to make 'just that small change' in their individual unit. It might seem like a small thing at the time, but it can have large unforeseen implications for the cost or timing of the whole project that can never be fully costed back to that individual.
- A few limited **options or appliance upgrades** can be offered to buyers prior to construction, designed and costed in from the start. Earthsong buyers were offered a choice of three different bathroom layouts, optional upstairs terrace and downstairs toilet, and shower rose and rangehood upgrades.
- **Futureproof.** When you can't include something to start with for budget reasons, consider putting in the infrastructure (such as spare conduits or access panels) that makes it easier to add later; while also realising that technology, regulations and requirements change, and that the infrastructure may never be used.
- If building in stages, do a **post-occupancy evaluation** of the built houses before starting the next stage. At Earthsong we surveyed the residents a year after the first seventeen homes had been completed, seeking feedback about what worked and what didn't. The survey showed a very high level of satisfaction with the design and performance of the houses, with only small changes suggested, such as an extra light or two, or minor changes to cupboards.

NAVIGATING DEVELOPMENT

8

STORY

While my boys and I settled into Tūī House, members would visit the land in the weekend. Over that summer we got into a rhythm of gathering around the fire pit for Friday-night fires. Sometimes there was a theme, such as the 'red-card party', for which everyone wore red clothes, brought red food and drink, and we spent the evening discussing our understandings of the red card in our decision-making system. The trees were laden with fruit; plums and grapefruit were dropping on the ground, apples and pears swelling and ripening, kiwifruit and feijoas still coming on. It was a very peaceful and lovely place to be.

Last year had been a hard year. The trauma of the architect selection process had been followed closely by seven months of such intense effort for the project that I'd had no time to process all that had happened. I longed for a period of deep and quiet reflection time but knew that was unlikely in the coming months. At least we had this time over the summer to connect in a different way, to start building our relationship with the land, deepen our relationships with one another, and quietly celebrate the progress we'd made.

Many new people joined at the end of January when we started accepting

The concrete garage

members again. The old concrete garage on the land became our meeting place and first common house. The walls were made of porous home-made concrete blocks, with translucent roofing that let the light filter in through the internal vines. It was rough, and funky, and it was our home.

The name 'Waitakere Eco-Neighbourhood Cohousing Project' had always been a mouthful, but we'd felt the need to know our land before we could choose our real name. In early February we felt ready. We brainstormed many possibilities, including 'The Orchard', 'Ranui Cohousing' and 'Heartland Cohousing'.

'Earthsong' as a name was initially resisted by some as a little flowery, but it caught the imagination of many. For me, Earthsong expressed the sense that we were now the guardians of this piece of earth, and that everything we created on it would be the song that the earth was singing in this place. Others had heard that when the ramming earth is being compressed into the boxing to form a wall, it starts to 'ring' when it reaches the required density, and that for them was the 'earth song'. After three meetings we agreed on Earthsong, with 'Eco-Neighbourhood' as an important descriptor of the community we envisaged. As someone said much later at a permaculture hui: 'Earthsong, that's a beautiful name for Papatūānuku'.

More conflict arose, however, in early February. Both Cathy and I received a page-long fax from two member couples, the gist of which was that they felt we had too much power, 'we don't think you trust us, so we don't trust you', and asking for a mediation. While things had never been easy for me with one couple, I wasn't aware of any difficulties with the other couple, and I was horrified at the timing: the very day before, I had deposited $150,000 from the sale of my house into that couple's personal bank account until needed by our company to pay for development expenses. This was a pragmatic arrangement suggested by them to save them a little mortgage interest and gain me a better rate than I would get elsewhere. And they were accusing me of not trusting them! I was angry that they hadn't revealed their conflict with me until after I had transferred the money, and I was terrified of losing that money that was crucial to our project's survival.

In their fax they requested that the matter be kept confidential from the group. I wanted to respect their wishes but felt strongly that this was against our group culture. One member of each couple was on the Development Team (DT) at that time, and we had a DT meeting scheduled for that same afternoon, the main purpose of which was an internal review of our work. We always began our meetings by checking in about how we were feeling and what was going on for us. I named my stress and worry, and the dilemma I was in. I felt strongly that Cathy and I shouldn't have to handle this in isolation, that the group needed to know and deal with this conflict together. Honesty and trust between us were vital for the huge work we were doing.

A special full group occasion had been scheduled for that evening, but feelings were running so high that instead of the planned events, we discussed what was happening. I found my power that evening, refusing to be cut down. What we were trying to achieve was *enormous* in its breadth and depth, and I was fulfilling my role with all the effort, integrity and generosity I could muster. What we needed to get this project built were more people stepping into their power, not me stepping back, and I would support anyone else finding their strength and leadership and contributing in healthy ways. Power is not a *finite* resource!

The conflict played out over the next three months, with several facilitated sessions in the group to address it. One partner in one of these couples was our

Treasurer. In the past he'd been treasurer of an incorporated society where the aim was to keep the books balanced, but we were a development company engaged in a high-risk venture, and he was feeling increasingly stressed about the budget.

Instead of working together with DT he became more and more distant and sent increasingly blaming emails. He wanted both Cathy and me to back off and give others more space. A third couple were also increasingly critical of how the project was shaping up. We were approaching the crunch point, when people would have to make the decision whether they were committed to buying a house and making the project work, or not, and those tensions surfaced in many ways over that time.

Amid these tensions progress was being made. We continued working on the design details, the water systems, the costs and financing. We were granted Resource Consent on 24 March 2000, and had our first major Open Day on 26 March, an important milestone. We invited a local kaumātua to give a blessing. The Minister of Housing and three other Members of Parliament attended. Bob Harvey, the charismatic mayor of Waitakere City, arrived. We had speeches, songs and a circle dance on the lawn in front of Tūī House. There were displays of plans and models in the tin garage, musicians playing, a piñata for the children and apple juice fresh

Members welcome guests at the Open Day

from our own apples. Hundreds of people wandered around the mown paths and building outlines in the orchard and imagined what it would become.

We had been interested early on in using earth construction and had been talking with Earth House Builders (EHB)[1], which specialised in rammed earth, for some time. In April we piled into cars and visited several of their rammed-earth houses. We were impressed with the look and feel of the houses, and from that point started working actively with EHB.

My experience designing earth homes as an architect had been that earth construction was more expensive than timber construction, due to the high labour content. EHB supplied the full construction accounts of one of their recent houses to Chris Ellis, our Project Manager and Quantity Surveyor (QS), and he verified that they could deliver a rammed-earth house for under $1000 per square metre, giving us confidence that building in earth would be cost effective. The builders met with the architect and me several times over that year to discuss their specific construction details and methods that allowed them to build cost effectively, and these were incorporated into our design plans.

The QS estimated the cost-to-build of our project several times that year as the designs firmed up, and he and I put together several versions of the development budget. This itemised all the costs of developing our neighbourhood, including land, buildings, services, professional fees, consents and financing costs. The total costs amounted to more than we wanted to sell the houses for, with the gap widening every time we looked at it. This was adding to the tensions in the group and required cuts where possible.

We identified several ways in which we could reduce costs and developed five versions of the development budget, from our preferred 'state of the art' budget with on-site wastewater, stormwater and rainwater collection and building the whole common house, to the 'hatchet job' with standard services and a reduced common house. We tried to strike a balance between the things that we had to build in from the beginning and were not willing to compromise on, and house prices that members could afford. Some things had to be left out in order to get our project built, with the intention of finding a way to build them later.

In late April the Full Group finally approved Development Budget C, which, along with other cuts, budgeted for standard potable water with a seed fund for future upgrades; standard wastewater with pipes for future on-site treatment; and building only a reduced common house to start with, using the existing old concrete garages as the teen room and laundry. This gave us enough reduction in the budget to allow an average house price within what our members said they could accept.

By May both couples involved in the conflict had resigned from the group, and another member, Gary Stewart, picked up the role of Treasurer. Gary came from a small-business background, and although he had turned his back on the corporate world to become an artist, he felt called to help the project in this way. His skills and experience were exactly what we needed at that time. He joined DT and became our Financial Coordinator for a small wage. I quickly came to appreciate his strategic thinking, and before long I was thinking of Gary as my right-hand man.

My mood that month alternated between exhilaration and excitement about manifesting a thirty-two-house neighbourhood with a solid diverse group, and continuing depression and exhaustion with the intense work and the ongoing conflicts with one couple. With regular evening and weekend meetings I felt sick at not having enough time with my kids, but it was a crucial time for the project and I just had to keep going.

We had the houses valued off the plans, and the result was depressing: the valuations we received were only two-thirds of what the houses were going to cost to build. This was a huge hurdle for us, and a problem also encountered by the first cohousing communities in the USA. Valuers, by definition, don't anticipate the market but base their figures on historical sales data. Because there was nothing comparable to what we were designing, the closest houses they could find to compare us with were standard townhouses in the surrounding area, which were not only built of far inferior materials but also did not have any of the substantial common facilities or eco-features that we were planning. We needed acceptable valuations for the development to stack up financially, and this was an ongoing stress during this time.

In late May we gathered on the land. The main path had been mown, and house sites were marked with string. We walked around the site by ourselves with a small site plan and each assigned a value to each house location. We considered aspects important to us personally, such as views, 'feel' and distance from the common house. For some, distance from the carpark was a plus, for others it was a minus. Generally, the houses furthest from the road were considered the most desirable, and end units were more desirable than middle units. The grades given by each person for each house site were then aggregated and averaged and became our 'location adjustment factor'. We applied these to the house prices assigned by the valuer according to size and amenity, to give our final house prices.

Many members felt very anxious at this time. We came to realise that we didn't have enough confirmed and able buyers to build the entire neighbourhood at once, and at one meeting in early June we floated the possibility of staging the project. The mood lifted as people began to see that we could get creative and make this work. At this time, we commissioned a young graphic design student, JJ, to do some perspective drawings of our future neighbourhood. His drawings were superbly evocative of what our neighbourhood would look like, helping to keep us inspired to bring the vision into reality.

Then in June it was time for buyers to choose their houses. We spent the morning in a circle listening as each of us told our stories of our involvement in the project. The afternoon was spent in wandering around the site, talking with one another, feeling, thinking, negotiating. We had a unit selection order based on the order of becoming a Full Group member, but we also wanted this to work out for as many people as possible. It became apparent that there was a demand for four-bedroom houses, and with some small adjustments it was possible in three cases to take the

Earthsong perspective

third bedroom from a middle house to make it a two-bedroom unit and add it to the end house to give four bedrooms.

I was number one in the house selection order, being the first member to have paid my $2000 Full Member fee back in 1998. There were three positions that appealed to me, two on the edges of the community and one in the middle. I kept being drawn to No. 14. It was at the centre, a pivotal place, right by the crossover of the figure-of-8 path, the energy centre in some ways. I knew I needed space and privacy and I didn't necessarily want to be in the centre of the community once this project was built. But I continually found myself walking to that place on the land, my eyes drawn to it on the plan. I decided that Unit 14 was about *engaging* with people, community, sometimes difficulties, learning and growing and finding ways through it. Engagement, love and belonging. That was my place.

In hindsight, one of the things I am so glad we did was to design the whole site layout and all houses to a detailed stage before any of us chose our houses. This meant that our focus was on designing the very best for everyone, with no house not quite as good as the rest. Although we had clear agreements about not customising houses to suit individual owners in order to keep costs under control, once people had chosen and started identifying with their future home, a subtle change happened where some individuals inevitably started paying more attention to their own house or wanting small changes made for their situation.

The frenetic pace continued. The architect, the QS and I had long meetings with the builders over house construction details and costs, and similar meetings with Alan Drayton, our preferred contractor for the siteworks. Alan was a builder whom I'd met some years before, with a construction company committed to natural building. Though perhaps more interested in building houses, he was keen to be involved in our project and willing to build the construction road, water tanks, underground services and other siteworks that were needed.

DT, by now a tight core group of Peter, Cathy, Gary and I, was meeting twice a week on Tuesday evenings and Friday mornings for four to five hours at a time. We felt a huge responsibility to pull the project together and were working on many areas at once. At times it seemed that the crucial threads of construction costs, valuations, house prices and house sales would never meet in the middle to qualify for a construction loan. We looked for savings wherever we could without compromising what was important. The siteworks costs in particular were much higher than we expected, starting at 50% over budget, and much effort was made to reduce this where we could. We cut out things that we wanted but felt we could complete later, such as secondary concrete paths and finishing the driveway.

Eventually we had a breakthrough, when we found a different valuation company that was willing to look at our project a little more creatively and include the value of the common facilities in the house value. The new valuations were still lower than we believed they should be but were sufficiently close to what we needed that we could move forward.

We had a crucial Full Group meeting in August with a proposal to stage the construction and to start building the first seventeen houses in November as Stage I. These were Units 1–17 in Buildings A–E,[2] a total of thirteen terrace houses and one fourplex of four apartments. The disaffected ex-members came, voicing angry words and determined to show red cards to stop the project. They believed we were going to fail, and they wanted Cohousing New Zealand Ltd (CNZL) to pull the plug and pay back to contributors the small amount of money left in the bank. The meeting agreed they could have speaking but not decision-making rights, as they had withdrawn from the project more than three months before.

People listened respectfully and then kept right on with the business of making decisions to go forward with the project. There was huge commitment and solidarity from those with their hearts in what we were doing, and a strong container that could listen to those who wanted out, yet not get diverted. If we had stopped at that point and paid out what money was left, we would all have got a small fraction of what we had contributed, but for those who had lost confidence in our ability to successfully complete the project, it would have been something. As for the rest of us – we were determined to carry on.

The conflicts continued, however, in different ways. The disaffected couple remaining in the group said they were not going to buy a house at Earthsong, and two attempts to have them removed from the membership list were blocked. The Process Task Group renamed themselves the 'Process Team' because they decided they were entirely about process and not about tasks, and became a place where members, including this couple, met to air their grievances about the conflicts they were involved in, without facilitating any healthy processing of the conflict in the Full Group. Fed up with what was seen as very destructive behaviour to our group endeavour, the Full Group passed a proposal to deregister the Process Team as an official task group of Earthsong. If those individuals wanted to continue to meet as a support group, that was their personal choice, but they were no longer contributing to the health of our very challenging project by attending to the processing and facilitation needs of Earthsong.

The twenty months of development leading up to construction were hugely challenging, and the stresses and worries of group members often came out as complaints, accusations and conflict. These settled down towards the end of 2000 when people had to commit, or not, to buying their houses. Several decided to leave; while new people continued to join as members. One of these was Lippy Chalmers, who later said that joining the group during those conflicts didn't put her off at all; rather she saw that even when feelings were high, there was an underlying culture of respect that she was drawn to.

By the middle of August 2000 we started signing the Agreements for Sale and Purchase (AGSAPs) for Stage I houses. With eleven out of seventeen AGSAPs signed by the end of September, we had a small celebration on the land. The house footprints had been marked out on site with string, and we walked around the mown path between the orchard trees, acknowledging the purchasers of each site, each of whom left a treasure on the site of their future home. For me it was a beautiful pottery cup that I used every day for my morning coffee, a real symbol of home. Bryan hung a bicycle wheel in a tree on the site of his future upstairs unit.

Work on design, consents and setting up construction proceeded intensively. As part of the permaculture design we still wanted to manage our water issues on site as much as possible, despite having agreed to budget only for standard water design. We saw rainwater as a resource and part of a healthy ecosystem, not a nuisance to be collected and piped off site as quickly as possible. As well as collecting roof water into tanks for our water supply, we designed the site plan, with the help of our civil engineer Alan Franklin, to allow the rainwater to be absorbed on site as much as possible. The carparks were designed with porous permeable paving to soak up the rainwater and remove pollutants. The shape of the land allowed water to flow naturally into vegetated swales, wide shallow trenches beside every path in which the water would run overland and down to the pond at the north end of the site. This would give it time to soak into the land, to grow water-loving plants, and would greatly reduce the run-off that could cause flooding problems to our neighbours downstream.

It took many attempts to finalise a stormwater design that fulfilled what we knew about swales and permaculture and was also acceptable to our engineer and Council in terms of volume calculations so we could get Building Consent for the siteworks. Even though Waitakere City Council (WCC) and its water entity Ecowater wanted us to build an on-site stormwater system in line with their eco-city policy, it was outside their current code of practice and therefore needed full documentation and calculations from first principles from our engineer to convince them that our system would work.

This cost us tens of thousands of dollars more in design and implementation work than the standard system required by Council regulations. Ecowater encouraged and supported us to apply for a grant from Infrastructure Auckland (IA), a regional funding body charged with solving Auckland's transport and water problems, to help cover this extra cost. Peter worked intensively with our engineer Alan Franklin, specialist stormwater engineer David Kettle and Ecowater to prepare the application, and we applied for this grant in September, just before lodging our application for Building Consent for the terrace houses and siteworks.

EHB twice required money in advance to buy timber and pay some of their upfront costs. Part of their strategy for reducing build costs was to purchase living macrocarpa[3] trees (usually old farm shelterbelts) and arrange for them to be cut down, transported and milled to size. This required considerable lead time in order for the timber to be sufficiently seasoned before it was required on site. We were committed to using them as the builders, and in order to achieve the build price we needed, CNZL took the risk of paying in advance for the purchase of these trees, backed up by clear agreements and a high level of trust. In August we paid EHB $5000 to purchase timber, and another $58,000 in November for more timber and to help reimburse their significant costs to date, ahead of the formal contract.

Two of the three disaffected couples, having been unable to stop the project in August, advised us in September that they had a dispute with CNZL, wished to recover their money from the company and initiated a mediation. Between them they had loaned $90,000. This had the potential to halt the project in its tracks, as it was crucial that CNZL had access to all the money which members had loaned in order to have enough equity to secure the construction loan. We had all signed the Cohousing Agreement, which stated that departing members could only withdraw their money at the end of the project for precisely this reason. Our former Treasurer had played a key role in writing the Cohousing Agreement, and yet he had now lost faith with the project and wanted his money out.

We engaged Helen Haslam, former WCC councillor and very supportive of our project from the early days, in the role of mediator. This mediation was a huge extra stress at the time when we were under enormous pressure to pull things together to start construction. Several members represented our group and met with Helen and the two couples over a few weeks, releasing me to continue setting up the construction. Agreement was eventually reached to pay them out in stages over the next couple of years, backed up by personal guarantees from six members; sooner than we had all originally agreed but without jeopardising the immediate needs of the project. Helen was so impressed with the group's willingness to make it work for the withdrawn members despite our clear legal agreement, and with the ability of members to stay focused on the issues without getting into destructive personal comments, that she resolved to live at Earthsong herself when the time was right.

Our original contract with the architect had assumed we would complete all design and documentation in time to start construction in October 2000. Given the complexity and size of the project, the leading-edge environmental criteria and the need to allow time for group decision making, this was probably unrealistic. The terrace houses and siteworks plans only went in for Building Consent in September 2000, and the fourplex consent application wasn't lodged until the end of November. This meant that both EHB and Alan Drayton began pricing on draft plans, which continued to change throughout the pricing negotiations. This hugely complicated the process for all concerned – the builders, the QS and me. I continually reviewed all of the plans carefully as they changed, and every time found mistakes that needed fixing.

We negotiated over several months with both EHB and Alan Drayton to come up with prices we could go ahead with, pulling things out of the budget, massaging and changing until Stage I was achievable. We had an agreed price on the terrace houses by November, but the price for the fourplex wasn't finally resolved until well into construction in June 2001.

One member, Bryan Pulham, a surveying technician by trade, surveyed and pegged all of the house platforms. As spring progressed, we started having working bees of members in the weekends, cutting down fruit trees that would be in the way of the buildings, and some large macrocarpa trees from the site boundary. We were determined to save as many trees as possible, but it often seemed that the healthiest trees were clearly in the way and had to go. For two or three years we had piles of fruit tree branches sitting near our outdoor fire pit, gradually being fed into our communal fire. It was exhilarating working together to prepare for construction, but because I lived on site it was difficult to feel any sense of privacy and rest in the

The first digger coming past Bee Cottage

weekends. At times I longed to have a quiet weekend with my boys, doing ordinary weekend things.

In October the two large packing sheds from the old orchard were removed by contractors. Seeing the huge digger coming down the drive was my first real glimpse that construction was starting, and it caused great excitement. Robin L had been living in Bee Cottage with his daughter for that year, alongside the large beehive that lived in the kitchen cupboard and out under the eaves. After they moved out, we engaged a beekeeper to remove the hive, but the bees became distressed, started stinging and had to be destroyed. Bee Cottage was taken down by local man-of-all-trades Axeman Jack.

On 29 October 2000 we had another pivotal event, our Turning the First Sod celebration. We didn't yet have Building Consent, agreed construction prices or construction contracts, enough buyers or a construction loan, but we knew we were going ahead! Many people came. We had models of the site and houses set up in the old tin garage, and Willow and his school friends gave a barbershop recital. Robin L was the Town Crier, calling us to gather. We collected by the pear tree at the crossover of the path, said some speeches amidst a light blessing rain and all dug our spades into the ground. This community was going to happen.

Turning the first sod

As well as getting everything else set up, we were considering how to manage the construction. During the design phase, I had handled a lot of the project-management tasks as the Development Coordinator, alongside Chris Ellis from Promanco Kenman Auckland Ltd (PKA) as QS and adviser. We'd been advised that the bank would require the project to be professionally project-managed before it would approve a construction loan. PKA told us they didn't want to do 'half a job'; if they were going to be involved during construction, they wanted to manage the whole project themselves.

I was exhausted, at the end of my stamina after coordinating the whole complex process through the design phase, feeding information in both directions between the group and our consultants, thinking and strategising and finding the path between maintaining our vision and remaining viable. I knew that it was just another job to PKA, and I would still need to be closely involved to safeguard our vision. But I was an architect, not a project manager. It was a relief to hand it over.

We had an auspicious beginning to construction, when the electrical utility company United Networks arrived in November to lay the power cable in from the street and install the electrical transformer on our site. We knew that a council sewer ran across the site somewhere through this area but needed to establish its exact location. The Kiwi digger bloke reached into the cab of his digger, drew out two bent wire rods, and proceeded to dowse for the sewer. I was astonished, especially when they dug down at the point he located and there it was!

We engaged a mortgage broker to help us put together the budget and other documents we required to get construction finance. Gary and I, with PKA's help, worked hard putting an acceptable budget together. We interviewed four bank managers, and by the middle of November had indicative offers of construction finance from three different banks. They all had conditions such as security over the land, professional project managers being employed, a Deed of Indemnity that made each of us liable for the entire loan and requiring the seventeen units to be sold prior to the first drawdown.

Others in the group had been working hard all year to enrol new members. One member, Lynette Loffel, had been in a paid role as Marketing Coordinator for some months earlier in the year, and the Marketing and Membership Focus Group worked with a consultant to put together a comprehensive marketing plan. Despite this, we only had thirteen actual sales by November, so we looked for people who were willing to sign an agreement to buy a house as 'placeholders' until a real buyer came along. I asked my parents if they would help us, assuring them we would have real buyers before they needed to follow through with the purchases. After some persuasion my folks eventually agreed to sign up for one house, and when pressed further, another, paying deposits to CNZL on both houses. I signed up to buy another of the houses as placeholder, and we kept looking for one more person to do the same.

By the end of November, we had finally agreed on the scope of works and the price for the siteworks with Alan Drayton Builders, though some aspects of the contract were not yet finalised. The Full Group agreed to spend $250,000 on construction ahead of signed contracts, and the siteworks began in earnest on 23 November.

The first worker on site was Carl, an artist on the digger. He stripped topsoil from the pond area, the main path and the building platforms. It was a joy to watch his precise and careful work around the survey pegs and remaining trees. A big mountain of topsoil started to grow on the front of the site by the road. The view of the digger filled my entire living room window when it excavated the road past Tūī House. Suddenly I was living in the middle of a construction site.

Gravel was laid on the main path for the construction road. Though we hadn't finalised EHB's total price, we had a clear enough agreement that they could proceed.

Siteworks begin

They started on site on 14 December, preparing one floor slab and pouring the concrete just before they went off site for the two week summer break. I watched it baking under the hot sun for days, and my heart sank. I knew it was best practice to keep the concrete damp and cool as it cured to avoid cracks, especially in that heat. With construction started and professional project managers on the job, part of me had begun to relax. I realised that relaxing was not an option. I gathered my strength again and insisted they set up sprinklers to keep the slab cooler as it cured.

Just before Christmas we heard that we'd got the IA grant of $93,500 for our stormwater system, and we also accepted the offer from The National Bank for $2.85 million of development finance. We were under way!

GOOD NEIGHBOURS WITH EARTH

9

THEME

We know ourselves to be made from this earth.
We know this earth is made from our bodies ...
We are nature with a concept of nature.

GRIFFIN, 1984, P. 226

'What's that beautiful smell?' asked the young visitor to Earthsong as she came into the common house, gazing around with a small, wondering smile. Those who live at Earthsong cease noticing the subtly fragrant, slightly spicy smell soon after moving in, but this is a typical first response from visitors.

New construction often smells strongly of chemicals and can precipitate a headache within minutes. Earthsong houses smelt beautiful from the beginning, a combination of the resins of the solid timbers, and natural tung tree oil and citrus thinners applied to the timber. Our noses are highly sensitive organs that have evolved over millennia to give us information about our environment, and especially if something is healthy for us or not. Trust your nose!

Cohousing is about rebuilding our relationships with *one another*. We also need to rebuild our relationships with *the earth* and the other species that we share it with. Let's face it: humans have not been good neighbours with the earth's biosphere and all the creatures within it.

What is healthier for us as humans is often also healthier for the planet. At Earthsong we have always had an equal emphasis on both social and environmental sustainability, people and earth; and we find – time and time again – that these two principles are complementary and mutually reinforcing.

Many of the sustainable design aspects of our neighbourhood were made possible not only in *addition* to a cooperative social structure, but *because* of our cooperative social structure; the two have always gone hand in hand. Living within a diverse and supportive neighbourhood increases physical and emotional wellbeing and makes it easier for individuals to make low-energy, sustainable choices. We learn a lot from each other, and there is a level of accountability to our vision and values.

Very often, these same values of social and environmental sustainability also support economic sustainability. Residents live in warm, low-energy houses with running costs significantly lower than those of a standard suburban house.

ENVIRONMENTALLY SUSTAINABLE DESIGN

The construction industry is a major contributor to the stresses on the environment. It is an enormous consumer of resources and producer of some of the worst pollution. Buildings last for a very long time, and determine transport needs, energy and water use over their lifetime. Standard house design, materials and services pay little regard to minimising these negative impacts.

In our age of easy access to information and relatively easy travel, we are learning how interconnected the world is, that activities in one place can have consequences far away. We can no longer throw things 'away' without ignoring that every 'away' is someone else's back yard. Choosing materials and technologies that do the least possible harm, either to our own back yard or someone else's, is a good start, but ideally our buildings should be restorative, and actively contribute to the ecological health of the whole ecosystem.

At Earthsong, the site, buildings, materials and services were all designed to 'the highest practical standards of sustainable human settlement'.[1] This chapter describes those elements. More than sixty-five people now live where only one did before, in a thriving and flourishing community that is nurturing the soil and trees back into health, valuing the water systems and providing a much greater diversity of plants and habitat than existed previously.

Buildings in a garden

Of all the communities included [in this series of case studies], Earthsong Eco-Neighbourhood has perhaps the most ambitious vision. The simple, pithy [Vision] statement encompasses ... a hugely rich and complex social and environmental agenda ... The environmentally sustainable technologies of this project are amongst the most comprehensive in cohousing and undoubtedly the best documented.   MELTZER (2005, P. 85)

Site

Location

The number one environmental design issue to consider when choosing a site is location. This will determine the need for transport for the entire lifespan of the community, and transport has a huge environmental cost. Transport of building materials and tradespeople during construction; travel of residents to schools, shops, workplaces, friends and family; transport of food, goods and people .... The choice of location either locks the community into high fossil-fuel use and dependency on private vehicles, or ideally is close to public transport, and is walkable or cyclable distance from shops and community facilities.

Landform

A key principle of sustainability and permaculture is to notice, respect and work with what exists, and the natural landform should inform the design at all levels. Soil is not an inert material to be unnecessarily pushed around; healthy soil is an ecosystem, full of organisms that create and maintain soil fertility. The land may need remediation from past toxic uses, instability or water flows, but designing buildings and paths to fit the natural shape and character of the land where possible is respectful and minimises the need for extensive siteworks and ground disturbance.

Layout

Placing the carparks at the entrance to the site, the community building at the focus and clustered dwellings along pathways, makes it possible to have a relatively dense neighbourhood that still feels spacious and relaxed. This has both social and environmental benefits – land area that would otherwise be used for driveways or road is freed up for productive gardens and community living space, for children to play safely and for neighbours to interact as they come and go from their houses.

Comparing Earthsong's site coverage with a similar area of land around a cul-de-sac in the adjacent suburban subdivision reveals significant differences. There are twice the number of houses at Earthsong than in the standard subdivision, even though the total house footprint is similar. Earthsong has less than half the total paved area for cars (parking, driveways and roads), and consequently much more land area available for open space (75% at Earthsong, and only 53% in the neighbouring suburb).[2]

Productive landscaping

Industrial food production has major negative impacts on the environment by using high levels of fossil fuels in fertilisers and pesticides, running machinery and transporting the food great distances. Growing food locally without chemicals is healthier for people and for the environment.

At Earthsong the original site was an old apple orchard. A huge effort was made to save many existing trees, which contribute to the established feel of the neighbourhood. Guided by permaculture principles, edible landscapes with vegetables, fruit and berries have been planted, and also native trees to feed the birds. Bees and chickens both contribute to a healthy, diverse ecosystem, and several methods of composting are used to turn green waste back into soil. Even small areas of land beside houses can produce plenty of healthy, fresh food, and this land use is usually beautiful too.

Productive gardens

Buildings

Size

Only build as much as you need. Even eco-friendly construction uses significant energy and materials, so building smaller houses and having shared facilities makes good environmental sense.

Individual houses at Earthsong are well designed but compact (100 square metres for a three-bedroom home). They don't need a spare bedroom for occasional guests, a living room large enough for large parties or meetings, or even a laundry, because these are available in the common house. By sharing resources, we have access to increased facilities and 'common wealth', while we use less overall.

Passive solar design

Designing buildings that work with their location and climate is the very basis of good design. All Earthsong buildings are oriented and designed for energy efficiency and natural climate control using passive solar design principles. In most climates, attention paid to these principles can reduce or eliminate mechanical methods of indoor climate control.

Here is a simple summary of what to consider for temperate climates.

- **Conserve** heat within the house with high levels of insulation, double-glazing, thermal curtains and draught-stopping of windows and doors.
- **Collect** sunlight/heat through north-facing windows (south-facing in the Northern Hemisphere).
- **Store** the heat in heavyweight materials such as concrete floors or rammed-earth walls.
- **Distribute** the warmth throughout the house through placement of rooms, openings and passive air circulation.
- **Protect** the house by shading windows from summer sun with appropriately designed overhangs, and screening from winter winds.
- **Disperse** unwanted heat through ventilation.

Behaviour of occupants

Ongoing choices by occupants also have a significant effect on the thermal performance of houses. Unless they are automated, climate-responsive design features do require us to be more aware of the rhythms of day and night, the seasons, the latitude at which we live and our local climate. Good information and ongoing education are required about such actions as pulling curtains at dusk to conserve heat, or avoiding the placement of furniture or carpets that shade a thermal mass concrete floor.

Over time owners at Earthsong have made changes to their houses to suit their own ideas and priorities. Many homeowners have covered their north-side timber pergolas with clear roofing to give sheltered outdoor space. While this extends the living space of a small house, it also reduces the solar gain from the north-facing doors and windows. Most such conflicts can be avoided with good design, but in a small house there are sometimes trade-offs between liveability and optimal design for thermal performance.

Materials

Appropriate sustainable building materials don't have to be expensive; many simple and effective solutions can be found using materials close to their natural state – cheap, beautiful and sustainable. The very effective acoustic ceiling in the dining room of our common house was created simply using spaced timber battens over hessian material, with insulation behind.

At Earthsong we used the following criteria to choose building materials and components:

- low environmental impact in its extraction or manufacture;
- renewable if possible, with steps being taken to renew the supply;
- low embodied energy (the energy used in extraction, manufacture, and transport of the material);
- low toxicity in manufacture, for builders and for residents;
- durable and fit for purpose without toxic preservatives;
- reusable and/or recyclable (not composite or glued).

Walls are either 350 mm rammed earth[3], or timber-framed and timber-clad with wool and polyester insulation, giving the Earthsong houses a solid and timeless feel. Plenty of windows let the sun warm the coloured concrete floors, which have a durable low-sheen finish of tung tree[4] oil with citrus thinners. The thermal mass of the heavyweight materials means that houses are naturally much warmer in winter and cooler in summer than houses built using the lightweight materials that are standard in New Zealand.

Solid, untreated, naturally durable timber[5] was used throughout for structure, cladding and linings, and timber joinery. We completely avoided particle board and other medium-density fibreboard, as these are full of glues and largely unable to be reused if removed. Internal timber linings are finished with tung oil and citrus thinners, and plasterboard wall linings to timber frames are painted with breathable biopaints. These non-toxic materials, natural oils and paints all add up to low-energy and healthy houses, and people with severe chemical sensitivities report much better health since living at Earthsong.

Common-house acoustic ceiling

Solid timber lintel set into the earth wall

The tuatara guardian of our common house

Materials such as these often require a high skill and labour content. One can argue, however, that using highly skilled labour is more sustainable and socially beneficial than using highly manufactured materials. Skilled labour usually makes possible the use of less-processed materials with a lower embodied energy and shorter travel distances. Working with natural materials is usually healthier for the builders, and much more satisfying than the standard high-volume low-skill technology that relies on fossil energy use and highly manufactured products.

Builders working with natural materials take pride in their work, and their skills are visible and valued. Skilled builders can respond to opportunities, working with the variable natural material to create something special. In our common house, one builder matched two pieces of wall lining with mirrored grain patterns to create a tuatara (native reptile) guardian for our dining room.

Externally we used CD50[6] oil on the weatherboards, the least toxic timber treatment we could find that still gave effective protection to the wood. Lightweight corrugated metal roofs are a very common New Zealand aesthetic and excellent for water collection. PVC[7] was avoided wherever possible and practical, and instead we opted for polypropylene downpipes for feeding the roof water into the tanks.

All possible materials from the two existing dwellings on the site were salvaged and reused, including the matai timber flooring and the frosted-glass 'tūī' front door, which were reused in the common house; rimu timber framing, which was turned into beautiful dining tables; and the old concrete cladding, which was crushed and used for the driveway base.

Using non-toxic materials and avoiding composite materials meant that much of the construction waste, separated at source, could be reused or recycled. For example, untreated timber offcuts were used as firewood, and plasterboard offcuts (mainly lime) laid over areas of subsoil to help break down the clay before the topsoil was replaced. Organic waste was composted, and metals and other recyclables were taken to the recycling station, greatly reducing the amount of waste taken to landfill compared with the waste generated by conventional construction.

Services

Power and water, phone and internet, and waste management are all essential to our modern lifestyle, but pipes and cables are usually buried in the ground or behind wall linings. Their invisibility doesn't mean they can be taken for granted, and the financial and environmental cost of supply and management of services can be considerable.

Many options are available to single households for generating power, collecting rainwater or managing waste on site. A cooperative neighbourhood adds many more possibilities for reducing consumption and reducing costs. Cohousing is essentially a mini-local-government system, with the capacity to both organise community-scale on-site services, and to bulk-buy services such as power and water from providers to on-sell to households.

Sustainability includes affordability, and our approach at Earthsong has been to achieve as much as we could across the full spectrum of environmental and social goals and be willing to let go of perfection in any one area. We couldn't include everything we wanted at the time of construction because of political or financial constraints, but where possible we built in the ability to upgrade later.

Energy

All buildings at Earthsong are designed for passive solar climate control, much reducing the need for heating in winter and staying cool and comfortable in summer. Supplementary space heating when required is from a range of heat pumps, high-efficiency wood fires (burning wood mostly from on site) and small electrical heaters.[8] Solar water heaters provide the bulk of hot water in all houses and in the common house. As a result of these measures, and with the information and support available within a community committed to reducing energy use, the average electricity use per household is half of the national average and costs householders less than one-third of the national average.[9]

We explored photovoltaic (PV) panels to generate electricity from the sun at the time of construction, but the cost was prohibitive. Instead we installed cables into the wall framing of each house to make it easy for an individual household to install PV panels later. The economics and technology have changed considerably, and we have now installed a PV system at Earthsong to supply 25% of our power needs. Many other alternatives could be explored for on-site electricity generation depending on the site. These include wind turbines, water generation and geothermal heat, though none of these was practical at Earthsong.

Water

We recognise water as a resource rather than a waste problem. Rainwater is collected from roofs into six 33,000-litre water tanks and piped back for use in houses. Because this is a multi-house neighbourhood, our drinking water supply comes under public health regulations, which are much more stringent than for a private house and would require some form of treatment. Instead we have a dual water supply to houses, with water for drinking coming from the council water supply and all other uses fed by the tanks. Low-water-use appliances and higher awareness of water use means that our total water use per household is much less than in a standard house.

During construction, a water-monitoring study[10] saw water meters installed to the pipes to each fitting in one house, extra water meters to the other six houses of that cluster, and several on the supply line to those houses, to monitor both tank and city water use. The meters provided monthly water use data which showed that Earthsong used only 72% of the average Auckland household use, and of this, 59% came from rainwater. Only 9% of the water used in the monitored house was for drinking and cooking. If this is typical of other households, it means that over 90% of water supplied to households in Auckland, treated to potable water standard, is used for non-potable uses.

Permeable paving to carparks allows stormwater from the driveway to soak into the ground. All surface rainwater and the overflow from the tanks flow into densely planted swales (shallow dish drains) beside the paths, running down the middle of the site to discharge into a large pond at the northern end, home to frogs and ducks. This overland stormwater system allows the water to soak naturally back into the ground, filtering sediments and nourishing plants, increasing biodiversity and reducing water run-off from the site.

Waste

All organic kitchen and garden waste is processed on site and returned to the soil. A variety of methods are used: aerated compost bins, the EM (anaerobic effective micro-organisms) bokashi system, and worm farms. Woody branches are chipped for garden paths, and larger branches are used as firewood for the wood fires in the common house and some private houses.

Our plan for an on-site wastewater treatment system was opposed at the time of construction by the regional water body, so we went ahead with a standard system. However, the pipes were located to make it relatively easy to divert the wastewater to an on-site system if this was implemented later. We have one composting toilet by the common house, built as a joint-venture demonstration project with our local council to trial its use in an urban area. Composted material from the toilet is used around ornamental trees and in private gardens.

Clothing, books, kitchen equipment and the like, in good condition but no longer wanted by a household, can be left at the Free Shop in the common house, to be picked up by another resident: one person's junk can be another's treasure. A comprehensive recycling collection for plastics, glass, metals and paper operates in our area. All of these measures contribute to the amount of rubbish put out by Earthsong households for council collection being less than one-third of the average for Auckland households.[11] Informal education of residents helps to maintain awareness of the need to reduce this further.

Communication technology

Communication technology changes fast, and we are dependent on local providers for this service. Initially each household bought their own internet service through their landline phone provider. However, spare conduits were included in all service trenches and under all paths at the time of construction to facilitate later upgrades as technology evolved, and these allowed the recent installation of fibre-optic cables running to all households. We are now able to have one main broadband service coming into Earthsong and distributed to each household, although it is still an option for households to choose an independent connection. Many households have now cancelled their phone connection and also get their landline through the internet service. This results in fast and extremely cheap internet and phone services.

Economies of a connected neighbourhood

Significant financial savings come with bulk purchasing of services such as electricity, water and internet. The service providers charge one fixed supply charge to our Body Corporate; higher than for a single house, but very much less than that for thirty-two single houses. The Body Corporate pays for the total amount used, then bills individual houses within Earthsong. Each house is metered and charged for its actual electricity, water and internet use, retaining the incentive for individual households to pay attention to how much they use.

Electricity usage can vary widely at Earthsong between identical houses with similar numbers and ages of inhabitants because of the habits and behaviour of the residents, such as how many appliances they use and whether they put on more clothing or turn on some heating. High individual users to some extent determine the overall cost to everyone at Earthsong, because the pricing plan from the supplier is determined by our overall use.

When the provision of services is managed by a cooperative neighbourhood, reduced use by residents can be facilitated and supported in several ways. Our internal governance means we can set our own priorities and manage these services to fit our vision. For both electricity and water, we had a two-step charge for many years: the first basic amount of electricity or water used by each household was charged at a low rate, with any use above this charged at a higher rate to encourage mindfulness around use.

Education is important, sharing ideas and tips about ways of reducing power and water use, and how to manage the systems more efficiently. There is quarterly feedback of consumption to each household, and accountability and informal competition by making individual house use transparent to the whole community. All these mechanisms have been in place in some form at Earthsong, with the result that thirty-two homes and the common house are functioning with an electricity supply of the size that usually supplies ten houses in New Zealand.

Cooperation between neighbours can reduce running costs in many other ways, as well as having immeasurable social benefits. Some tasks are shared formally, such as the cooking of common meals, organising the organic vegetable cooperative and the lawn-mowing roster. Informal cooperation, such as childcare or checking on a sick neighbour, also plays a part. Bulk buying of food items, seedlings or compost happens often.

With good systems of management, equipment such as lawnmowers, garden tools and workshop tools can be shared. Car-pooling and car-sharing are much easier to organise and manage when we already know and trust one another. Members swap or trade skills, such as dressmaking, house maintenance or IT support. The Free Shop allows circulation of goods no longer wanted by one household but useful to another, with no money changing hands. Social, environmental and economic sustainability go hand in hand.

Maintenance information and records

Part of being a mini-government and having our own shared internal services is that the responsibility for maintaining those services remains with us. If someone puts a spade through a stormwater pipe leading to a tank, it is not the local council that pays for the repair. Because our building construction was staged over eight years, our underground services and systems were also installed in stages, sometimes with accompanying changes in thinking and materials.

Documenting exactly what is built and where during construction is vitally important for on-going maintenance. The neighbourhood will still be here in fifty or a hundred years' time, when everyone who remembers the construction will be long gone, and future residents will be very thankful for this information.

During construction I took thousands of photos of pipes and cables in walls and in the ground, measured and documented positions and depths, and collected information on all our systems. I compiled these into six large folders or Maintenance Manuals. Ideally these are kept updated and all repairs and replacements are logged. They are consulted often.

Water pipes, telephone and data conduit leading to four units

(See Appendix 7 for notes on compiling maintenance information.)

KEY CONSTRUCTION LEARNINGS

- Construction problems can occur with even the most standard designs and are more likely when unusual materials and systems are used. We had more than our share of construction challenges. While some of these problems were more painful than others, we found solutions for them all and carried on.
- Do we wish we'd chosen more standard construction? No. We have beautiful, solid, timeless buildings, with good thermal performance, that are lovely to live in. The smell of wellbeing still infuses our lives fifteen years later.
- Is it possible to use sustainable materials and stay affordable? Yes. Many sustainable materials don't cost more than standard materials, although they might require more research and more effort to obtain. There will often be a higher labour content, but also lower material and maintenance costs. It's a different aesthetic. Solid, natural timbers gain character with the knocks and bangs of age, unlike painted plasterboard which just starts to look shabby. Purchasers paid more money for the added costs of construction challenges, but our houses still ended up affordable relative to the standard housing market.
- Does group consensus mean compromise, or more courageous choices? This depends on the strength of your vision and group commitment to sustainability. In our case we held each other to account and pushed each other further to uphold our vision than we might have done individually. The consequences of the difficulties were held by the group, not by individuals, and together we stood stronger.
- How much risk is reasonable for a group to take on? Again, it's up to the group to decide. Balance your vision and commitment with sensible, well-researched decisions. We went out on a limb by choosing unusual building systems, but they were backed up by solid research and professional support. We certainly had our issues, but those few challenging years have produced lovely buildings that will last for generations into the future.

CONSTRUCTION UNDER WAY

10

STORY

Over that summer of early 2001 I watched the orchard slowly transform into the paths and houses I knew so intimately on paper. I propped a ladder against a large eucalyptus tree on the edge of the bush overlooking the future pond and climbed high into the tree for a grand view of the entire north end of the site. I watched in awe and excitement to see men starting to build this place that I'd spent so many years imagining.

My whole life was bound up in the project; I was thinking and problem solving day and night. My office was in the small sunroom at the back door of our home Tūī House, and the siteworks contractor Alan Drayton would come to my door at 7 a.m. every morning to talk through the day's work. He was on site most of the time, constantly thinking ahead about the timing and logistics of the work, and we worked very well together.

It was exciting to be under construction, but it was not an easy life for my little family. Willow was in his last year at high school and Erin in his first. We were living in the middle of a construction site, and it was very difficult to feel we had any kind of private family life together. With no private space at all outside our house, I would

The wall panels rise

stumble out to get the newspaper in the morning past builders arriving for work. The builders' portable toilet was placed outside my bedroom window for several weeks. There was constant noise and bustle of men and machines, dusty in the summer and muddy through the winter.

And then members would visit in the evenings and throughout the weekend, excited to see our neighbourhood taking shape and wanting to talk about the progress or ask questions. There were no clear boundaries for me between work and my private life, and that took its toll. For a time, I trialled a coloured flag system on my door in the weekend – green when it was fine for someone to knock, or red if I just needed some time to myself. Once it was dark and the builders and members had gone home, I was the only adult on site, the night watchman, alert to sounds and conscious of the vulnerable semi-built houses and all the expensive machinery.

Earth House Builders (EHB)[1] were skilled at building rammed-earth walls. Heavy plywood formwork was erected on the new concrete floor slabs, ramming earth was mixed with lime and cement and tipped into the formwork in layers, and a strong young builder rammed it firm with a hand-held pneumatic ram. It was hot, dusty work, but steadily the solid wall panels rose on their concrete slabs and the site started to resemble an ancient stone ruin.

The Development Team (DT), and the Full Group to a lesser extent, was still working hard. DT now met only once a fortnight, but meetings still continued at times until after midnight. It was complex, detailed, highly responsible work, but all four of us were very engaged and meetings often erupted in laughter. The Full Group of members met every second Saturday afternoon, back at the church hall in Avondale, and the meetings were followed by a shared meal. The concrete garage was now in the middle of the construction site and used for storing materials.

In January 2001 we were working on the unit title plan and easements. This included subdividing off 1 acre (0.4 hectares) on the road frontage of the site to help to make the project financially feasible. We planned to sell this site to a new company to be set up by some of our members, who would develop it as a sustainable commercial enterprise in keeping with the values of our neighbourhood.

Our member surveyor Bryan and I pegged out the trench lines and manholes for the underground services and realised many more fruit trees would have to go. We were still trying to sell the last Stage I houses, still finalising prices and contracts for both the siteworks and the house construction (though both had started), still working on legal agreements to go with the bank loan. It was unrelenting, but very rewarding work.

Stage I roof shout

Some of the major balls in the air didn't land until the middle of March. After five design iterations we finally got approval from Council for our overland stormwater system. Building Consents for the terrace houses had been granted in late November, but it took until March to finally agree on the total construction price. The first wall framing was installed upstairs on two units in early March, and suddenly they looked like real houses, high and light and lovely. The first roofs were installed two weeks later.

We were still negotiating the fourplex price, but we signed the contracts between Cohousing New Zealand Limited (CNZL) and Alan Drayton Builders[2] for the site-works, and EHB for the houses on 16 March, combined with the roof shout for the builders. One member, Chris Free, made a cake in the shape of one of our houses, and lots of builders, the architect and engineer, project managers and members mixed and mingled outside Tūī House.

A few days later, twenty-seven members sat at long tables in our lawyers' office to sign Deeds of Indemnity, personal guarantees and other legal documents as security for the bank. This fulfilled the last condition for the bank loan to CNZL, to enable us to make our first bank drawdown as planned on 20 March.

In late March we had a weekend hui at a local retreat centre where strong respectful sharings helped to air some painful episodes and begin the process of healing. We spoke of the sacking of the Process Team and expulsion of one couple. I shared some of my pain about the architect selection process. Peter spoke after me, saying he now thought he had been wrong to believe that the group didn't have the maturity to handle me being the architect; it was an important moment for me. There were still unresolved and messy feelings, but the group as a whole felt solid and strong, willing to look at the difficult issues and unwavering from the vision. I felt proud of my community.

EHB got into a rhythm. I kept ahead of them all year organising hundreds of decisions from members about details, from floor colour, to toilet seats and basin shape, stoves, rangehoods and door handles, as well as ongoing construction issues and decisions to be made about such things as timber choice and fire separation between units.

The construction drawings for the fourplex Building A³, one of the five buildings to be built in Stage I, had not been completed until late November 2000, delaying the finalising of the contract price and Building Consent for this building. This was a handicap that caused enormous headaches for Gary as the Financial Coordinator, for me as the Development Coordinator (DC), for the project managers, and for the builders. Our project was a much bigger job than EHB had built before, and as well as managing the logistics of building several buildings at once, they also had to concentrate on pricing this last building. We had little room to move as our bank loan approval was conditional on their price being within a certain range. EHB's quotes kept coming back too high, and it took several revisions of both the design and their pricing before we could agree on a construction price for this building.

The architect was also working on the construction drawings for the sixplex Building I and the common house throughout this year, with many decisions needed from us on design, planning issues and details. One member, Rose Christie-French, took real leadership over the detailed design of the common-house kitchen, proposing a layout and organisation of workflow which was enthusiastically endorsed by the group, and which has subsequently been a joy to work in. We were drafting the Body Corporate rules, and still organising marketing events to bring in the last few real buyers.

Site Meetings were held once a week, led by the Project Manager John Murphy, with the quantity surveyor (QS), builders, architect, engineer, and me as DC and client representative. While the building of the rammed-earth panels was efficient and fast, delays started happening as the builders got into the carpentry. The building programme started slipping, and increasingly they complained in Site Meetings of their difficulties and delays in getting adequate dry timber in time.

EHB needed to source and buy trees well in advance of when the timber would be needed on site. We had already advanced them substantial money to buy trees before they started, but they regularly asked for money to buy more. It was a constant dilemma for us as we had very little security over the timber until it came into our possession on site, but it got clearer over time that they didn't have the cash flow to fund the timber they needed, and the delays were causing problems for us too.

By the end of April the stress was building again, with delays in construction, the fourplex price still not agreed, timber framing being exposed to wet weather for too long, and constant mistakes with construction. EHB seemed to be struggling. The project managers worked with them to train and guide them in their management systems and documentation to cope with our large project, but they didn't seem very organised. We had expected both directors to be on site most of the time, devoting their entire working week to our job, but we rarely saw one except at Site Meetings, and the other was mostly at his yard working to source timber and manufacturing the water-based glue-laminated mill flooring that formed the terrace house upstairs floors. The site management was not good enough and many building mistakes were made.

I prowled the site every day, checking each of the seventeen houses against the plans. I constantly picked up issues that weren't built right or weren't done at all. I noticed there was no roof bracing to one building as they were installing the roofing, and the engineer had to redesign the roof bracing so it could be installed after the roofing was on. Peter was also a regular visitor to the site, and several times alerted me to something that needed addressing, such as a party wall between two units being lined without the acoustic insulation installed. I was disappointed in the level of supervision of construction by all our paid professionals: architect, engineer and project managers. I was chasing up the builders, architect, and engineer, a job that should have been done by the project managers. Sometimes I felt I was doing everyone else's job as well as my own.

I felt like a strainer post, being pulled from different directions without any support or bracing. I was the pivot point between two extremely challenging worlds – between the Earthsong Full Group, my community, the world of relation-ships, consensus, anxiety and conflicts; and the hard-edged world of construction,

The muddy building site

consultants, development, money – I was the translator of one world to the other and back again. I lived in cold and uninsulated Tūī House. My beautiful curtains, hand-painted for me by a very dear friend who had recently died, grew mould. The toilet walls ran with water every time it rained. The bathroom was black with mould and had a fist-sized hole in the rotting wall just above the bath. My back gave out in April after several weeks of stress, and I was sick for weeks through that very wet winter.

Permaculture teacher Robina McCurdy ran a permaculture workshop for our group on a weekend in May to design the basic permaculture layout of our site. There was rain, mud and cold, but we worked together envisaging the growing systems of our new shared home, getting to grips with the reality of how much food we wanted to produce on site and how much energy we were willing to put in to growing it. After this workshop future residents felt a real ownership of their future gardens, and a new Permaculture Group was set up to oversee the creation and implementation of the permaculture design and management plan.

Mistakes and delays continued in June. Winter was bitingly cold and very wet and at times some areas of the construction site were knee-deep in mud. At every Site Meeting the builders complained about the difficulties in sourcing sufficient timber and getting it dry enough. This constant problem with unseasoned timber was slowing things down, so Cohousing New Zealand Ltd (CNZL) agreed to lend

EHB $5500 to buy a dehumidifier large enough to dry substantial volumes of timber in their yard.

Even though the programme was slipping badly there didn't seem to be many builders on site, and EHB acknowledged they didn't have the cash flow to pay for more labour. Normally the cost of the labour was paid in arrears on a monthly basis with the rest of the contractors' monthly claim, but CNZL started paying for labour on a weekly basis so they could employ more staff. This became a sum of $15,000 to $20,000 per week for labour alone. We knew this project was a challenge for them and tried to help where we could to keep them building.

Despite the delays, two buildings neared completion, and we scheduled a major Open Day for 8 July to launch two units as show homes. There was frenzied activity during the weeks beforehand by both the builders and by members in order to finish the houses in time. Members of the Marketing Group worked hard on arrangements for the day, sending out invitations and media kits, and organising signage, displays, information stations and the official speakers. The very day before the Open Day, builders were finishing the pergolas to these houses while paving was being laid below, and members were shifting topsoil, planting trees, cleaning the houses, hanging curtains and arranging furniture.

Earthsong started to feel like a village, with houses along pathways, the pond taking shape and members working together. People arrived in droves on the day, walked around the paths and looked through the houses. We had speeches and were presented with a BRANZ (Building Research Association of New Zealand) Green Home Scheme 'Excellent' rating for the homes.

In my speech I said that, just as it takes a village to raise a child, it takes a group to build a village; a group of ordinary, extraordinary people. The arrangement of our buildings around common space, very different from the normal rows of houses facing a street with a garage at the front, described our choice to place a higher importance on our relationships with one another than on our relationships with our cars. It was the physical manifestation of the social relationships we had grown together as we'd worked to build this neighbourhood. And our environmentally responsible construction was not only *in addition to* our social and cooperative structure, but it existed *because of* our social and cooperative structure; the two went hand in hand. The day was a great success and we made it onto national TV news that night.

Work continued on the houses. While Buildings C and D were nearing completion, E and B² were much further behind. Since the cost-to-build of the fourplex Building A had not been finalised until June, the ramming of the downstairs walls of this building had only just started. Siteworks were also behind schedule, with trenches open and mud everywhere. The pond was excavated in June and July, creating a huge mountain of soggy non-compatible clay stockpiled on the front of the site.

Because we had wanted to save fruit trees and disturb the site as little as possible, we had only removed the topsoil from the immediate vicinity of the building platforms. This proved to be a mistake, because through that winter trenches were dug; trucks delivered materials between the buildings; stockpiles of scoria for backfilling drains were dumped on top of the topsoil; builders' vehicles drove over it all; and topsoil, clay and scoria were all churned into a puggy mess. There was mud and slush everywhere. It was an awful building site to work on and caused future problems for our gardens and soil fertility.

Too many mistakes were happening. The builders continually placed untreated pine framing directly on concrete or rammed earth without a DPC (damp-proof course – a waterproof layer), and I was really dissatisfied with the frequency with which that and other construction defects were missed. At every site meeting I brought questions and concerns about construction that no one else had picked up. It was true that I lived on site and could check on the buildings every day, while architects and project managers are not expected to be on site more than once a week or so. But builders need to be held to account for shortcuts or lack of care, and it wasn't my responsibility to do that; we were paying consultants to monitor the quality of construction. The project manager, architect and I started regular sessions in between the site meetings walking around the building site together in a bid to pick up construction defects sooner.

The programmed completion date for all seventeen houses in the contract had been September 2001, but by the end of July only two houses were finished and the rest were well behind schedule. EHB started talking about how much more the construction was costing than they'd estimated, and saying that they needed more money. They were clearly in some trouble, and the last thing we wanted was for them to fail. We were prepared to consider paying more if mistakes had been made in the costing, though that would hurt. However, we needed proper documentation to substantiate their claims, both before the bank would agree to fund the increases during construction, and for our own members to understand and eventually pay for the increases.

The QS, Gary and I met with the two directors of EHB several times over the first two weeks of August. We were joined at one meeting by EHB's and our accountants, and at another by their lawyers and the whole of DT. At each meeting the amount they demanded grew larger and larger, from $150,000 to eventually $500,000. At every meeting Gary and I asked for documentation to back up their claims, and none was ever produced. We asked for a list of their creditors and how much was owed to each so we could see the extent of their financial problems, and this was never supplied.

DT had been dealing with this issue in confidence from the rest of the group for the two or so weeks over which this unfolded. We were desperately trying to find a way to keep the builders afloat and knew that one sure way to tip them into liquidation would be for word to get out to their subcontractors or suppliers that they had financial problems. Our group was large enough that, especially with a few people on the fringes, we weren't confident that everyone would keep the information to themselves.

It was a painful dilemma for those of us on DT: we were part of a consensus group, committed to total transparency and all information being available to everyone; at the same time we had a responsibility to the viability of the project meaning that in this case we felt compelled to keep this information confidential. It was one of those hard places where we sincerely felt that our obligation to the group was such that we had to keep information from the group. This dilemma was particularly traumatic for those in DT who couldn't share their worries with their partners.

It got to the stage, however, where there seemed no way out other than EHB going into liquidation, and at that point we needed to let the whole group know what was going on. A special Full Group meeting was called at short notice and almost everyone turned up. Members of DT explained to the group that the builders had serious financial difficulties, and that we'd been struggling with this for the last two weeks. It was a huge relief to share that knowledge, and the feeling in the room was of concern, but also overwhelming support and determination that we would find a way to complete our project. There was sympathy for EHB's plight, and various possibilities were floated about how we could help without jeopardising our own position: from buying them out, to putting in a micromanager of finance and labour on site. The feeling of trust in DT and solidarity in the group was palpable and gave those of us in DT a real boost of confidence to continue acting in the compassionate but firm manner we had adopted.

The next day, 21 August, Gary and I had yet another meeting with one of the directors of EHB at PKA's office in central Auckland. He repeated his demands for more money, and Gary and I repeated our request for proper records documenting the extra costs. During that meeting the director took a phone call, and then quickly left. Shortly after that another phone call came through, from Peter, who said he was on site watching the builders throwing their gear into a truck and leaving the site, and what should he do? The project manager advised that they were entitled to take their own tools and property, but nothing else. Gary and I raced back to Ranui as fast as we could through the slow evening traffic, but by the time we got back the builders were long gone. Peter had ended up blocking the driveway with his little car, with his seven-year-old son inside, to stop the plumbers removing four solar panels and cylinders that we'd already paid for and which had been stored in the garage ready to install. The word went out and other Earthsong members arrived, we got the locks changed on the garage, but there was little else we could do at that time but huddle in shock.

I spent the next day phoning the builders' subcontractors and suppliers, assuring them that we had paid EHB up to date for their services, but hearing from most that they had not been paid in turn. Some were angry, others just shocked. We were told by one sawmill in Northland, which had not been paid for timber supplied to EHB, that they would send the local motorbike gang to our site to recover it. We put up a chain at the end of the drive, and members took it in turns to talk to anyone who turned up and to let no one through. Bryan took to sleeping in one of the unfinished houses in his sleeping bag. It was a great relief not to be the only person sleeping on site.

Things went terribly quiet for a week or so. Occasionally a subcontractor would turn up at the gate, wanting to know what was going on. We were in shock and weren't sure what to do. On 30 August we heard that EHB were officially in liquidation, but little else seemed to be happening. A couple of days later Gary and I went over to their yard to see what was happening. We found the gate wide open, and the builder white as a sheet. The Northland supplier was there with a forklift removing stacks of timber from the yard, and threatening to run the forklift over the builder if he tried to stop him. This was timber that he'd supplied but had not been paid for; timber that we'd paid EHB for but which was not in our possession. The builder looked totally freaked out, having been abused by this and other suppliers and feeling completely out of control.

We phoned the liquidator, aghast that he hadn't secured the builders' yard. He arrived a little later with an assistant, and Gary and I stayed with them for most of the day, cataloguing materials in EHB's yard that we believed were ours, and having them trucked away to a safe location until the legal ownership could be established. There was not much left, just some insulation, small piles of timber, cement, brackets, one set of stove and hobs, some internal doors. We had paid over $180,000 in advance to EHB, and we were desperate to recover as much of that as we could.

I did a detailed inventory of the building site, estimating volumes of timber and sheets of plaster wall lining remaining in stacks in the unfinished buildings, and the work needed to complete each house. There were seventeen houses in seventeen different stages of construction. I went through each house, scheduling in great detail what work had been completed on each house and what was yet to be done; which hardware had been installed and which was missing; which rooms had doors, and which didn't. I worked with the QS to put together an estimate of how much we'd lost and how much it should cost to get the houses finished.

We were bleeding money. The interest on our construction loan was over $4000 per week at that stage. We desperately needed to complete the houses and get them sold to their buyers to pay back the construction loan. The project manager talked to one of his mates who owned a middle-sized building company, Akita Construction, and after some persuasion he agreed to take on the job of finishing the houses. They were standard builders, not skilled in natural materials or non-toxic construction, but we had few choices by then. They had to pick up a large construction project, seventeen houses in different stages of completion, built of unusual materials, and with all the risks and unknowns associated with picking up another builder's uncompleted project.

Akita's first quote to finish the job was over $1 million, which was $200,000 more to complete the houses than we had budgeted to receive from selling them. I dreaded having to tell the group, and I anticipated anger and blame from members fearful of the project's failure. But the energy from the group this time was of huge faith and trust, that we were all in it together and we would work it out.

We went through a huge cost-cutting exercise with both the houses and the siteworks, deleting everything we didn't feel was absolutely essential to getting the houses finished. We had limited choices about this, because Council required completed buildings before it would issue the Code Compliance Certificate, which was needed to get titles under the Unit Titles Act, which were needed before CNZL could sell the houses to the buyers and repay the construction loan with the sales

Siteworks in the mud

proceeds. We took the painting, oiling and final clean out of the contract for owners to complete themselves. We substituted plasterboard for some of the timber linings and deleted bathroom cabinets, wardrobe doors and house patios.

Alan Drayton's builders and subcontractors had kept working on the siteworks throughout this time, installing the power, water and phone lines into the trenches, installing and connecting up the water tanks, and completing the pond work. We took everything out of the siteworks contract that didn't have to be finished at that time, including the main paths and swale bridges, the driveway and carparks.

In addition to the money CNZL had already paid for things we didn't end up getting, there was the cost to CNZL of the delay before Akita started on site, the extra cost of their contract over what we had left to spend, and the cost of the extra time taken to finish the job, both to CNZL in extra bank interest, and to individual members who were renting temporary accommodation. The contract with EHB had been due for completion by September 2001; Akita finally went off site in July 2002. We figure CNZL lost in total at least $500,000, maybe closer to $1 million. If we'd thought that giving EHB $500,000 extra was going to be all they needed, it would have been worth doing that just to keep them going and get our houses finished. But we suspected that their problems were larger than that, and the liquidation report eventually said that they owed a total of $1.58 million. EHB's financial problems were much bigger than just our project.

Painful as it was, the group really pulled together through this process. If anyone had lost their nerve and reneged on their commitment to buy their unit, it would have put the whole project in more jeopardy. But Gary, our Financial Coordinator, remained calm, the group stayed strong, and even though we were making painful decisions to cut more things out of the budget, we came through with little conflict. We even gained two new members and buyers at this time, one of whom, Margaret, had come from Scotland to check us out. She felt that everyone was so positive of outlook that she was confident it couldn't possibly fail.

By the middle of October, we'd made enough cuts to get Akita's price down just below $1 million, although many of the costs were not fixed due to the uncertainties of picking up unfinished work. The National Bank could have insisted that the unfinished houses be sold in order to recover their funds. However, given that shareholders of CNZL were also the purchaser group, they agreed that CNZL could engage Akita to complete the houses, provided that CNZL met the $200,000 shortfall in funding. This we covered in the short term with a loan from Prometheus Ethical Finance, backed up by $5000 guarantees from forty-eight members, friends and family, who pledged to contribute that money if there was any shortfall at the end. The support we got at this time from many people, some only distantly associated with Earthsong, was incredibly gratifying. The shortfall was covered at the end of Stage I by increasing the house prices of all units by between $10,000 and $13,000 each, depending on size.

During this whole time, while we were desperately trying to get construction restarted, there was also pressure to get the unit plan finished in order to apply for titles, so CNZL could sell the finished units and start paying back some of the bank loan. The individual unit boundaries had only been in draft form until then, and the north yard sizes of the six houses in Buildings C and D had been sketched by the architect a little larger than we had earlier agreed in principle. Design Task Group put a proposal to the Full Group to standardise the yards of these units to match other units, effectively reducing their north yards a little and increasing the common space in the orchard and meadow.

There was an uproar. What some people expected would be a straightforward fine-tuning of unit boundaries before the survey plan was finalised turned into a conflict about both physical and interpersonal boundaries. Drawing the line between private space and community space became a very charged issue, until eventually the group agreed to leave the original draft lines as the agreed boundaries. In some ways this issue was an outlet for the anxiety in the group at this time. We hung together extraordinarily well through the external threat, but people were stressed, and this probably exacerbated the strong feelings about this issue.

Akita Construction started on site on 23 October 2001, only eight weeks after EHB had left. Those eight weeks had felt like years. The responsibility, largely borne by Gary and me, of pulling our project away from the precipice and back onto the tracks had taken a huge toll. Life felt bleak. I was short-tempered and grumpy, hating myself and others. I took myself off to the countryside to stay with friends for four days, slept, ate and sat gazing into space for hours. I started to come alive again.

On the way home I stopped to meet with my group of friends for our regular seasonal ritual. It was Beltane, midway between spring equinox and summer solstice. My friend Deanne had made the centre table a riot of colour, with a Pacific-print tablecloth, vibrant irises and daffodils, oranges, strawberries, beans. She led us in a gentle meditation focusing on our senses, ringing a little bell by our ears, feeding us strawberries, wafting lovely smells under our noses. It was a celebration of the senses, of being alive, and the perfect end to my four days of replenishment, feeling anchored back in the lush and beautiful physical present. I felt the spring come back into my step.

Hearing my story of the last few weeks, Deanne invited me to stay with her on Waiheke Island for some more rest and replenishment, and I phoned her a few days later to organise the stay. She didn't answer the phone. The next day, five days after our sensory celebration, another of my friends phoned to say that Deanne had committed suicide. She had planned it carefully, and clearly had known, at that ritual which had felt to me like such a celebration of life, that it was in fact her farewell to us. None of us had known of the depth of her despair, and I was completely shocked. I sat on the bank above the pond, alone in the night with the deserted building site around me, and howled.

When Akita started work in October, Building A was a single-storey rammed-earth shell with the concrete upper floor in place; Building B had its roof on but no windows or upstairs wall cladding; E was closed in except for the third bedrooms, and Buildings C and D were very close to completion[3]. The top priority was to get C and D finished so people could move in. Work on Buildings E and B also started advancing again, as wall cladding, plumbing and wiring were installed. Some wall framing had been exposed to the weather for months, so it was a relief to get the cladding on.

I started to ease off from the intensity of work, telling the group I would give the job 100% but not 150 or 200%, and would take six months off after the houses were finished. It was spring, and my beautiful new house was slowly forming into a real house inside. Members were spending more time on the site clearing out construction rubbish, sanding and oiling windows and timber boards, and painting walls in their own houses. I came home to Tūī House one afternoon and found someone had left food on my doorstep. Some pot plants had been arranged in a semicircle to create a small defined outdoor space for me outside my back door; the beginnings of having my own patch again. I felt blessed by belonging to a community at last.

In the middle of December, the first three households moved in. Earthsong started to come alive as a neighbourhood. I could still flick in my mind between the two images, of the orchard that was and the neighbourhood that was becoming, but the balance was changing. The shape of the village was becoming the foreground, with houses nestled into the shape of the land, the main path looping around the walnut tree, and the swale swinging around and down to the pond. I visited two of my neighbours before Christmas, and they each had lovely things to show me – a Christmas tree at Geraldine and Gary's, and one of Chris's cakes at Lynette, Mary and Adelia's, with little marzipan figures of all three of them sitting in the middle. So this was cohousing. So lovely.

It was January 2002 before work restarted on Building A, after difficulties in

From left: Robin Allison (DC), Bill Algie (architect), Chris Ellis (QS, PKA), John Murphy (Project Manager, PKA), four members of Akita Construction and Tony Nash (PKA)

finding someone who could complete the upstairs rammed-earth walls. This and other construction proceeded much slower than expected. It was a stressful time, with the cost of construction increasing with the delays, bank interest by now running at a horrendous rate and several households in temporary accommodation until their houses were finished.

Finally, in March, my boys and I moved out of Tūī House into our new home at the crossroads. It was beautiful, solid and warm, though there was still oiling and other jobs to finish in the house, and the garden was bare clay. To convert Tūī House into our interim common house, the wall between a bedroom and the living room was removed to create a space large enough, albeit squashed, for meetings and dinners. I was adamant about creating the clarity of separation by not bringing my work into my new home, so the DC office moved into a larger room in Tūī House. A communal laundry was set up in the old concrete garage, nominally sharing the space with an area for teens.

By the end of March there were eleven households living on site. We started having a section for residents' issues in the Full Group meetings and we built a sandpit for the kids by Tūī House. Common meals began, though the meals were cooked in member's homes and carried up to Tūī House for dinner.

Although it was satisfying to have my community move in around me, it did present different stresses. I worked hard to keep my personal life separate from work issues, and tried to make it very clear whether I was emailing the group or interacting one-on-one as the DC or as a neighbour. Out of work hours I tried to be just another neighbour working on my house or relaxing around the fire, but often fielded questions from others about their own houses or other work issues.

My primary focus remained on the development of the project, and it was hard to maintain friendships with individual members while also having a role for the group. Sometimes I had to say 'no' when someone wanted 'just one small change to my unit', and this was seen as a personal 'no' rather than a job 'no'. We were all exhausted, and it took energy to hold the boundaries between being a friend and neighbour to individuals and still working for the good of the whole; between giving my all to the work and still safeguarding a little space for my private family life.

Living in closer proximity than we were all used to also brought up differences in privacy needs, and we had a couple of sessions together to share our assumptions and needs around privacy and socialising, how much interaction with others was appropriate for us when we were in our private yards and how to indicate this to others. For a time, I trialled the coloured flags again outside my front door to indicate whether I would welcome visitors at that time or needed time alone.

Despite the financial troubles, members had still been joining, including Pat and Helen Haslam (our mediator of the year before), and Glenys and David Mather later that year. We had found real buyers for all the Stage I houses by the time of completion, relieving my parents and me from completing the purchase of the three houses we had signed up for. It was a huge relief when titles finally came through in April 2002, enabling us to settle many of the house purchases and start to repay the bank loan. At the same time, I was still liaising closely with the architect over the design and documentation for the common house and Building I, preparing to lodge the Building Consent application. Gary and I were also working on the development budget and logistics for Stage II so we could set house prices and start signing people up.

Twenty members including me had formed a new company, Walk to Work Eco-Developments Ltd (W2W), in July 2001 to buy the section on the front of site that we had subdivided from Earthsong, and in April 2002 the sale price of $220,000 was agreed (with CNZL leaving $70,000 in as a loan), enabling CNZL to pay back another chunk of money to the bank. W2W raised a mortgage to fund the purchase, and for many years members of W2W paid monthly contributions to pay the interest on the mortgage. We were committed to eventually creating a sustainable commercial development that would complement Earthsong and contribute to the local social economy.

In June 2002 Building A was finally finished enough for those four households to move in. The bollard lights along the paths had been installed and were fired up for the first time, revealing a fairyland in the low light of evening. On 22 June, seven years after the first public meeting that had launched the project, we had a celebration dinner. Forty members were seated around two horseshoe-shaped tables in the Tūī House large room, packed in like sardines and very happy. We had a delicious dinner, Chris had made a wonderful 'rocky road' cake, and I showed seven years of photos of our journey to date. We talked and danced into the night – we'd pulled it off, we'd built Stage I, the hardest part, all the preparation and the major siteworks and the first houses. We'd arrived. We were elated and exhausted. It would take some time to sink in.

GETTING IT BUILT

11

THEME

Though every journey is different,
it helps to have a map.

'We've found a promising site, and we want to build a community. What should we do next?' I've lost count of how many times I've been asked variations of this question. Few of these projects survive beyond ideas into built reality. In order to increase the odds, I offer what worked for us.

Every housing development involves three main areas of work: finding a site and designing and constructing the buildings; setting up the legal and financial structures that support the development; and marketing the project to achieve sales.

These three areas of work are also essential in cohousing projects, and it is useful to keep them all in mind throughout the whole process. However, in cohousing they are more complex and much more intertwined, and they usually happen in the reverse order to the process for a more conventional development: the people come first; then the systems between the people; then the site, design and construction.

Earthsong required a large investment of time and money to adapt the cohousing concept to New Zealand's cultural, legal and financial framework, and to attract potential residents and buyers. This chapter considers the whole of the Earthsong development history and highlights the key stages and learnings along the way, in the hope of assisting other collaborative housing groups.

FIRST STEPS

The first steps are briefly repeated here in the context of outlining the whole development process.

Period of research (see Chapter 2)

The Auckland Ecovillage group was, in effect, the 'research phase' of the Earthsong development journey. While it did not lead to a single ecovillage as envisaged, it informed the subsequent establishment of several large and small communities around the North Island.

The openness of the group provided a valuable learning environment to explore the breadth and depth of eco-community, but it became a challenge that eventually stalled progress and led to the group's slow demise. It's hard to build a sense of shared endeavour and trust when there is uncertain commitment and a continual turnover in those attending. It became frustrating when new people wanted to go over the same ground that some of us had already discussed several times.

The key learnings I took from this time were the importance of refining your vision, articulating it clearly, committing to working towards it and avoiding going backwards to accommodate new people with very different ideas.

Articulate and claim your vision (see Chapter 3)

We all have ideas about the world we'd like to live in. A key step in taking action towards that world is to clarify and articulate the vision you have for the future you want, and then take whatever steps you can to move towards it. Cohousing and many other initiatives start with one person, a 'burning soul' who prioritises that project over whatever else they are doing.

After the Ecovillage group dissolved, I clarified the key elements of the future I wanted and wrote a five-page proposal. It started with a Vision Statement encapsulating the main elements into a short, dense and inspiring sentence, and then explained in more detail the various elements of cohousing, permaculture and eco-design. This proposal formed the basis for the neighbourhood that slowly coalesced over the next few years.

Find your core group (see Chapter 4)

> Every cohousing group needs *'One burning soul and six dedicated participants'*
> MCCAMANT AND DURETT (2011, P. 26).

It takes one person to start … and it takes a group to build a village. The core group is that small handful of people who are so passionately aligned with the same vision that they are willing to put in significant time and effort to bring it about.

At the inaugural public meeting in June 1995 I described my vision for an urban cohousing neighbourhood, and two people with very similar values and aspirations answered that call. Over the next year our small core group of three learned how to work intensively together, and worked on internal organising agreements, legal structure, land acquisition and design; but ultimately it was the relationship building between us and the culture building for our neighbourhood that were the most significant achievements of this time.

It can be helpful to think of a triangle, most of it buried deeply in the ground. Only the land, houses and the living community are visible, but they are supported by a crucial foundation of relationships, agreements, systems, research, design and culture building – invisible but essential to the stability of the whole.

BUILD MEMBERSHIP

It felt important for a time to safeguard the small core group of very committed members until we had worked out the basic framework. However, a cohousing project also needs to build and retain a strong membership group to make the project viable and have committed buyers ready when the time comes.

Find potential members by getting the word out in whatever ways you can, through friends and networks, events, social and formal media. Many people first heard about us by word of mouth. We also set up stalls at festivals and markets, and several times a year we featured in newspaper or magazine articles and radio interviews. We put notices in the local paper and ran orientation evenings once a month. We put out a simple newsletter to our growing database of interested people and set up a website. Regular Sunday lunches once a month were open to all, and we hosted public events such as occasional speakers or an afternoon discussion forum. Many people were interested, quite a lot came to check us out, and a steady trickle of people joined the group for short or long periods. The group gradually expanded.

Putting the word out

Build relationship between those in the group – this is the bedrock that will carry the group forward through the challenging effort of working together to create cohousing. In those early years, we always had a shared meal and social time before we did the business of meeting. Occasional camping holidays together were useful mini-experiences of living beside one another, cooking communally and thinking together in a more relaxed setting.

There is tension between *process* (i.e. the relationships between people and how things are done) and *task* (i.e. progressing the project and getting things done). In my experience they are both vital, and both need attention. Meetings need to be both enjoyable and effective for people to keep coming, and good meeting processes are essential.

A great way to build group relationships is to learn skills together that are needed for the project. This could be study groups focused on researching and discussing aspects such as sustainable design or legal structures, or workshops led by skilled professionals in areas such as facilitation, group skills or permaculture. Consider making cohousing seminars or decision-making workshops a condition of membership. This helps to build shared understanding, nurtures a shared culture and trains all members in skills useful for your collective project.

It is exhilarating working together to create new forms that better fit your values. Make sure that, as well as contributing to the end result, the effort you are putting in is also satisfying and worthwhile at the time. Always remember that the sense of

Camping holiday to build community

community among those in the pioneering group as you work together is one of the 'products' or benefits of the work.

Establish the membership process (see Chapter 5) with a threshold so you all know who is committed to your shared project and who can therefore participate in the decisions. Decision-making rights go with responsibilities to the project. You are engaged on a large and complex project, and you need to all be travelling towards the same agreed vision. You can't afford to be slowed down or taken on side journeys by those not willing or ready to commit, and who carry few of the consequences of a stalled project.

Establish core governance agreements (see Chapter 5) such as agreeing the decision-making structure, communication agreements and conflict-resolution agreements. You are a group of diverse people, and clarity around expectations of behaviour helps to build your unique culture and to avoid some of the bumps.

Keep articulating your project as it evolves

As ideas developed in the three main areas of membership and marketing, legal and finance, and site and design, it was very helpful to articulate the key aspects that we wanted people to know in an Information Booklet.

It was extremely satisfying to produce such a booklet, and the booklet was invaluable when it came to explaining our intentions to Council and other bodies, and for recruiting new members. It was another 'product': a tangible reminder of the clarity and progress we had made to date.

The Information Booklet we wrote in 1998, not long before we found and bought our site, included information on:
- Vision Statement
- what is cohousing?
- design principles – environmental, social, economic
- decision-making method
- Communication Agreements
- membership structure
- contact information.

Assess members' financial commitment and contributions

The reality is that any cohousing project needs money. You may find an external funder, in which case you will have much less financial stress but probably also less influence over the design and development of the community. There is risk in any development, and those willing to take the risk and put up the money need to have an appropriate degree of control over decision making.

Before we purchased land, we had assessed our own individual and collective financial capacity with a Financial Questionnaire. This was a useful step that gave a readout of our collective resources and helped bring a sense of reality to everyone in the group. Ideally, we needed enough equity between us to purchase a site freehold, because we knew loans to purchase bare land were difficult to obtain, and we would need this equity in order to proceed with construction.

Earthsong Financial Questionnaire

If your concerns were met to your satisfaction:

- How much would you be willing to loan or invest (as a deposit) to the project?
- Would that come from liquid assets, selling existing house, increasing mortgage, bridging finance, etc.?
- When would that money be available to the project?
  - now as seed money
  - deposit on site
  - to fund development costs up to Resource Consent
  - to settle the land purchase
  - to secure a construction loan.
- What is a conservative estimate, and an optimistic estimate?

A strength of having a cohesive group, with a level of relationship and trust among members underpinned with robust agreements, is that it unlocks other ways of helping. Not every individual needs to have both enough equity and enough income to finance their house purchase. Many younger families struggle to accumulate enough equity to qualify for bank finance, even if they have a good income and many years of working life ahead to pay off a loan. Older people may have the equity but are at the end of their working lives. Some might have funds invested elsewhere that they would be willing to lend to the project with appropriate terms and agreements. Others may be willing to act as guarantor to someone else's loan. There are many ways to contribute, and the combination of these circumstances within a cohesive group committed to a joint project means that collectively there can be enough equity for the project to proceed.

Many people are more comfortable if their financial situation remains confidential from the wider group. The small financial task group needs enough detailed information that they can be confident the group is financially viable, but the results of the questionnaire can be summarised for circulation to the whole group in a way that does not identify individuals.

Another useful step would be to request that each household obtain pre-mortgage approval from a bank. In that way the details remain between the bank and the individuals, while giving confidence to the group that each household has a realistic chance of financing the purchase of a house once it has been finished.

BUYING LAND

By this stage all the three main areas of endeavour need to be sufficiently developed.

- **Marketing and membership** have established the foundational membership agreements (see Chapter 5) and built the membership numbers and relationships to a viable level to consider major financial outlay, including land purchase and engaging paid consultants.
- **Legal and finance** have considered who or what legal entity will buy the land, and how the purchase will be funded. A lawyer and an accountant are on board to advise on setting up the legal development entity and tax implications, and to provide clarity on the preferred ownership system when the project is completed.
- **Site and design** have clarified the overall goals and qualities of an appropriate site; have agreed on the site criteria (see Chapter 7); and have been researching, visiting and assessing promising sites.

Site feasibility (see Chapter 4)

A developer will have in mind the kind of houses she/he knows will sell and the likely configuration of density, house size, roading, amenities, materials, etc. that will create a financially successful project. She/he will then test this against what is possible on a specific site and crunch some numbers to see if a development on that site is financially feasible. A cohousing group is likely to want a different housing layout, but this still needs to be financially feasible and achievable.

When we found the site in Ranui it fulfilled most of our site criteria, and an initial scan of site information and Council requirements looked good. We then did a detailed feasibility design and costing to make sure it was possible to build what we envisaged on the site, and that it stacked up financially.

We had less than a week to confirm our offer to buy the site, so I was commissioned by the group to do a sketch 'bulk and location' site plan for the site to see how many houses we could comfortably fit in, in the configuration we wanted, including carparking to one side, a common house, and individual houses with north solar orientation and good community spaces between them. I also drew up an indicative house design and materials schedule.

This gave a Quantity Surveyor (QS) experienced in multi-unit development enough information that she/he could estimate the cost of development and construction of our proposed neighbourhood, including siteworks and all services, houses and common house, based on our site layout and other site information.

We also commissioned a registered valuation of the site to confirm its market value. Our requirements – and therefore the value of the land to us – were different from those of other developers, but we didn't want to pay too much in case our project didn't proceed, and we needed to sell the land. We asked the valuer to include a generic valuation of the proposed houses from the indicative house plan and materials, to get an idea of what our houses would be worth in that area.

Using this information and with the advice of a developer, we put together a financial feasibility budget which included the cost of the land, the cost of construction of buildings, siteworks and services, professional fees, local authority consents and financial contributions, as well as costs of marketing, bank interest on the construction loan, and an appropriate contingency. The total costs were divided among the units to give proposed sale prices for different-sized units and these were compared with the valuations.

The key was to compare the expected costs with the final expected value in order to determine if the project would work financially, and to be sure that the price of the site was appropriate. This was only the first of many iterations of design and budget, but by using our best knowledge and educated assumptions we got a good reality check to guide future planning.

Buying land is a huge milestone, and a real expression of determination and intent. Once a site has been secured it is a good time to do a membership drive, as there are likely to be people interested who have been holding back until they know the location.

DEVELOPMENT STRATEGIES

Developing a cohousing community is not for the faint-hearted! It requires large sums of money; a range of skills; and engagement with the highly complex, highly competitive and high-stakes building industry. Any multi-housing project requires the willingness to take risks. This is why standard developers build in a substantial profit margin, because it is skilled and complex, and not all projects end successfully.

Developer-led strategy

If a cohousing group wants speed, efficiency and little risk, the group should consider finding a developer to build the project for them. Developers have experience, track records with financiers and networks of professionals they are used to working with. They can work fast and efficiently, making decisions as required and taking all the risk. However, developers who carry all the risk of designing, building and selling completed units will make decisions based on their assessment of what the market wants, and not on the specific needs of a cohousing group, because the speed with which they sell the completed units has a direct bearing on the profit they take out.

Self-development strategy

It is possible for a cohousing group to act as their own developer. Earthsong did, because we couldn't find a developer willing to work alongside the group. Self-development gives the group a lot more control, because they can make decisions based on their specific needs and wants rather than on what 'the market' requires, knowing that members have committed to buy the units once complete. However, the group also take all of the financial risk, and the development will almost invariably take longer (because the group haven't done this before, and they work by consensus) and cost more (because they are trying to meet a range of needs, and the project takes longer).

An extremely useful planning process called the 'Timeline Game'[1] was developed specifically for cohousing groups. It addresses all the major areas that require attention: group formation; legal, financial, marketing and membership issues; site, design and council consents. Working together as a group, members identify and understand the steps needed, and arrange them in order and relationship with each other to

Playing the Timeline Game

create a map to guide progress towards a completed cohousing neighbourhood. It's an enjoyable and enlightening process.

Using the self-development strategy is only possible if there is the expertise and willingness within the group to navigate the complex world of building development. Being our project's own developers required a huge time commitment and was a huge responsibility – and it was the most thrilling and satisfying project any of us could imagine being part of.

Joint-venture strategy

Perhaps the ideal scenario would be for the cohousing group to partner with an experienced and open-minded developer in a joint-venture project. This has advantages for both parties. Risk and control can be shared, as the cohousing group's commitment to buy the completed units gives them the right to help shape the development. The developer provides the experience, access to finance, contacts and project management that allows the project to proceed, in return for guaranteed sales.

Committed buyers may put in significant money up front, further reducing the risk and the costs. Very clear roles and agreements need to be negotiated and recorded between the group and the developer, but with the right people and agreements in place, this strategy can be ideal.

COORDINATING THE PROJECT

Building projects are enormously complex and challenging even when using standard systems and materials, and more so when the design goes outside the norm. In such circumstances there is a continual gravitational pull-back to doing things the known and therefore easier (and less risky) way. At Earthsong we have learned over and over again of the value of having strong, knowledgeable leadership representing the client group when dealing with outside consultants and contractors. An innovative project needs people with the skills and background to drive the project, to look closely at what is being proposed at each step of the way, to ask searching questions and to keep ensuring that the decisions made by consultants or on the construction site are those that best serve the vision.

An efficient structure is required to manage any multi-unit housing project. A diverse decision-making group adds another layer of complexity, and there is the potential for hugely complicated relationships and miscommunications with outside professionals, contractors and Council unless one person from the group is mandated to interact with each. The liaison person is a conduit of information – in both directions – between the group and the outside consultants and needs to champion the group's vision in all aspects of implementation. During the construction phase, even with a strong commitment to full participatory decision making within the group, the liaison person also needs to have the mandate to make some decisions quickly when that is in the best interests of the group and the project.

Self-developing required Earthsong to organise the various tasks ourselves and led us to establish paid roles within the group. We identified three key roles (outlined following) needed over the whole development period, and members with the appropriate skills were given these roles and paid a small fee to enable them to prioritise the project over other paid work.

- **Development Coordinator (DC):** Overview and coordination of the entire project; liaising with all building-related consultants, contractors and officials; developing and monitoring development budget and timeline; coordinating tasks and decisions by group members related to development.
- **Financial Coordinator:** Financial overview and planning; liaising with banks and other finance consultants; monitoring cash flow; financial aspects of contracts and sales.
- **Legal Coordinator:** Legal overview and planning, including legal obligations and internal structures; liaising with lawyers; legal aspects of contracts, titles and sales.

Other paid coordination roles were required at different stages, as follows:
- **Planning Coordinator:** Liaising with the town planner; overseeing land use and subdivision consent processes, including water collection and on-site stormwater design.
- **Marketing Coordinator:** Coordinating marketing strategies; managing enquiries and membership processes.
- **Landscape Coordinator:** Liaising with landscape consultant for Resource Consent.

A detailed job description was developed prior to each role starting. These job descriptions itemised the role's key responsibilities and duties, its mandate and authority, and the terms of engagement (pay and hours). The paid work didn't include Full Group meeting time, attending specific task groups associated with the role, or other work considered to be the voluntary contribution of a member. Full reporting to the group was expected with notes of all meetings and phone calls. Detailed timesheets were required, itemising time spent on each specific task.

While in theory these job descriptions were written for the role, not for the person, in most cases there was only one person within the group who was both able and willing to take on the role, so we didn't face the situation of having to choose between members. We were clear that anyone paid for a role at Earthsong had to have already put in substantial voluntary hours and shown dedication to the project and was expected to continue doing this.

Except for the Marketing Coordinator (who reported directly to the Marketing and Membership Focus Group), all other paid coordinators met as the Development Team (DT) twice a week to coordinate all aspects of the development as it progressed. We also established an Employment Team (ET) to act in the role of employer, overseeing the contracts and performance of paid members and being arbitrators of any difficulties concerning paid work. ET was the interface between the group and those in paid roles, receiving any complaints and feedback, and both supporting the workers and holding them accountable.

See also Chapter 13 for a discussion of hiring from within the group.

LEGAL AND FINANCIAL STRUCTURES

Most legal entity and tax laws are written either for individuals or for corporations. Cohousing has elements of both and is different from both. To ease our interactions with Council, banks, and other building-industry organisations, we chose legal structures that were known and familiar in that world. Internally, however, the non-incorporated membership of Earthsong Eco-Neighbourhood has always been the key decision-making body that directs our official entities.

Development Legal Entity

On advice from developers and lawyers, Earthsong formed a limited liability company called 'Cohousing New Zealand Ltd' (CNZL) to be our development entity.

CNZL was not set up to make a profit, merely to be the legal vehicle with which we could develop our cooperative, inclusive community.

We then had to grapple with all the regulatory issues associated with being a company, including tax and GST requirements, and with the question of how to put our money into the company without triggering onerous requirements designed for corporations. Tax and securities law assumes that companies are profit-driven and requires detailed disclosure documents if companies are seen as soliciting investments from strangers. Instead, we emphasised the fact that we were known associates who lent money to the company to spend on the development of our own houses. Members who lent money became shareholders in the company, at the rate of a $1-share per $1000 lent.

To define the relationship between members of Earthsong Eco-Neighbourhood and our company CNZL, we worked with lawyers to draft our major internal legal document, the Cohousing Agreement. Members pledged to lend varied amounts to CNZL at nominated key times, recorded in a schedule of contributions. We built in agreed rates of interest, payable to contributors at the end of the project. This interest helped to balance out the financial impacts on those who put money in early and thus enabled the project to proceed, with the financial advantage to those who came along once the houses were built. In return for the loans, CNZL undertook to build the houses.

Financing the project

CNZL had enough funds pledged by members under the Cohousing Agreement to pay for the development costs right up until the beginning of construction. This is how it worked.

We had signed the Initial Organising Agreement (IOA) and had developed the culture and structure of our project such that when the land was found, we had the substance and confidence to take the next step. The cost of the land was $660,000. Five members agreed to sign the sales agreement 'on behalf of a company yet to be set up' and put in equal amounts of money to pay the 20% deposit or $134,500 required to make an unconditional offer to buy the land. Those five were confident that either the project would proceed and others would come in to help complete the sale, or they could borrow enough money between them to complete the sale on settlement and then sell the land to recoup their money. If not, they would lose their deposits.

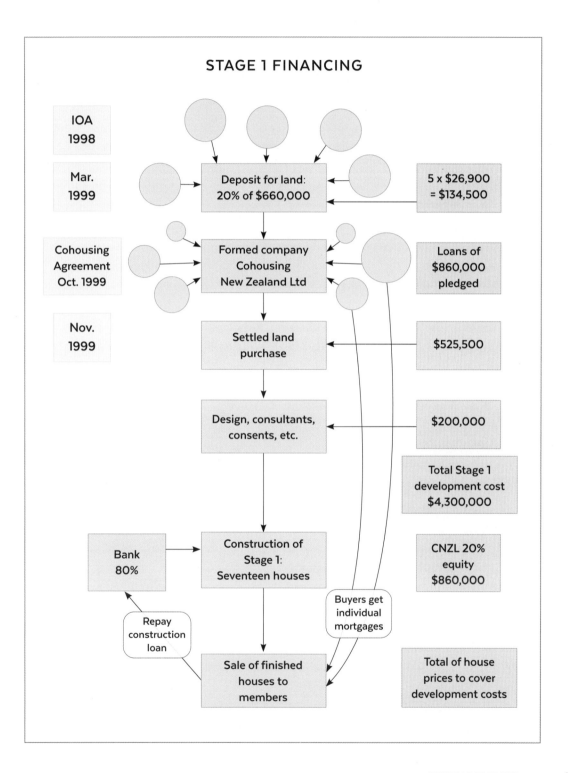

STAGE 1 FINANCING

IOA
1998

Mar.
1999

Cohousing
Agreement
Oct. 1999

Nov.
1999

Deposit for land:
20% of $660,000

5 x $26,900
= $134,500

Formed company
Cohousing
New Zealand Ltd

Loans of
$860,000
pledged

Settled land
purchase

$525,500

Design, consultants,
consents, etc.

$200,000

Total Stage 1
development cost
$4,300,000

Bank
80%

Construction of
Stage 1:
Seventeen houses

CNZL 20%
equity
$860,000

Repay
construction
loan

Buyers get
individual
mortgages

Sale of finished
houses to
members

Total of house
prices to cover
development costs

We had negotiated an eight-month settlement period, in which we wrote the Cohousing Agreement. The twenty-seven members who signed it in October 1999 pledged to lend to CNZL a total of $860,000 (including the $134,500 deposit). CNZL was able to draw in the money required from members to settle the purchase, which left $200,000 still available to CNZL to pay for all the costs of development, including design, consents, project management and legal fees up to the beginning of construction.

With the help of our QS, we kept track of the estimated cost of construction as the design evolved, and constantly updated the development budget. The development budget, similar to the site feasibility budget, includes all the costs – land, consultants' fees, construction of the buildings and services, and bank interest. Our development budget included a contingency but no profit, and the costs were divided up among all the houses so that the total of the house prices covered the costs.

Once we were ready to begin construction, much larger sums were required, and we turned to the banks for a construction loan. The equity we had put in amounted to 20% of the total development cost of Stage I, and we needed a construction loan to cover the other 80%. With the help of our project managers and a mortgage broker familiar with development finance, we put together a proposal and interviewed four bank managers. One of these came through with a loan offer with conditions we felt we could meet.

These conditions included:

- 100% pre-sales off the plans – this was achieved only with the help of three 'placeholder' sales, legally binding to those who signed, but with the expectation that real buyers would take over those sales before the houses were finished
- Professional project managers – expensive for us, but a safeguard for the bank that the project would be well managed
- Cohousing Agreement – this gave the bank confidence that the legal and financial situation between us was clear
- Deed of Indemnity – tying all members together so that we were each and all liable to repay the bank if things went wrong
- Development Budget – showing that all the development costs would be covered by realistic house prices
- Valuations – that showed that the houses would be worth at least as much as the total cost to build them.

It can be a real challenge to pull all the threads together to create a financially viable project. In our case, valuations were a real problem, as valuers by definition don't anticipate the value of a new form of building. With no other examples of cohousing in New Zealand, they simply compared our houses with similar-sized houses in the local suburb, without including any added value for shared facilities such as the common house, or for the energy efficient, healthy buildings or the use of eco-materials. The valuations came back lower than our predicted construction cost.

Valuations are important both for the company to get the construction loan, and also for the individual buyers to get their own mortgage finance to buy their houses once these have been completed. A bank would only lend CNZL up to 80% of the total value of the project. When the construction costs were higher than the valuation, the 20% that CNZL had to find as equity became more like 30% of the total costs of the project. A low valuation also affected the individual buyers' ability to get a pre-approved mortgage to buy their house off the plans, and thus the number of confirmed buyers dropped off as costs rose further above the valuation. We were in trouble!

We needed either lower construction costs or higher valuations, or both. We didn't want to cut too much out of the design to reduce the construction costs, as this might have reduced the valuations and also made the houses less desirable to the buyers. We didn't want to lose any buyers because we needed 100% pre-sales. In the end, we found valuers who were willing to include added value for the common facilities, and with a combination of slightly reduced design elements, tighter construction costing, higher valuations and enough buyers, we did manage to meet the bank conditions and were able to proceed.

CNZL contracted with the builders to construct the siteworks and buildings, and on completion sold each house to each member buyer, who secured their own mortgage to finance what they still owed CNZL for their house. As each house sale was completed, CNZL was able to repay a portion of the construction loan. Subsequent stages followed a similar pattern.

Two major grants and an interest-free loan contributed towards the costs of our project:

- a grant of $93,500 from Infrastructure Auckland for on-site stormwater management (see Chapter 8)
- a grant of $203,000 from the ASB Trust to build the common house as a venue for education for sustainability (see Chapter 12)

- an interest-free loan of $300,000 for three years from Waitakere City Council to help build the common house as a venue available to community groups, and for education for sustainability (see Chapter 12).

Ownership Legal Entity

We wanted a legal structure that would allow owners to buy and sell their houses easily without undue complications of collective ownership, and that would be acceptable to the banks so owners could get individual mortgages. Unit titles combine elements of both private and common ownership, and as such are a very good fit for cohousing.

Each owner gets unit title to their own house, small private garden, and one carpark. All owners also get a 1/32nd share of the common land, common buildings and facilities. Under the Unit Titles Act 2010, all unit proprietors are part of the Earthsong Body Corporate. Body corporates typically elect a committee to manage their shared facilities. At Earthsong, however, all aspects of our neighbourhood are managed by the appropriate Focus Groups and the Full Group of members according to our decision-making procedures. Even our legal entities take their instructions from the unincorporated body of members of Earthsong Eco-Neighbourhood, unless this proves to be incompatible with their legal obligations.

There are some implications of the unit title system for development that are worth noting.

- The project needs to be designed and gain Subdivision Consent and Resource Consent as a single development, including house footprints, plans and elevations.
- Building Consent can be granted at different times to separate buildings, and it is possible to build separate buildings in different stages.
- Titles are not issued for individual dwellings until all the walls and roofs of that stage have been built.
- Unit title boundaries are typically defined by the walls and roofs of buildings, and any additions or alterations that would breach those boundaries require the written consent of all the other unit owners and interested parties (including any bank with a mortgage over a unit). Logistically this makes any alterations very difficult. In our case, the unit title boundaries were drawn at the outer edges of the individual gardens or yards, giving a lot more flexibility

around additions and changes later on. Some units have added small porches to their entrances. One owner with an upstairs unit was able to push up the roof to give added headroom upstairs.

- Unit title boundaries between the yards of attached units mean that any additions within a certain distance from the unit boundary are restricted. Additions and alterations may also impact on common services within the individual unit area (such as stormwater pipes), so appropriate approvals and oversight of owners' works by the Body Corporate is necessary.
- Unit title developments come with obligations of all proprietors to the Body Corporate, i.e. to all the other proprietors. It recognises that each dwelling is not only individually owned but is also part of a larger entity of many dwellings. Homeowners must consider their neighbours to a much greater extent than is the case for owners of stand-alone houses, and this requires agreed systems to maintain the integrity of the whole. This, of course, is entirely congruent with cohousing.
- Body Corporates have regulatory requirements under the Unit Titles Act. Focus Groups such as ABC (Admin Body Corp) and Site Management (including design review) handle these regulatory requirements on behalf of the Earthsong Body Corporate.

We also established a charitable trust, the Earthsong Centre Trust, to manage the ongoing educational objectives of Earthsong, and to apply for grants for this purpose. One third of our common house is owned by the Earthsong Centre Trust in recognition of the grants that helped us to build it.

KEY DEVELOPMENT LEARNINGS

- Existing systems such as planning rules or legal systems may unnecessarily hinder cooperative developments. Decisions must be made about when to try to change the system or challenge specific roadblocks, and when to work within the existing constraints, because the effort of trying to achieve everything you want may mean that the project fails to materialise at all.
- As money is spent on buying the site, paying consultants and other costs,

time increasingly has an impact on *costs*. Those liaising with outside professionals need to get clear estimates of time and must follow up to ensure the professionals deliver – or at least keep you, the client, informed of delays. Paid consultants need to be clear with the client group about when an instruction from the group might hold things up. .

- I have no doubt that we were demanding clients. The whole project was hugely challenging, and we were much more demanding of ourselves than we were of others.

- Members in paid positions must keep clear boundaries between their personal wishes and the wishes of the group, and must be willing to sometimes enact decisions with which they might personally not have agreed. And those in the group need a level of trust that the person in the paid role has sound reasons for advocating a line of action, based on prior experience or deeper understanding of the issue gained in the role. It's an edge, a contestable space, which requires both robustness and sensitivity.

- Think ahead to when an owner wants to move on and sell their house to someone new. We were so focused on the challenge of getting our project built and selling houses to individual members that we didn't pay attention to the financial and social implications of future sales.

- CNZL sold the houses to the first buyers at cost, many of whom have since on-sold at market value. There is an opportunity in the development phase to consider building in a mechanism to keep the houses more affordable.

- When an owner on-sells their house, they are selling both an individual house and a share of common land and facilities. Consider building in the requirement for a percentage of the increase in value of the house to go back to the commons, in recognition of the increased value of what you continue building together.

- When houses are sold to new people, pay attention to enrolling and integrating those new people into the culture of the community.

What we are selling is community;
and by the way a house comes with it.[2]

LIVING ON A
BUILDING SITE

12

STORY

That winter of 2002, Heart Politics for me was a place to celebrate powerful mani-festation, and I was given a standing ovation at morning circle. Earthsong is a fruit of Heart Politics, and that recognition touched me deeply. In August I attended the first wānanga at the Tauhara Centre, a seven-day gathering that had grown out of Heart Politics. It was a transformative experience that gave me time to reflect on the journey of the last seven years.

We had some good news in August, when Waitakere City Council (WCC) agreed to reduce our reserves contribution by $30,000 after considerable work by Peter. Housing developments were usually required to pay 6% of developed land value towards Council's cost of providing reserves or open space. Peter's persistence and skill in making the case that we were providing substantial areas of common open space and recreation facilities within our own development, which reduced the need for Council to fund public reserves and facilities, finally paid off.

Payment of coordinators stopped in September but I kept working, unpaid, compiling information for the Maintenance Manuals, working on figures for Stage II, liaising with the architect to complete the common-house drawings, dealing with remedial issues in the buildings, and organising the digging of the swales, the final site shaping and truckloads of topsoil around houses.

With Stage I construction finished and the pressure off, we finally had time to catch up on years of deferred group and interpersonal processing. Group psychotherapist Margot Solomon held a series of group processing sessions over four months to talk about what we had been through, and to start to build community in a new way now that we were living together as neighbours.

In October members gathered to tell one another our collective story. I had mapped out our development process, covering long sheets of paper with the parallel processes and milestones of our timeline. The chart papered the walls of the Tūī House living room, and members added photos, documents, and sticky labels to show when they had joined the project. Many newer members heard the history for the first time and understood the years of effort that had led to getting these first houses built.

Akita Construction went into liquidation in October. This was a nuisance for us but not the disaster that Earth House Builders (EHB) had been, as the houses were complete except for remedials. It did mean, though, that all the final defects and details were left unfinished. CNZL picked up the responsibility for any serious issue, but owners were left to complete the last items themselves.

I was desperate for a break, and watching my summer disappearing yet again into Earthsong work. A low point was supervising the digger as the contractor shaped the main swale and rock wall footings through the middle of the site. That day it became clear that 500 mm had to be chopped off the side of my own private yard so that the main path and swale would fit through the gap between my house and the neighbouring building. In my role as Development Coordinator (DC) I had to make that decision to take half a metre off the side yard of an individual owner, me, for the good of the whole, knowing that few in the group would even know this had happened. I desperately wanted to do things differently but didn't know how.

As we had deleted the completion of the paths as one of the cost-saving measures, residents negotiated loose gravel paths to get from their houses to the shared laundry or to their cars, often wearing gumboots to get through the muddy and rough conditions. Laundry, groceries and even children were carried by wheelbarrow over the gravel, and Rose started making little badges for 'the falling-over brigade'. We agreed in December that the cost of the paths would be covered by Body Corp levies, with a small extra capital levy from Stage I owners. There was increasing pressure from the group to get the work done in early January; but those of us at the sharp end of the development process had had a hellish couple of years and were desperate for some respite over summer. I said I wouldn't be available during January to organise it, so Cathy agreed to get quotes and organise the contractors, though I would still need to be involved because the positions and levels of the paths were critical.

I completed the Stage I House Maintenance Manuals just before Christmas that year. They were folders of very detailed information about the systems and specific details relating to each house; photos

Typical mode of transport post-Stage I

of positions of pipes and cables in the ground before being backfilled and in the wall framing prior to the linings going on; information about the solar panels, how to repair the earth walls, and any issues for each house that didn't get completed when Akita went into liquidation. As an architect, I knew these were essential manuals for future maintenance. I handed over the responsibility for each house to its owner/s, with information to help them.

The day after Christmas I started building my rock wall. While I loved my house being in the middle surrounded by my community, the position meant that my 'private' garden, being right beside the path and teardrop garden, was one of the most visible places on site. The ground dropped away to the swale, and the site plan had included a rock retaining wall beside the swale to support my yard level with the house. This rock wall had been cut from the siteworks budget after EHB fell over but it needed to be completed before I could plant a hedge for privacy.

I knew the only way it would get built was for me to build it. It was hard, heavy, dirty work, and so much slower than I anticipated. Others around me were establishing their homes and private gardens, but again I was slogging away on common work before I could even start my private garden.

In some ways that was a terrible summer. The extreme pressure was off but that gave space for all sorts of other issues in the group to come bubbling up. Gary's

Working on 'the wall'

personal relationship broke up, in part a consequence of the stresses of the last year, and Gary moved out. I was still doing essential work for Earthsong, and recognising the toll it took to carry so much for the group through extraordinary challenges, with so little emotional or physical support.

The new year, 2003, started off badly, with conflict around concreting the paths, a process now led by Cathy and Lynette. Despite the extra stress generated by trying to get contractors on site in January, work didn't start until late February and the job wasn't completed until April. With seventeen households now living on site there were lots of opinions about how the paths should be done.

We had two systems to accommodate. Our commitment to wheelchair accessibility required the paths to start close to floor level at the front doors and fall in a gentle gradient away from the houses; and our swale system required a constant fall at the bottom of the swale, so the water ran downhill as it travelled north towards the pond. There was a swale beside every path, and sometimes these two requirements meant that the swale ended up much lower than the path. I constantly defended the care that had gone into planning the location and levels of both the paths and swales for our swale system to work, and for the paths to have appropriate gradients for wheelchair access. Feelings ran very high through this period.

Working bees of members were held on weekends over March and April to set rocks in concrete under the edge of the new concrete paths to prevent erosion from the swale undermining the paths. Several of us were oiling our houses for the first time, cleaning off the blackened surface and applying a benign copper-based oil called 'CD50'.

Having had a bit more space to myself over the last couple of months I felt a little happier. I began thinking about what else I wanted to do with my life. For the first time in three years it felt possible to take up my architectural practice again. I asked myself what, when I was 80, I would wish I had done. The answer came clearly: to have completed Earthsong thoroughly and well; to have harvested the best learnings and understandings, and to have kept applying those to other ventures.

I had a strong yearning to write and reflect about the intense journey of Earthsong and applied for a grant from the Social Entrepreneur Fund (SEF) run by the Community Employment Group of the Department of Labour to encourage social innovation. I requested $20,000, enough to fund me for two days a week for a year to write the history of Earthsong, and to attend the USA Cohousing Conference in Boulder, Colorado in June 2003.[1]

In March I started saying we should work towards commencing Stage II in the spring, and the Development Team (DT) was ready to consider this. Helen H had joined DT, and Cathy had withdrawn after feeling burnt by the path conflict. With all the experience of Stage I under our belts, DT felt we could manage to set up the next stage of development without expensive project managers and were keen for me to take the overall managing role. Helen was instrumental in arguing that the pay and conditions should be a lot more supportive than they had been in Stage I, and Gary and Peter agreed. Recognising the ongoing stresses of having to manage my relationships within the group of being both a neighbour and a key employee, DT also recommended that my conditions of employment include regular supervision sessions with an outside supervisor.

Most in the wider group were also enthusiastic about moving forwards, though there were some who just wanted to settle into their new homes, and even some who argued that we should stop at seventeen houses to avoid further liability.

In April the Full Group agreed to employ me for four months to do the feasibility study for Stage II. It felt completely different from last time. Peter was especially supportive, saying in the Full Group that he felt I'd handled the wearing of different hats well, over and over again. I was finally getting support, recognition and backing to use my energy and talents for Earthsong, without feeling there were people trying to pull me down. We'd been on a long journey together, we'd learned and grown up a lot and life was starting to feel good and nourishing at last.

I started work again in high spirits, eager to begin strategising and planning for Stage II. I set up the Design Focus Group again and initiated a post-occupancy evaluation of the Stage I houses to see if any changes were required. I started talking with Alan Drayton about doing more building for us. I was poring over the plans for the remaining houses and the common house, before commissioning a feasibility costing to complete the project. At this time Lippy Chalmers took over as Financial Coordinator from Gary, and Pat Haslam, an accountant, stepped into a support role.

The relationship between Earthsong and Council moved to another level. Helen

Haslam had been a WCC councillor in the early 1990s and was a great supporter of the Earthsong idea when I approached Council in those early years. She had since moved into Earthsong and became a key broker of relationships with Council which led to many useful outcomes for Earthsong. Helen and I met regularly over several months with Council officers to draft a Memorandum of Understanding (MOU), recognising Earthsong as a key partner in demonstrating sustainable homes and communities, and a recognised provider of advice and expertise to Council. The MOU was finalised and signed in July.

Through this MOU connection I was asked to represent WCC on the design team of a different project, the NOW House, a research house being designed as a typical first home but incorporating as many sustainable features as possible. The NOW House aimed to provide an example of an environmentally sustainable, affordable and desirable home built using design concepts, products and materials which were widely available at the time. My work on this project continued for the rest of the year.

As if life wasn't busy and exciting enough, I was elated to hear that I'd been awarded the SEF grant to go to the cohousing conference in Boulder in June and to write up the history of Earthsong. The conference was a real highlight, at which I shared insights and learnings with others passionate about cohousing.

I gave a presentation at the conference about Earthsong, and the feedback from other conference attendees was very affirming. We were the first cohousing community in New Zealand, fitting the concept into our legal, financial and cultural framework, and without any of the experienced professional support that was by then available in the USA. We were self-developed and had incorporated sustainable architecture and services to a much greater extent than almost all other cohousing communities at that time. We had weathered setbacks during construction, we had beautiful houses and we still liked each other (mostly)! It was good to get a wider perspective and feel that, overall, we had done really well in 'only' eight years. I felt proud to belong to this impressive international community of cohousers.

Things were looking up in my personal life, too. I had been spending time with a woman, Robin M, and she came with me to the winter Heart Politics gathering in July 2003. She was a scientist specialising in genetic engineering (GE), and on the face of it an unlikely partner for me, the driver of an environmentally sustainable community, but we shared many other values. That winter at Heart Politics, she bravely held a space to talk about GE, an issue that had become extremely polarised in the media and other public discourse. It was a very fruitful conversation as people talked about their fears, the unknowns and the possibilities. The culture of Heart Politics is to remain open-hearted and work to find connection rather than separation, so that issues that affect us all can be addressed together, rather than by one opposing camp or the other. The idea arose of hosting a gathering of people of diverse views and skills on the subject of GE, and a small group including Robin M and me started meeting to organise a GE Dialogue, planned for April 2004 at the Tauhara Centre in Taupō.

As Earthsong was now a residential community while still being a development company, with very different concerns and drivers, we had engaged an organisational consultant to facilitate a review of our internal structure in April. As a result of this, a small team of members worked on a new structure of working groups. In July we agreed to set up a pair of teams, the Management Team (MT) to attend to issues involving membership and residents, and the Construction Team (CT) which would take over the development and construction focus of the old DT but without having overall responsibility to manage internal issues as well. A new Personnel Team was established to liaise with and support any paid members. In a departure from the largely self-select method we had used to date, a selection process was agreed to fill the positions in each of these three teams, with suitable liaison and overlap between them.

Gary had stepped into the breach as Financial Coordinator in that critical pre-development phase of Stage I, and he and I had worked closely together through the enormous challenges of the previous three years. I hugely valued his support, knowledge and strategic thinking. But those construction challenges had had personal costs within the group, including his relationship break-up. He had resigned as Financial Coordinator after Stage I was complete and had moved out of Earthsong, but he was committed to continue supporting the project for his own satisfaction and in service to a project he believed in.

The new teams were selected on 26 July. The meeting started with a level of tension, much of it directed towards DT, and towards Gary in particular. As both Cathy and Peter had earlier declared that they were stepping back, Gary and I were the only members who had front-line experience in getting our project built and were willing to carry on, and for a time through that meeting it looked as if Gary did not have enough support to be selected for the new CT. In the end Gary, Lippy, Bryan, another member Wendy, and I were selected onto CT by the group; but I was unhappy about the process and the risks to our project if we did not have Gary's experience and wisdom from Stage I. The thought of being the only previous DT member on CT, and having to reinvent, re-explain or revisit details and ways of working that we'd already worked out, filled me with dread.

I felt people had little understanding of the ongoing responsibility, overview and detail that DT had managed in Stage I. Some expressed a need for a clean sweep and sharing of the power; but CT was the management team of a development company, with all the risks and challenges faced by developers, and we were working towards signing a contract worth $1.4 million in the next few months. We needed the best and most experienced people for the job to take us through successfully. Suddenly I wasn't feeling so positive about Stage II any more. Why did we have to make it so hard?

Later, at a debrief about the process, it was clear people were seeing the power, authority and recognition of members of DT and wanted to spread that around, but weren't recognising that DT's 'power' came out of an enormous amount of work, commitment, passion and responsibility, and the ability and willingness to make decisions, to stick our necks out, to go the extra 100 miles. The re-organisation of Earthsong teams meant that the visible power and responsibility was now spread more widely, but without recognising the underlying work and commitment required, it risked sucking energy out of the 'doing'. Several people on MT began to feel overloaded and stressed as they shouldered some of the burden and responsibility and realised the amount of work involved.

By August I was working hard on development budgets, the construction timeline and construction prices. Based on the numbers of members ready to buy houses, we made the decision to build only the next seven houses in Buildings F and G² as Stage II(a). I started meeting with Alan Drayton and his site manager Ross Davidson to go over the plans and get them started on pricing.

It was a time of great change in the New Zealand building industry. Major defects had become apparent in standard timber-framed construction techniques, details and materials, leading to mould, rot and other weather-tightness issues in recently completed buildings. This 'leaky-building' problem had prompted a huge shake-up of the industry and a tightening of codes and requirements. Local city councils were also tightening up their requirements, as they were increasingly considered liable for approving inappropriate details and faulty construction and being required to pay huge costs. Even though we had Building Consent for both Buildings F and G from

2000, Council insisted that we follow the new updated requirements, all of which added to the construction cost.

The money issue was again extremely challenging, the problems seemed formidable and my stamina was run dry by years of effort. We were back into full establishment mode, with meeting after meeting trying to pull all the pieces of the project together. The budget looked bad and the prices we needed to sell the houses for had risen hugely, but members were surprisingly upbeat and optimistic. One by one each potential buyer came around to accepting the higher prices.

Since we had established a track record with the bank from Stage I, it required only five of the seven houses to be pre-sold. On 10 October we had a house-choosing night, and four members put their names on the houses they wanted to buy. I was one of those buyers. I didn't have the funds, but I knew we needed more sales before we could start building, and I also wanted to safeguard a place in case one of my sons chose to live at Earthsong in the future. Having sufficient dependable income at that stage allowed me to obtain a mortgage on my existing house for the deposit, though I didn't have a plan for how I was going to manage the full price once the house was finished.

We needed one more sale before we could get bank finance for the seven houses of Buildings F and G, and at that meeting a consortium of five members put their names on a fifth house; they were people with spare funds who agreed to buy the house together to hold the place until someone else bought it. We'd done it – we'd jumped the last major hurdle that meant we could go ahead with Stage II(a). Construction could start in spring.

As part of strategising to complete the building work, we had brainstormed how we might fund the building of our common house. The cost of building a reduced common house was built into the Stage II budget, but it could only be built after all of the houses were completed and sold, and would be an incomplete version at that. We invited Bob Harvey, the charismatic mayor of WCC and champion of its eco-city direction, to visit Earthsong to discuss how we might fund our common house, which was essential to the educational role we had committed to through the MOU. His suggestion was that we set up a charitable trust focused on education and apply for funding, and indicated that WCC might be able to help.

We had another permaculture workshop with Robina McCurdy, focused on designing several areas considered a high priority. I worked with two of my neighbours on a beautiful koru design path for the teardrop garden, which was later built.

Permaculture workshop

I had been working on the rock wall all year but taking it more slowly and learning to feel the satisfaction of building it. My neighbour Chris often helped by mixing the concrete. It was finished in October and I spent a long weekend shifting topsoil and planting my garden. I could finally plant a hedge to give some privacy to my back yard.

At CT we talked about how to manage the construction this time. I'd learned a lot from our project managers during Stage I. I'd also built a strong relationship with Alan Drayton[3], and we were negotiating for his company to build both the houses and the siteworks for Stage II(a). In November the Full Group approved my revised job description as DC to include project management, and my role moved again into construction mode.

I was aware that having seventeen households now living at Earthsong adjacent to the building site could cause more tensions for everyone: for the builders, for the residents, and for me. Once again, I was wearing two hats – both a member/neighbour and managing a huge contract on behalf of all members. As DC I needed the authority to carry out my liaison role with the builders as efficiently and effectively as possible, while remaining accountable to the group. Any confusion, mixed messages or even too much friendly chat between residents and the builders as they worked risked delaying the work and costing us all. As Robin the neighbour, I needed at times to be totally at home, not dealing with questions and problems when I was off duty. At this point Lippy was the only other member in a paid role, working ten hours a week as Financial Coordinator.

As the first step in preparing the site for Stage II(a) construction, we removed some of the enormous clay piles from Stage I stored south of Tūī House. They soon grew massively bigger once the builders started clearing the sites for the next houses. We had put huge effort into saving the old fruit trees in Stage I by clearing only minimal footprints for the houses, only to find that many of the old trees we did manage to save died anyway, and we also had all the problems with gravel, clay and topsoil mix-ups. For Stage II(a), we made a pragmatic choice to cut down all the old fruit trees and let the contractors strip off and stockpile the topsoil, which gave them a clean and clear site to work on.

Bryan and I surveyed the main driveway and digger driver Carl built it. It sloped gently in from the road, higher and wider than before but following the same graceful curve as it always had. Site manager Ross boxed and poured the concrete footpath crossing. Even at this early stage I could see the care and thoughtfulness with which he approached the job. Stage II(a) felt in good hands.

During December we heard that Council had approved a $300,000 interest-free loan to help build the common house as a venue available to community groups and the wider public, and for education for sustainability. This was fantastic news and meant we could start working on other funding applications, and plan to build the common house as soon as Stage II(a) was completed, before building the last houses. After a hiatus of over a year, several more people joined as members. Things were moving again, and life was looking up.

In January 2004 the builders were back on site: men, machinery, noise, dust, action … we were happy! The tumble of grass and old trees to the south of Building E was transformed into bare clay and openness, and gradually houses grew out of the wasteland.

The MOU with Council started to bear fruit. One joint project was construction waste monitoring for Stage II(a), with waste separated, measured and much of it used on site, meaning very little waste left the site. All 500 employees of Council came to Earthsong in February on a site visit as part of their eco-city orientation process, to better understand aspects of sustainability that they themselves were promoting. WCC also assisted us by designing and producing an Earthsong flyer and interpretive posters for tours, with content supplied by us.

The concrete floor slabs for Building F were poured in January, and in March the earth-wall ramming started – music to our ears! As well as managing the construction, still negotiating the price and contract with Alan Drayton and working on council issues, I also started working on the decision log and other documentation as part of my SEF funding. In my spare time I was planning the GE Dialogue with Robin M and several others. I was busy and happy.

The SEF funding turned out rather more traumatic than should have been the case. Some of the grants made to other people in New Zealand were publicly challenged and questions were raised in Parliament. Then on 20 March the *Sunday Star* newspaper ran an article based on comments by one of the directors of EHB, who said that our company CNZL still owed him money, and as a director of CNZL I shouldn't be getting a government grant. The journalist had tried calling me only the night before to get my side of the story, and as I was away from home that weekend, I hadn't got the message. I was devastated to read the article. It brought up old grief and trauma from the EHB disaster, and I felt my reputation was maligned.

Because of this article, my name became one of those mentioned in the newspapers and on TV as examples of how the government was wasting money. Our advice from many sources was not to respond because it would only inflame it more, so I wasn't able to defend my name. Because of this media attention, the Minister of Social Welfare requested an audit of my grant. I put together an interim report of my work on the history of Earthsong. Three officials flew up from Wellington in May and spent a morning asking me questions. They were mostly interested in the story around EHB, which was painful but ultimately good to tell. The audit eventually concluded there was no wrongdoing on my or our part, but of course this was not newsworthy and was not publicised as the slurs had been.

The GE Dialogue was held in April. People from diverse viewpoints were invited or chose to come: GE scientists, doctors, organic farmers, social scientists, anti-GE activists, an ex-Governor-General. Forty-nine people came for four days of dialogue, an open structure but strongly held as a safe space for people to share their individual beliefs, questions and concerns, and listen deeply to others. The scientists believed their work was contributing positively to knowledge and society. Few people have the skills to argue the science, but many at the gathering believed there was a wider context within which decisions about science should be made.

This gathering was a profound exploration of the wider context, and one scientist acknowledged some feeling of relief, that he could share the responsibility for decisions around GE in this context of respect for different perspectives. A highlight of the gathering was seeing Greenpeace Steve and gene scientist Richard, from opposite poles of the debate but who had listened respectfully to each other and even shared a bunk room for three nights, singing a version of David Bowie's 'The Jean Genie' together on the last evening. The public debate had focused on the incompatibility of the polarised views, but we were finding many shared underlying values that opened the door into a deeper understanding and therefore a place from which to find a way forward.

The GE Dialogue had arisen out of the connection between Robin and me despite differences in our environmental beliefs; learning to build relationship and understanding while holding difference. It was a deeply significant and transformative experience. But perhaps our relationship had served its purpose, because our lives seemed to diverge after this, and things became increasingly problematic between us.

We finally signed the building contract with Alan Drayton in April 2004, three months after construction had started. The cost was far higher than we wanted, but they were doing a good job and we felt we would get what we paid for. This allowed us to sign the bank loan documents in May.

We also started working towards building the common house. The cost was built into each house price, but the collapse of the builders had left us with no funds to carry over from Stage I for the common house. We had agreed in January to accept the Council loan offer and to establish the Earthsong Centre Trust as the entity that would carry forward the third part of our Vision Statement: education for sustainability. We had also agreed to engage an internal Funding Coordinator with the brief of raising a further $500,000 by June. The Design Focus Group began

Stage II(a) framing

to review the plans and to make any changes required so that, as well as being our common house, the building could also be an educational centre and public building.

From the beginning, the group had not been totally aligned behind the idea of sharing our common house, the central part of our collective home, with external community groups through an educational agenda. We had ongoing discussions, goal-setting processes and some conflict in the group for the rest of the year about how the dual use would work. There was still internal debate about the structure of teams and Focus Groups, and regular Community Building workshops with Margot Solomon were ongoing, recognising that we still needed help with our group dynamics and had years of emotional processing to catch up on.

I had also been talking with Tony Miguel of Ecowater, WCC's water division, about joint water-monitoring projects through our MOU relationship. The largest project involved installing more than twenty-six metres to collect monthly water-use data. Our previous attempt to treat wastewater on site had been opposed by the authorities during the design phase, so we were delighted to include a composting toilet by the common house, as a trial for Ecowater to assess whether a composting toilet could be appropriate within the urban drainage area.

The Design Focus Group was working hard fine-tuning the common-house design and making many decisions for the working drawings in order to get Building Consent. There was real urgency to also get the Building Consent approved for the six units of Building I by the end of June, before a huge new Council levy of $9000 per unit, called 'Developers' Contributions', came into being. Buyers started oiling the outside timber cladding on their units in the weekends as it was installed.

We had contracted a professional fundraiser in March to raise funds for the common house, and she worked with the Fundraising Group and our Funding Coordinator over this year to plan funding applications and internal fundraising events. A movie fundraiser brought in nearly $1000 for new chairs, but a lot of effort was put into planning a fundraising dinner and art auction, which eventually foundered on the rocks of unresolved agenda differences and interpersonal issues.

Though the construction of Stage II(a) proceeded well all year without any major hiccups, by late July I was exhausted and again very stressed. I spent a few days almost immobile with back pain, before blacking out and crashing my head against the bath edge, giving myself a black eye. I spent a few days on Waiheke Island to recover.

And then, on Sunday, 29 August 2004, I was having a peaceful day working in my garden when the phone rang. My son Willow answered it and handed the phone to me with a worried look. Dad said my name, and then choked up. Mum came on the phone. 'What's up?' I said. She replied, 'We're at Lesley's place. We think she's had a heart attack. She's ... gone'. 'Gone where, to hospital?' No. Gone. It took my brain a few seconds to catch up. It was such a total shock, so unexpected, so unbelievable, so permanent.

My parents had been worried when they hadn't heard from my sister that weekend, had gone to her home and found her body on the floor. My sons and I jumped in the car and rushed into town. It had been a normal quiet Sunday, but two hours later I was being driven in a hearse to the morgue with my sister's body in the back. All our lives changed in an instant.

My sister had been diagnosed with muscular dystrophy in her late teens. The disease mainly affected her upper body, but it hadn't stopped her living a full life, becoming an accountant, travelling and buying a home. In the last few years she had bravely taken a new direction, leaving her highly paid job and returning to university to study for a property degree. She had graduated just three months before, winning the top prize for a graduating student, and was about to start her dream job in the property industry. She had a whole new life ahead of her ... but unbeknownst to us all, her heart muscles had been weakening, and suddenly her life was over. She was forty-six.

The next few weeks were a blur of deep grief, organising Lesley's funeral, sorting out her stuff, selling her house, trying to comprehend. Mum blacked out as we were sorting through my sister's house a few days after she died, and we called the ambulance. My uncle had a heart attack in October and was in hospital for a few days. My family was in deep stress. And construction carried on, and I did too – on the surface – with a huge despairing hole of blackness inside.

There was no time to stop. Seven houses were nearing completion, and needed oiling, painting and paving. I was setting up the common-house construction to happen as soon as Building G was finished in December. The group was grappling with committing to build the common house when we didn't have all the funds we needed. We considered staging it, only building the dining room and kitchen, or building the shell only and finishing the internal fitout as and when we had funds.

There were major conflicts between the Promotions Team, Management Team and Personnel Team. Lippy, who already played a key role as the Financial Coordinator, was chosen as the new Marketing and Membership Coordinator. There was strong feeling from some within the group that key roles should be spread across several people and a request was made for her to relinquish one role if she wanted to take up the other. Others saw this as a personal attack on Lippy and defended her right to keep both roles. Feelings ran high.

Three new households moved into Building F in November. I inherited some money from my sister that enabled me to complete the purchase of the house I had bought. I was relieved to be able to follow through on the purchase but felt gutted that my sister's death had made that possible.

In December, a big garden party I had planned at Earthsong for my fiftieth birthday still went ahead. People drifted around the paths and sat above the pond listening to the band play in the late afternoon sunshine. My neighbour Chris made another wondrous cake, a tall rainbow tower, and we gathered on the common green for speeches and acknowledgements, my family seated around me. It was a celebration of community and our village. I felt loved and appreciated but was terribly unhappy inside.

With my sister dying so soon before my fiftieth birthday, I felt a visceral change in my life: from expansiveness – still opening to limitless possibilities – to passing the mid-point and looking towards my old age – a narrowing down to death. Not a happy change. The suddenness of her death prompted me to start living each day as if it were my last.

Things had become distant between Robin M and me over the last few months, and we left each other just before Christmas. I came home from a short summer holiday to find that, in my absence, two members had dug a trench through my garden to the swale to install a drain, damaging some of my plants, including a little kōwhai tree that had been my sister's. It was rage-inducing, a violation of my personal space, when I so desperately needed to feel in control of my own home.

After a brief pause in January it was all on again with the next phase. The garage was built to provide storage for the builders. The just-completed Unit 21 became our temporary common house, 'Tūī Two', for the next year. I moved my DC office again, this time from Tūī House to the south bedroom in Tūī Two.

In early February 2005 Tūī House was demolished. It had been my and my sons' home for more than two years, and then our temporary common house for nearly three years, but I had no love for that cramped, mouldy building. It was built of home-made concrete blocks tied to a timber frame. It felt like justice when I drove the big digger and gave the edge of the parapet the first whack with the bucket to bring it down. The concrete blocks were crushed to become hard fill for our

The common house footprint taking shape

driveway, and the rimu framing was stockpiled. Peter later made three beautiful tables for the common house out of this timber.

In February we signed the contract with Alan Drayton Builders to build the common house for $1.13 million, with the understanding that we only had half of the funds and might need to call a halt before completion. The site was cleared and the outline of our community home was marked in lime on the clay – another huge part of our vision beginning to take form.

In February my elder son Willow, by then twenty-two years old and doing a post-graduate diploma in teaching at The University of Auckland, left home to share a house with three friends. Two weeks later my younger son Erin also left home to study at The University of Otago in Dunedin; one more goodbye. I went off to the WOMAD music festival in New Plymouth in March, and while there I got a phone call to say that Erin had been hurt. He had been to the pub in Dunedin with some mates to celebrate his eighteenth birthday (and the legal drinking age), and had got caught up in a fight outside the pub. He copped a flying fist to his jaw, which was broken in four places. I was devastated. My sister's sudden death was still raw, and this was my precious boy, my youngest who had just left home, and he was hurt, and far away.

There was grief and loss within the group through that time too, as my immediate next-door neighbour Narelle had been diagnosed with a brain tumour in 2003. She had been declining over the summer and died on 1 April. She and her two children had been part of our lives and an active and valued member of our project for more than six years.

I was arguing with Council over using non-treated timber for the upper deck of the common house, managing ongoing decisions by the group about things such as kitchen design and equipment, putting together the Stage II(b) budget to build the last eight units, getting expressions of interest in buying those units and working with the architect over finalising the drawings for pricing and construction.

There was ongoing conflict and resistance in the group over several issues, including the internal structure review and the relationship of our educational trust with members and residents. There was also conflict within the Construction Team and with the Personnel Team, all of which led the Personnel Team to resign in July.

Construction of the common house continued without a lot of drama, thank goodness, because by this time I'd also taken on the job of being the supervising architect for the construction of the NOW House – the research house for which I'd been on the design team representing WCC in 2003. The builders for this house were nowhere near as competent or careful as our builders at Earthsong and there were ongoing problems and worries with the quality of construction. I was working hard, and it had been a difficult few months. I felt all scattered out around the edges and empty in the middle.

The Funding Subgroup worked hard for most of that year making funding applications. In May we got a huge boost, with the ASB Trust granting us $203,000 to help build the common house as an educational venue. We'd applied for more funding from the licensing trusts but heard in June that they'd turned us down. A total of eight other funding applications had been made, but most philanthropic funding organisations didn't prioritise sustainability as one of their areas of focus and none of these applications was successful. By that time, we were halfway through building the common house and had no other likely sources of major grants.

We briefly considered whether we should stop, but there was strong support from the group to carry on. At one meeting a member, Margaret, expressed her worries and doubts about how we'd fund the common house, before saying, 'Then I remembered I'm at **Earthsong**, so of course we'll find a way to do it!' It so completely

Lifting the main beam in place

expressed the spirit of how we'd come so far, and the determination of the group to complete our neighbourhood.

In June the roof went on the common house and members spent a hectic couple of days oiling the battens for the dining-room ceiling before they were installed. We had a roof shout for the builders, and the next night we hung fabric and ferns over the empty wall framing and window holes, covered tables with cloths and greenery and had a candle-lit midwinter dinner – our first dinner in our beautiful common house. In the bare shell of the building and with no electricity, it was lit only by candles and very cold, but everyone glowed with pride and achievement.

One of the award applications I'd put in earlier in the year came to fruition when we won an Auckland Regional Council Environment Award, which was good for morale but didn't come with any funding. With no further grants expected, we predicted a half-million-dollar shortfall. Walk to Work Eco-Developments Ltd

Midwinter dinner in our common house

(W2W), the separate company some of us had set up to own and develop the land at the front of site, was asked to buy out CNZL's $70,000 share to help bring in funds. The group also decided in October to levy all units around $3500 each to make up the remainder of the money required to complete the common house. A loan was set up from an ethical finance company, secured over one unit, to pay for the shortfall in the short term and allow the completion of the building.

Work continued all year by the Marketing and Membership Focus Group to bring in new members and pre-sell the last eight houses. Work got increasingly busy with setting up to build these houses as Stage II(b), wrestling once again with budgets and costs, and oiling the common house in the weekends. It was constant rush and scurry – there never seemed to be a time to stop and recharge. By September we had a price from Alan Drayton Builders[3] to build the eight houses, an indicative loan offer from the bank and five serious buyers. We started working bees to clear the last of the trees towards the front of site and set out the positions of Buildings H and I.

The common house was nearing completion, and I organised the siteworks to dig the swale past Buildings F and G and reshape the common green in preparation for final paths and paving. The extent and design of paving and paths around the common house became another contentious issue. The original site design had two paths connecting the main path with the rotunda, but one of these had been deleted in February in favour of a ramped path between the rotunda and the grapefruit tree. This path, which connected Buildings E and F directly with the common house along a route that had been in place to Tūī House, became increasingly contentious, and the issue came to a head in November when the decision to build it was deferred. To me it felt like a casualty of increasingly fraught relationships within CT as we struggled with the problems that continued to come our way as we tried to get Earthsong completed.

We had heard that the commercial land between us and the Ranui shops had been sold and was likely to be developed, and around October I started representing W2W in meetings with other central Ranui landowners and WCC, a group that became the Ranui Central Development Network. We continued to meet for several years and were an active part in shaping the future of our suburb through a consultative process that produced the Ranui Action Plan in 2008, and ultimately led to the new library and other development.

By November the common house was very nearly finished, and the builders were gradually moving over to the Stage II(b) site. The outside paving around the common house wasn't included in the main construction contract, so I started organising contractors to lay the concrete patio outside all the doors and on the north side. An unusual detail had been used at the base of the building in order to insulate the concrete slab without using polystyrene; the detail involved a timber wall plate at the slab edge, protected from outside moisture with a solid zinc flashing, which was then covered by the cedar cladding. The site manager Ross told me then – in November – that concerns had been raised in June about compatibility issues between the zinc and the cedar cladding, and he believed the zinc also needed to be protected from uncured concrete. The architect had verbally given the go-ahead in June, but both he and the builders had failed to mention these concerns to me as DC at that time.

I phoned the zinc supplier to ask for advice on how best to separate the zinc flashings from the new concrete. I was told that zinc should never be placed adjacent to concrete. Over the next week this unfolded into confirmation that it was a very serious problem, and zinc shouldn't have been installed at ground level at all. Zinc is not compatible with concrete (fresh or cured), bitumen (in the malthoid damp-proof course), red cedar timber or any underground situation where it will stay wet. All these conditions applied to the common house.

It just knocked me over. We were so close to having our beautiful common house finished. I was utterly exhausted and had been running beyond my stamina for so long. I kept on coping, but inside I was a mess. I started seeing a therapist, recognising finally that I needed support in more ways than I was getting. It had been such a huge journey. I needed to dig into some of the unresolved issues and climb back out of the hole.

Everything that could be finished in the common house was done by the end of December, leaving the rotunda floor and the paving unfinished while the architect, the builder and I struggled in Site Meetings to find a way through. A report from a corrosion engineer recommended complete removal of the zinc. This would have required removal of the timber cladding covering the zinc around the entire building, been hugely damaging and costly, and still not addressed the protection of the timber plate in the floor slab.

Despite these unfinished items, the common house was given practical completion in December. Council were happy for residents to use it in a limited capacity as our common house, but not for any public use. I moved my office yet again just before Christmas, cramming my desk, bookshelves and files into the narrow office upstairs.

It had been another huge year, with joys, satisfaction, conflict and connection. I still felt I was camping in my house. I hadn't had time or energy to make it into a home; it was just a place to go when I wasn't working. My energy and focus were still on the building of Earthsong. But every step brought us closer, and even coming up against obstacles that we couldn't see past, there was now no doubt we would find a way through.

POWER AND LEADERSHIP

13

... authentic citizenship ... is to hold ourselves accountable for the well-being of the larger community and to choose to own and exercise power rather than defer or delegate it to others.

BLOCK, 2008, P. 55

It was March 2000. The Development Team (DT) was working intensively to pull together the design, legal structures, budgets, consents, builders' quotes and contracts, buyers, and all the other aspects that were essential to have in place before we could begin construction of our multi-unit neighbourhood. One Earthsong member was very stressed about both timeline and budget and sent increasingly unhelpful emails to the DT.

In particular, he had a problem with Cathy and me, felt we had 'too much power', wanted us to 'Back Off!!' and give others more space. I felt he was pulling in another direction, had become more and more distant and anxious and was hindering rather than working with us to pull off this huge project. Which did he want, to try to meet the timeline and budget, or for us to back off?

I sent him some questions. I was genuinely curious, as well as feeling frustrated, attacked and battered.

Do you believe our project needs leadership?

If no, what other group can you name that has successfully completed a project of a similar scale and complexity to ours without leadership?

If yes, what is a model of leadership that you see as appropriate? What group, organisation, or political body uses an appropriate leadership model effectively in your opinion?

No answers were forthcoming.

I am still curious. What does healthy leadership look like, particularly in the context of a large, complex project where the decision making lies with an empowered group? This is largely new territory, and we are inventing it as we go. We need to keep talking about power and leadership in groups and in society, keep having the collective enquiry about how to work most effectively and in a way that feels healthy for ourselves individually and collectively, and for the planet. It is hugely important work for our time and continues to be my learning edge.

LEADERSHIP

Group situations with some form of hierarchy are familiar to most of us, whether it is in a family, or in a work context, or in an elected committee. Leaders usually have that position through structural authority, family position or personal charisma.

I have also been part of 'leaderless' groups that are not focused on getting anything done but have the aim of sharing and support, processing and thinking together, and these have been extremely important and valuable for me. Even in a process group such as this, however, in every case I can think of, someone initiates or convenes each meeting of the group, pays attention to what is needed and sets it up. Even if this role is rotated within the group, when there is a task to do someone needs to take it on – and that is leadership.

Because of our familiarity with hierarchies, we tend to put people in that position, and then often rebel against them. This is ultimately unhelpful to the wellbeing and purpose of both the group and the individuals, and one of the tasks of any group is to pay attention to when this might be happening. If we focus more on 'acts of leadership' rather than on 'having a leader', the landscape for action changes considerably.

The major mechanism by which new things happen is individuals taking initiative. It is my experience, over and over again, that even well-supported ideas don't become reality unless someone takes the action to organise them. Such action can be anything from creating a beautiful arrangement for our central table at Full Group meetings, to coordinating the project to install photovoltaic panels to generate electricity, to setting up a car-share scheme. Things are achieved because someone takes leadership, with the clear vision of what is needed and the drive to organise the steps to make it happen.

In cohousing or other community projects with collective responsibility and decision making, this leadership is always in the context of and accountable to the group and must always be coupled with the consensus of those affected. It is easy to assume others want the same thing. At Earthsong we each continue to learn, sometimes to our surprise, that others may have very different perspectives, and actions that affect the group must get agreement of the Full Group.

'Gravity' is continually at work, pulling back into what we already know, the usual way of doing things, whether of hierarchical decision making or standard building practices. When you are trying to do things differently, it requires huge leadership to resist that gravity constantly pulling back into the norm, to question and think through afresh time after time, with your eyes on your vision and wanting to do it better. The extent to which other people step into their own leadership to champion the shared vision and values is the extent to which the leadership is shared. It's a dance.

POWER

Power is the ability to effect change.   MARTIN LUTHER KING

We need powerful people in this world to work for the common good, to champion change to our destructive behaviours, to create different models of how we can live in respectful relationship with one another and the rest of earth. We need people standing in their own power, using self-awareness and love in service to the whole.

Power itself is neither good nor bad; it is a force that can be used in many ways. It is not a coincidence that we use the word 'power' to also mean electricity, a hugely useful force that powers the appliances and machinery that support our lives. Of course, power (or electricity) can also be highly dangerous without appropriate attention, behaviour and safeguards. Power can be used for good or evil, as so many things can.

Most of us grow up to understand power as 'power-over'. Power-over is unaccountable power, used by individuals or corporations for personal or corporate gain without responsibility to those affected. Most organisations and many families are based on power as control and compliance. Power-over is finite: the more power A has over B, the less power B has; the less power B has, the more A can have. When a group of people meet, even when there is a strong belief in power sharing and consensus, these old and dominant patterns of power can re-emerge, and we can find ourselves struggling.

There is another belief system around power that acknowledges that for each of us to be fully engaged in our lives, we need to find our personal power. There is an enormous difference between personal power – or 'power-with' – and power-over. Power-with is an infinite resource: being in one's personal power does not mean there is any less for others. Power-with, for me, has a connection with the spiritual. Those times when I feel most fully alive, inspired and powerful, are when I am most in touch with my relationship with Gaia, my place in and connection with the living system that includes us all.

Power of any kind is never evenly distributed. The idea that we should have equal power is an accountant's concept that requires continual auditing. We have all experienced times of being more powerful or less powerful than those around us, so we can understand how it feels from several perspectives. In a typical power gradient or hierarchy, it is also important to remember that those who are higher on the power gradient are less aware of the gradient; for instance, if you are a confident speaker, you are less aware of the difficulty others might have with speaking in a group.[1]

It's often safer in a group to be perceived as having less power. It can be a challenge to be in a visible leadership position and stay open and loving while still growing a thick enough skin not to be damaged by the flak that that position attracts. As Laird Schaub has remarked,

> In cooperative culture, there's a strong tendency to criticize people filling leadership roles far more than to appreciate them. Where that's the case, assuming a leadership role can feel like wearing a t-shirt with a bullseye on it.[2]

Issues with power happen in every group, and it's important to keep talking about it as a group. Pay attention to overt power and covert power, such as the power of passive aggression. Developing power consciousness will help to keep power moving within the group. Power with transparency and accountability, with connection and relationship, with responsibility to those affected, is a force for positive change.

At the end of 1994, having reached a deep clarity and passion to build an urban cohousing eco-neighbourhood, I knew I would need to step beyond my shy and introverted self and find a strong sense of inner power that would enable me to take action. The ceremony and intention of my fortieth birthday party was designed to support me to 'step into my power' for the work I wanted to do in service to the planet and was crucial in giving me the confidence to take the next steps.

I absolutely support others, in their own way, to step into their own power around working for the common good. Effective leaders need power and influence and also have a responsibility to use power well. It serves us better to strengthen the weaker rather than knock down the stronger; we need more and more people stepping into their own power, not any of us stepping back. The work of creating a flourishing and sustainable world needs empowered and caring people.

As Nelson Mandela, quoting Marianne Williamson, said in his inaugural speech in 1994:

Our deepest fear is not that we are inadequate.
Our deepest fear is that we are powerful beyond measure.
It is our light, not our darkness that most frightens us.
We ask ourselves, who am I to be brilliant, gorgeous, talented, and fabulous?
Actually, who are you *not* to be?
You are a child of God.
Your playing small does not serve the world.
There is nothing enlightened about shrinking
so that other people will not feel insecure around you.
We are all meant to shine, as children do.
We were born to make manifest the glory of God that is within us.
It is not just in some of us; it is in everyone and as we let our own light shine,
we unconsciously give others the permission to do the same.
As we are liberated from our own fear, our presence automatically
liberates others.[3]

LEADERSHIP IN AN EMPOWERED GROUP

Most of us are more familiar with leadership than we are with working in an empowered group. I believe *both* are important and desirable for achieving social change. Empowered groups are groups in which members are not (or not only) followers, or audience, or 'consumers' of the process, but are participants fully engaged in the process: contributing ideas, being part of decision making and taking responsibility for the outcomes. Empowered groups also need leadership, and ideally they help to grow participants into acts of leadership – this is a very different dynamic.

> Leadership is best thought of as a behaviour, not a role.
>
> JANOV (1994) IN WHEATLEY (2006, P. 24)

Cohousing communities, by definition, are empowered groups, with a participatory process, consensus decision making, complete resident management and a non-hierarchical structure. This has huge benefits – more ideas, more alignment and buy-in from members, more energy, more creativity, more support of projects. There are also significant tensions here which are both creative and challenging, and particularly around leadership. The challenge is how to manage these tensions to best serve our projects and planet.

In the last few decades there has been much emphasis on self-awareness, self-actualisation, discovering the hero within, becoming a whole person. This is essential work to conscious evolving; and we also need to pay attention to how that works *between* people. How do we transcend the myth of independence into healthy interdependence; not giving up the self-actualised individual but making the shift from the competitive I-centred culture to a more we-centred culture? Like the jazz player, keeping attention on both the music we are making individually and the music we are making together.

There is an analogy about geese that circulated among my friends in the 1990s. I have no idea if this is true goose behaviour, but there are some helpful messages here about both leadership and an empowered group. Here's how it goes:

> Geese fly in a 'V' formation, each taking advantage of the uplift from the bird in front, and by doing so they can travel much further as a group than when they travel alone. The goose at the apex works hard, cutting the wind for the others

in their slipstream. The other geese make encouraging honks to the one at the apex to keep her going, because they know it's such hard work. When that front goose gets tired, she moves back in the V formation and another takes that hard role. If a goose can't keep up the pace, they drop away and go down to land to rest or die, and two other geese always go down with them to support them when they need it, so no goose must recover or die alone.[4]

People inevitably bring their lifetime experiences of power and authority into new contexts. Some people are damaged by their experience of power-over and reject all leadership or bring a tendency to resist authority. In a group context it's important to become aware of attitudes to power, and part of the commitment to living in community is to be prepared to work on it. What is important is to grow an understanding of group dynamics so we can work it out together, and not perpetuate the old in the new context. This is part of the work of community, and an essential aspect of working towards sustainability.

Others may bring their version of the hero archetype, seeing themselves as the champion to slay the dragon of the status quo (Campbell, 1949). When the status quo at Earthsong is a set of values that are inclusive, innovative and committed to sustainability, throwing out the old may mean a reversion to what is more normal in society rather than a progression towards doing things even better.

In an empowered group, leadership is spread widely, and many varieties of leadership are supported and grown over time. This does not mean, however, that anyone can step into any position. We come with different skills, abilities, inclinations and priorities. In a project as complex, demanding and technically specialised as the development of Earthsong, it required leadership with the skills, training and experience to manage it. The lead goose can only rest if others have the appropriate skills to perform the task at hand.

If being skilful is seen as being (too) powerful, people may withhold their skills from the group for fear of negative projection or reaction. This denies the group the full benefit of those skills, and the group is the poorer for that. A group that values diversity recognises and supports each person to do the work for which they feel called and qualified.

The construction phase and the living phase of cohousing require different skills. Earthsong has moved into being an ongoing residential community, and we are still evolving ways of mentoring and encouraging one another into sharing roles and responsibilities at different times and building in succession planning. We make sure there is a co-facilitator at every Full Group meeting to support the facilitator. We try to ensure there is an 'apprentice' for every key role, someone who is learning and can take over when required, and that someone who moves on from a role continues to mentor the person who has taken it on.

An empowered group that generates ideas together is wonderfully fertile ground for nourishing leadership and helping the seeds of those good ideas to grow. An example at Earthsong is our annual winter hui. The initial idea, of having one weekend every year when we spend time together as a community, came from an individual. This idea was taken up by a Focus Group which discussed the overall shape of the weekend and assigned a budget. The call went out for others to be part of organising the hui, and several people with ideas for different activities within the overall shape stepped into leadership to organise those parts. This annual weekend, full of different activities, including community connection and reflection time, delicious food and intergenerational play, reminds us how good it feels to connect with our neighbours and belong to a tribe.

SERVANT LEADERSHIP

Servant leadership (Greenleaf, 1977) may sound like an oxymoron – but many acts of service are also acts of leadership, and some forms of leadership are certainly acts of service. The difference perhaps lies in the motivation – whether the leader is acting to maintain or grow his/her position of power or a rigid status quo; or whether the leader is a servant first, wanting a better outcome for all, understanding what could make a situation better, then taking action towards that goal.

Servant leadership could also be called 'stewardship', or 'kaitiakitanga'. Stewardship is defined as 'the careful and responsible management of something entrusted to one's care'.[5] Kaitiakitanga, in te reo Māori, can be understood as 'looking after that which nourishes'.

Margaret Wheatley talks of self-organising organisations as living systems, based on a collective purpose and the relationships between people, that can adapt and change in relationship with the environment it is within. Leaders within a self-organising system begin with a strong intention, not a set of action plans, and have confidence in the organisation's intelligence.

> The potent force that shapes behavior in these organisations and in all natural systems is the combination of simply expressed expectations of purpose, intent and values, and the freedom for responsible individuals to make sense of these in their own way.
>
> WHEATLEY (2006, P. 129)

A servant-leader observes, pays attention to the situation, then asks, 'How can I use the opportunities available to me to serve best?' Each of us has ideas which, at the best of times, may only be partially correct or useful. By working together, even challenging each other at times (with awareness and compassion), we can discover which ideas or actions best suit our collective project. We never have all the information, so a servant-leader is open to insight and intuition to bridge the gap into foresight and inspiration. A leader then gives guidance by going in front, and takes the risk of failure along with the chance of success.[6]

The capacity to serve requires a reasonably secure level of personal power, or we end up taking energy from those we seek to serve despite our intention to give. Using our power to serve means participating in the clear purpose and values of an organisation, supporting people's choices about how they can best serve that organisation, and being willing to be accountable and to hold others accountable for their actions.

Peter Block writes about reconstructing leader as social architect.

> Not leader as special person, but leader as a citizen willing to do those things that have the capacity to initiate something new in the world. ... the task of leadership is to provide context and produce engagement, to tend to our social fabric.
>
> BLOCK (2008, PP. 86 AND 88)

PRIVILEGE

One reason that power gets such a bad reputation is its association with privilege, or unearned power. This is the power or advantage we gain by being born with a certain colour of skin or the 'right' gender, or into a well-resourced family, or in a prosperous country.

I know myself to be incredibly privileged. I live in a beautiful, healthy and relatively egalitarian country; I am white, educated, able-bodied and middle class. I am also a woman, a lesbian and was a solo mother for a long time; not such privileged states.

I decided back in the 1990s that feeling guilty about my privilege was a waste of opportunity. There is no shame in being who I am and with the life I was born into. The shame would be in using that privilege only for my own personal or family wellbeing. I had the capacity and circumstances to think beyond just surviving, and I felt a responsibility to use the opportunities I had with awareness, to best serve our collective life.

That led me on the path to build Earthsong, to demonstrate more cooperative and sustainable housing and social systems. Earthsong is undeniably middle class, needing individuals with sufficient resources to purchase their houses. Being middle class meant we had the opportunity to trial different models of organisation and construction that those less privileged wouldn't have the resources to try in the same way. I felt I could be most effective by using the skills and resources I had to demonstrate how other middle-class people could live more sustainably, and by doing that, to trial aspects of healthy housing that could then be applied to more affordable housing, or papakāinga housing, or for others with fewer choices or resources.

I believe we all have a responsibility to use the opportunities we have to reduce our environmental footprint, to trial new and better ways of doing things that don't deplete life for anyone or anything else, to make choices that help move us all towards more sustainable practices that contribute to a flourishing world.

SUPPORT AND ACCOUNTABILITY

It is hard work being in a leadership position, as that lead goose knows, and those putting in the skill and effort on behalf of a group need the support and encouragement of the group. In addition, people taking leadership within an empowered group must also be accountable to the group. It's both/and again: both support and accountability, both accountability and support; recognising when someone has skills and energy for a task or direction and supporting them to step into their power to carry it out, while also holding them accountable for how it impacts on the common good.

A sports team is selected based on skills and motivation, and they are sent out onto the field to play on our behalf. And we cheer them on. That's the encouragement that keeps them going and inspires them to greater effort. Showing appreciation is an act of leadership, but is often left to the perceived leaders, who themselves also need appreciation. The geese know how to honk to support those at the front line.

Sometimes, during the development of Earthsong, we encountered obstacles that seemed insurmountable. I was on the front line researching, negotiating and arguing with Council, architect or builder, trying to keep the built reality matching our vision. Though it didn't happen often, occasionally other members, who were removed from the battle and the energy it took, continued to be staunch about an issue when my tendency at that time was to concede and go with what was possible.

This is the power of accountability to a committed group with a shared vision. If I had been answerable only to myself, no one would think I didn't try hard enough, but with a group there is peer pressure and accountability, and ultimately, the effort was worth it. But it is exhausting to fight these battles, and the one at the front line needs adequate support from the people holding him/her accountable. Those who share the vision and hold so firmly to the principles need to also support the people who are doing the work.

Support and accountability can come from outside the group as well. Peer relationships, both one-on-one and in small groups, can be vital. For several years I met with two friends once a month in a 'peerenting' group. Every month we would take time to each talk about what was happening in our lives and work, the challenges we were facing, and issues we valued getting other perspectives on. Sharing my experiences with friends who knew and valued me outside the Earthsong world helped enormously.

The bi-annual Heart Politics gatherings were extremely important, too. There I met with a group of peers whom I got to know over many years, all engaged in their own explorations of social justice and sustainability. Heart Politics both supported me to be the biggest I could be and was another accountability check. I knew I would return to the gatherings twice every year and say, 'this is what happened, and this is how I dealt with it'. The consistency of these gatherings held me to be totally in integrity in my Earthsong world because I held myself accountable to my Heart Politics peers.

HIRING FROM WITHIN THE GROUP
(See also Chapter 11)

Perhaps the edge between leadership and the empowered group comes into sharpest focus when considering hiring people from within the group for key roles. A group may not face this issue if it outsources all the professional roles to outside consultants, and if group members are able and willing to do all the internal organising, including liaising with the outside consultants, as voluntary contributions. To some extent it depends on the breadth and scope of the vision, and the availability of professionals experienced in implementing such a vision.

In our case we were adapting the cohousing model to the culture and structures of New Zealand for the first time, and needed to think together with lawyers, accountants and project managers about the best ways to set that up. We were designing for community and also incorporating sustainable materials and construction systems and needed to play a highly active role in the design, local authority consenting and construction processes in order to see that this was carried through. And we were developing an unusual form of housing that needed publicising and marketing in order to attract enough purchasers, who understood and actively chose that model, in order to make it viable.

In all these areas, no local professionals had the appropriate experience and values such that we could hand the work over to them. We therefore paid members to take on several roles throughout the development and construction of Earthsong, for longer or shorter periods. Paying group members is a very delicate and charged issue, fraught with dangers, but being a coordinator/liaison person for a development of our size was not a role that could be done only in the evenings and weekends.

There was huge anxiety in the group about potential conflict of interest and power differentials within the group when we were considering whether a group member could or should take on a key role. I see this as operating from the old patriarchal paradigm of separation, objectivity, how things work in the world we know, rather than the paradigm of connection, how things could be, valuing spiritual and emotional connection and inspiration. If the focus is on either/or, one inevitably sees a conflict of interest. If we are willing to hold the complexity of the edge, of both/and, it opens new possibilities – a synergy of interest.

When looked at from the perspective of strengths and gifts, rather than problems and conflicts, the picture looks very different. If we had approached the architect's selection from the perspective of 'We value this member, how can her skills and strengths be best used in service to the project?', if we had had honest conversations about the implications and whether I and the group could handle the stresses, we may well have decided that in this group, at this time, for this project, the most useful role I could play was as overall coordinator, which was the role I ended up playing. But we would have decided that together, and I would have had the support of the group to bring my architectural knowledge in service to the project.

Issues of group dynamics and power relationships will inevitably arise when paying members for key roles, and guidelines are needed to deal with decision making, disagreements and conflict. Set up internal support and accountability for the paid member/s, so that those working intensively for the group can focus their energy on the job. Channel any individual complaints about their work through a small team who can assess whether the complaint results from an interpersonal difference or whether it needs to be addressed as part of the role, and how best to do that.

KEY LEADERSHIP LEARNINGS

- Talk as a group about how you can sustain yourselves and support one another in the challenging endeavour you are all engaged on, and especially how you can support those taking leadership. A supportive community is not just something you are working towards; you are building community now.
- Consider the benefits as well as the challenges of a group member playing a key role. If a group member is willing to put themself forward for a key role, have honest conversations as a group about what the project needs and what would be the most useful roles for that member.
- Create a small employment group to provide support and accountability and be the interface between the paid member and other members around employment issues. You want your paid member to be working most effectively for the project, not dealing with a myriad of different approaches from other group members as to whether they are doing their job well.
- Group members who are paid to work for the project wear many hats, and the pressures can be enormous. It can also be confusing for other members and maintaining clarity of roles is essential. One way to make

it clear whether someone is speaking in their paid role or as a group member at any time is for them to wear a 'paid-role hat' in a meeting when speaking in their role. When I emailed the group, I always signed the email either as 'Robin, DC (Development Coordinator)', or 'Robin, your neighbour'.

- Consider building in regular supervision sessions for those taking leadership roles. It is common knowledge that leaders in any context receive projections and sometimes challenges from others in the group simply because of their position – something commonly known as 'tall poppy syndrome', or putting someone on a pedestal. Having a regular place and a person skilled in group dynamics to talk things through with and put things in perspective can be very supportive and help to keep a wider vision.

- Everyone who takes on a sustained role of leadership faces the question of when to hold on and when to let go: when to defend the vision against subtle or overt attack, fiercely advocate the highest good and resist the constant pull-back into the path of least resistance; and when to let go, step back, trusting there is a strong enough culture to hold it. This is a dilemma faced by every parent: when to guide and defend your child from attack or danger, and when to recognise that your child has grown into their own life and no longer needs your fierce protection or hands-on guidance. There is no right answer, just a continual enquiry informed by connection and conversation with the wider group.

- A flourishing mature ecosystem contains a wide variety of plants and animals at different stages and niches. We could chop out the mature trees to give light to the new seedlings, or recognise the strength and beauty in diversity, how much life the mature tree supports and nurtures, the seeds it sows, the shelter it gives.

CHALLENGING TO THE END

14

STORY

The year 2006 started as usual for me at the Heart Politics gathering, finding haven amongst my peers, not holding any responsibility or role this time. I was worn out, empty and low. I had an image of a didgeridoo player, who uses circular breathing to sustain a continuous outbreath to keep the instrument singing. Earthsong had required such a long period of giving out my energy. My circular breathing had only just kept me going. The Finn Brothers' song was played one morning as we danced before morning circle: '... I won't give in, won't give in, and everyone I love is here ...'.[1] My cracks opened and I just sobbed. I won't give up; I'll take it through to completion. And joyfully, if I could find my joy.

My son Willow and his love Karen were married that January. They asked each of their parents what role they wanted to play in the ceremony. I wanted to walk my beloved son up the aisle. So I waited in the back room with Willow, Erin and two of his friends until his music started playing. One by one his groomsmen walked solemnly in. Then Willow and I went through the door, arm in arm, to a church full of expectant people, all looking around. We slowly paced up the aisle, my heart bursting, my boy on my arm, the celebrants smiling from the front. I hugged him and took my seat, and then the bridesmaids came in, and Karen on her dad's arm. The wedding was beautiful, simple and heartfelt, with lots of laughter and stories at the reception. I felt such pride and joy and love that my cheek muscles ached and my diaphragm hurt the next day.

There was rubble outside all the common-house doors and no floor to the rotunda, but we all came together on 22 January for a ritual of celebration of our long-awaited common house. This claiming and inhabiting was hugely important emotionally to the whole group, to embrace and welcome the central place of our community, after all the long years of effort and challenge. It was not complete, but it was extraordinarily beautiful, and we were awestruck that this was our place. The first common meal was cooked that night by a group of members, the Kitchenettes, in our beautiful kitchen. There was still a lot to sort out, ongoing disagreement in the group over the shape of the common green and design of communal washing lines, whether to buy furniture and what that should be, but for now we were aligned in wonder and exhilaration at our common heart place.

Common-house celebration

At the end of January, we set up a Zinc Task Group consisting of David M, Helen H, Lippy, Gary and me, to support the Construction Team in our negotiations with the architect, builders and Council, in the expectation that there would inevitably be arguments over liability.

Though the common-house zinc problem wasn't reaching any resolution, progress was fast on Stage II(b). Work on the Building H earth walls had started before Christmas and was completed in January. I was concerned about the somewhat crumbly surface of several walls, and two of the earth lintels were removed and replaced. I reluctantly agreed to keep the other walls because the worst ones were internal and largely covered by stairs or tiles. In response to this problem more cement was added to the ramming-earth mix for Building I's lower walls. At the Site Meeting every two weeks, as well as discussing Stage II(b) issues, we would come back to the common-house zinc problem and try to find a way forward.

We had half the buyers we needed for the final eight houses and new people were joining. The delays in completing and opening the common house to full public use, however, were by now deflating the ideas for fundraising, and the Funding Subgroup started running out of steam. Several applications had been made over the last year, all without success except for the ASB grant. The grand opening of the common house was put on hold, a gala we'd planned for March was shelved and the planned fundraising dinner had by this time become a distant memory.

On Waitangi weekend[2] in early February I joined a group of friends for a two-day walk around Mt Taranaki, culminating in a climb up to a sacred waterfall. On the second day I skidded on a loose rock near the end of the walk and fell onto my ankle, hearing a crack as the bone broke. I was deeply in need of spiritual replenishment, but I didn't make it to the waterfall. I spent the next few weeks on crutches, finding things even more difficult than they'd been before.

I kept up with urgent desk work as the builders carried on with Stage II(b) but couldn't visit the building site for several weeks. My ankle was too painful to clamber over rubble with my crutches, and the builder felt it would compromise his safety requirements because I couldn't move out of danger fast if I needed to. The floor slabs had been poured and the builders were making good progress ramming the Building I downstairs earth walls.

When I was finally able to go back on site in early March, I was horrified by the state of the new walls. One wall in particular had a very pitted and crumbly surface, and many others had crumbly seams or hairline cracking. Over the next few days the extent of the problem became apparent as I constantly pushed the engineer, the architect and the builder to fully test the walls to determine whether they were fit for purpose. The crumbly surface was initially considered by them all as an aesthetic issue only, and they jumped straight into solving the problem of crumbliness. But further testing at my insistence revealed significant porosity of the walls to water penetration, a much more serious long-term problem and not one we wanted to live with for the life (500 years!) of the buildings. Two walls were considered substandard and taken down. Despite the gravity of this situation, there was mutual goodwill, liking and respect between the builders, Alan and Ross, and me, and we all wanted a good result.

Earth-wall testing

I still wasn't confident that enough attention had been paid to the other earth walls, so I spent several hours doing my own detailed wall-by-wall visual assessment, sending a schedule of what I found to the architect and engineer. They organised more testing, and the next two water-penetration tests failed badly. I was sick with worry. The problems with the Building I walls were worse than the crumbliness on the Building H walls which I had reluctantly accepted in January, and I felt badly let down by them all – the builders, the architect and the engineer.

A stop-work was placed on the ramming until the extent of the problem had been assessed and a remedy agreed. Now we were spending time at the Site Meetings on not just the zinc problem but on the earth-wall problem too. More testing was done, and Graeme North, a leading New Zealand expert in earth building, was called in. Graeme's advice was to protect the earth walls from weather with hoods or eaves and to consider an earth-compatible protective surface coating.

A meeting in late March was held to assess the walls and try to determine the best thing to do. There were two builders, the architect, the engineer, the Quantity Surveyor for the bank, Graeme North and his offsider. And me. I knew the builders were worried and that if I insisted on taking more walls down, not only would it delay construction and cost both us and the builders hugely, but there was a possibility it might send the builders into bankruptcy. I was the sole client representative, and I felt enormous pressure to accept the walls and let construction proceed; but also a huge responsibility to make it right for us, the purchasers. I didn't want the solution to be a coating on the outside, I wanted a long-term reliable solution. After the meeting I fell to pieces in the privacy of my own home, feeling the stress and the fear of a repeat of Stage I and the builders falling over.

It was really tough trying to work out the best thing to do. Gary started coming voluntarily to all the Site Meetings to support me, so it wasn't just me standing up to all those men by myself. It felt hugely supportive having someone else there at meetings to hear what was said and to talk it through with later, and who could help translate that back to the group, be a back-up and share the burden of responsibility for decisions.

A design for hoods to Building H and lower Building I walls was eventually agreed as being satisfactory to meet the New Zealand Building Code, and construction restarted in early April. In the meantime, work was being done to identify an acceptable earth mix for the upper Building I walls to avoid repeating the same problems.

Another family crisis had happened in March when Dad was diagnosed with lymphoma, a form of leukaemia. After initial worry, the prognosis didn't seem too bad, so we carried on with relief. But the stresses of the last few months had taken their toll, and in early April I ground to a complete halt. I was so burnt out, I just ran out of steam, cogs all gummed up, couldn't move, tears running down my face. Several of my neighbours stepped in and organised a collection of money from my community to send me to a retreat at Piha on Auckland's wild west coast for the weekend, and I slept, read, walked and stared into space for several days.

I came back for another Site Meeting but still felt exhausted so went back to Piha for the rest of the week. During that week away I got a phone call from my nephew to say my brother Everard was sick in hospital. The rest of his family were away, and my nephew needed support. My brother soon recovered, but that meant my entire immediate family, except for Willow, had been seriously sick or had broken bones or had died in the last twenty months. I couldn't understand why these things kept happening. Event after accident after loss after work disaster after illness, on and on. I felt by then I was running, not on replaceable energy, or long-term stamina, or even blood or muscle, but on *bone*.

Helen H had an image of everyone else at Earthsong having moved on with their lives, and me plodding up the rear carrying all the heavy bags and needing to organise the food and the hotel. And that felt true. For Stage I, although I had played the major role, everyone else had also been deeply involved in the process and mindset of getting their houses built. This was much less the case for Stage II(a) and became even less so for Stage II(b), as the buyers were all newer members who hadn't been through the initial development work and were much less involved in the development process, even for their own houses. Most Earthsong members were settling into their new homes and creating gardens, glad that the last houses were being built but with this work being largely peripheral to their lives, because their part was over and someone else was handling it.

The zinc issue was grinding slowly onward. The architect, the builder, Council and Cohousing New Zealand Ltd (CNZL) were the four stakeholders or interested parties, and a building inspector from Council attended most Site Meetings. Because the design of the foundation wall plate and flashing was outside the acceptable solutions of the Building Code, Council required an independent expert report to certify that a proposed solution would meet the requirements of the Code.

It was decided by all parties to detail three options (known as 'status quo', 'bandage' and 'total replacement') and commission an independent report from BRANZ, the Building Research Association of New Zealand, to determine the best solution that would meet both the Building Code requirement for a fifty-year life, and Earthsong's requirements of environmentally sustainable construction. A BRANZ materials scientist visited the site on 23 May, and patches of zinc flashing were removed at several locations around the building for inspection. The news just kept getting worse as we discovered patches of white corrosion on the zinc's inside surface where it touched the timber plate. Instead of protecting the timber from moisture, the zinc appeared to be trapping moisture, and the timber plate was very damp. The whole detail, not just the use of zinc, was seriously flawed.

Back on Stage II(b), test walls using new earth mixes kept failing, and ongoing work was done trying to understand the problem. Eventually analysis of the soil composition showed that there was very little clay content in the ramming earth. Earth suitable for ramming requires a range of particle sizes from quite large (gravel) to very fine (clay). Some clay content is important because clay, being the smallest soil particle, helps the wall resist water penetration.

Because the ramming earth is a natural material dug straight out of the earth, there is natural variation in its composition. In the few weeks between the initial testing at the start of Stage II(b) construction and the bulk excavation of the ramming earth for II(b), the part of the bank being excavated contained significantly less clay content. Once this was understood, a 50/50 mix with a different ramming earth and a change of lime was proposed, tested and finally accepted, and work on the upper Building I walls could commence.

Because of the delays, it was well into May (early winter and therefore wet weather) before the new soil was excavated, and the high moisture content of the soil caused problems with milling, which required a different and more labour-intensive process on site, causing further delays. Despite this, the new mix produced generally high-quality walls to the upper level of Building I.

I finally felt able to relax and sleep at nights knowing I'd done everything I could. I'd resisted

Alan Drayton builder and Alan Franklin engineer

great pressure yet again and insisted all our professionals do a thorough job of making sure these walls and buildings were built to a high standard and were fit for purpose. The site foreman, Ross, acknowledged to me that it was good that I'd insisted on those first tests, that we'd learned something, we'd found the problem and worked out how to remedy it.

In August, I attended the eight-day wānanga at the Tauhara Centre in Taupō. We had been struggling at Earthsong for nearly a year with the problem of the zinc, and were not getting any nearer to a solution. Things seemed so slow and difficult. I started thinking that the (potential) rot at the base of the common house could be a metaphor for rotting stuff that needed to be expressed at Earthsong. For me it was around the architect's selection.

I talked with another attendee at the wānanga, Juliet Batten, and her insight was that our community was mirroring the history of this land. Many pākehā aren't too worried about the history of land wars and confiscations in New Zealand: they want to move on, not dig up the past. But Māori are living with the hurt and injustice.

We needed to bring this out in our community, not to scratch up old wounds, but because the common house was requiring it, was asking the question: 'What do we need to address in our founding, that is causing the rot?'

We held a sharing circle at Earthsong with this theme: 'What do we need to heal in our community to open up the energy again, allow the glow of the vision and inspiration to connect all the way down to the base of our community?' This shifted the energy for the group; allowed a much deeper connection between us; and opened the space for me, seven years later, to share my experience of the architect's selection process and hear others' stories, though there were few people left who had been part of the group at that time. There was so clearly a mismatch between what it meant for me and for others. There was huge love, appreciation and healing in the room that night. We subsequently held a further evening of telling each other our whole Earthsong history – another chance to weave ourselves together a little more and process more of the journey.

The zinc issue ground on with little progress. In August, after another difficult Site Meeting at which we grappled with this issue and were by now considering whether to rip up the timber plate completely, the builder Alan told me of his plans for his business, linking up with other builders to build eco-buildings. He said he'd like me to be on the team as a clerk of works. Here we were, in the middle of a painful process of contemplating destroying and re-doing his building work and arguing over what needed to happen, and at the same time he recognised that I was firm and fair, and he wanted me to bring those skills into his camp.

After further delays and many more meetings between all parties, we eventually agreed on a pragmatic solution: cutting and removing the lower 300 mm section of all the common-house weatherboards, removing the zinc flashings where we could and replacing them with stainless steel flashings installed over a small ventilating cavity. A drainage channel would be created around the base of the building where paving was close to floor level, effectively lowering the ground level to 450 mm below the floor level so that the flashing could be ventilated behind, and still maintaining the minimal thresholds we wanted for wheelchair access by putting timber decking over the channel.

Meanwhile construction on Stage II(b) continued apace. Building H was nearing completion, and we had the Building I roof shout, the last one for the project, in late August. Stage II(b) felt so different from the earlier stages when the buyers were much more involved, making timely decisions and available to do small urgent jobs to smooth the way. At this late stage we had sold only four out of the eight Stage II(b) houses. Buyers of two of those houses were overseas, and the others weren't available a lot of the time. It all meant much more work for me, because I still had to consult each one about issues and choices to do with their individual units, but they weren't around to do anything that contributed to the process.

I summarised the issues we were facing to the Full Group meeting in October: how the common-house flashing issue was dragging on; the H and I buildings were nearing completion but few H and I buyers were able and willing to pick up tasks; the need to prioritise finishing the swales so we could collect the Infrastructure Auckland (IA) grant money; that if everything went really well we might break even financially, but we could be in debt at the end depending on who paid for the zinc and the earth remedials, and whether and when we sold the last houses. The very best thing we could be doing for ourselves financially was selling the rest of the houses by Christmas. A last big effort was needed by everyone to get us through to the end.

It had taken all year to get our compost toilet commissioned, but on 6 November we had a ceremonial opening masterminded by Helen M and Barbara. Robin L dressed up as Lord Muck in a grey tailcoat and a Union Jack cravat. He did a hilarious Governor-General opening speech and read some Spike Milligan poems with suitable toilet themes. Barbara and Helen M handed around prunes, we all came up with a hundred names for poo, ate turd-shaped chocolate brownies and drank wee-coloured lemonade, and Robin L cut the toilet-paper ribbon amidst much laughter and hilarity. Then the fire was lit on the meadow and we relaxed with Guy Fawkes sparklers and chat, while enjoying the neighbours' fireworks from above the pond. That was a very happy night.

With completion approaching we started strategising about renting out the unsold units to pay the interest on the construction loan. However, all except Unit 31 were spoken for by December.

Lord Muck opening the compost toilet

Building H was handed over by the builders in November, Building I by early January, and more neighbours started moving in.

After a full year of debate, the architect, builder, Council and CNZL had finally agreed on the solution to the zinc issue, but not on who was to pay for it. In November, the Full Group approved CNZL commissioning the builder to do the remedials, whether or not liability had been established by then, and to pursue recompense later.

> At every stage of the project we've gone ahead before we've known where all the money was coming from. It's that kind of project. We'd never have these buildings if we hadn't, we'd have damp old Tūī House and a paddock of trees. It would never have been built if people weren't prepared to take calculated, informed, inspired risks. Not silly risks, but not steps that an accountant would take. It's not 'safe', it's not retrospective, the numbers in the columns don't add up yet; it's future oriented. We believe this will come together in the future if we go ahead now.[3]

The year finished on a personal high note with my selection into the New Zealand Social Entrepreneur Fellowship, a three-year fellowship with fourteen other movers and shakers around New Zealand. The work I'd been doing for so many years was recognised as significant beyond our own neighbourhood; it was of value to the country and the planet and worth all the hardship.

All Stage II(b) buyers had moved in by January 2007. We had sometimes talked about how things would be between the 'old' members, who had worked for years planning and living through the excitement and crises of the early development, and the 'new' members, who bought the last houses and moved into an almost completed neighbourhood. There were also changes in ownership of some earlier houses, so around one-third of the community was new at this stage, and there was a certain amount of turbulence with so many new residents at Earthsong finding their place. Two couples had become members from overseas and migrated to live at Earthsong, so they had missed all those steps of gradually getting to know our Earthsong culture by observation before participating as members. Others had not participated much until they moved in, so we had a bunch of new people with fresh energy ready to participate fully, but without the integration, understanding and relationships that had previously smoothed the bumps.

At the first Full Group meeting of the year, all Focus Groups and teams reintroduced themselves to members, saying what areas of Earthsong life they managed and what issues they were involved with: Management Team, Construction Team (CT), Promotions Team, Permaculture, Design, Common House Management, Kitchenettes, and the Earthsong Centre Trust.

The first issue that many of those new residents were involved with was the design and use of our central common green. Spatially and emotionally it was a powerful metaphor for group dynamics. The group had struggled with this issue before and opinions on the shape, and particularly whether there was a path across it or not, had become entrenched and divided. A special Full Group meeting was held on a Saturday afternoon in February, and two outside colleagues facilitated the process.

There were many old and new members at that meeting, a large excited group, all shuffling and jostling a bit, finding their place. A couple of members spoke strongly of ripping up the existing gravel base to the path, put in place a year before, and converting it to lawn, and this idea found favour with others. For the new members it was a simple design question, and since they all lived in the last row of houses, it wasn't a path they would use. But there was so much more going on than was visible on the surface. For those of us who had carried the weight of the difficult development, 'the path' had become a lightning rod for the conflicts and stresses of the past challenging years, and a place of opposition and resistance.

For me the path was deeply important. It was the final unbuilt section of the figure-of-8 path, designed to weave through the centre of our community, that was such a rich metaphor for the endless loop and overlap of both/and; the two equal emphases at Earthsong of sustainable physical infrastructure and cooperative relationships; the roles I played as both a member of the group and Development Coordinator (DC); the different path I had travelled from any of the group through the development and construction process; the path I still travelled several times a day between my house and my office in the common house.

There wasn't the space at that meeting to really talk it through. I found myself isolated and alone in my viewpoint, and the decision was made by the group to remove the vestigial path. I knew there would need to be a transition from the development phase as we completed the project and I expected that to be challenging. But I had hoped we had the process skills to do it with awareness and compassion, acknowledging all it had taken to get to that point, and moving forward together.

We still had unresolved issues from years before, especially those of us who had paid roles during construction and were also neighbours. There was still grumpiness about the setting up of the Earthsong Centre Trust and use of the common house. Disagreements continued through the year around trying to get consensus on furniture for the common house. There was ongoing discussion about our Community Building workshops with Margot Solomon which had continued several times a year, but several of those who were involved in conflicts or had the strongest feelings about issues were now refusing to attend. The community was in transition, finding its way, generally in good heart but with some rough and jagged edges.

The first couple of months of 2007 were busy for me with detailed earth-wall checks and final building checks for H and I, getting Code Compliance Certificates and titles. Deficiencies had been identified in the tank system design, so float switches were installed to each tank and flush points to each downpipe line. Topsoil was delivered and spread to the north of H and I in February, and the new residents started their gardens.

Work finally started in March on the repair of the common-house flashings. The lower portion of the vertical board-and-batten weatherboards was cut and removed to allow the zinc flashings to be replaced with stainless steel flashings. A channel was created outside all of the doors, the concrete paving for the common house was finally poured and timber decking installed over the channel. All was completed by mid-year, and the common house's construction was signed off by Council in July. Finally, after one-and-a-half years, we could use this building as we intended – for tours, educational events and use by community groups, in line with our vision.

We also decided in March to schedule working bees every second weekend to complete the overland stormwater swales and other landscaping, a rather massive task. These were tasks we had chopped from the budget in earlier phases of financial stress, but they needed to be completed before we could access the Infrastructure Auckland (IA) grant which covered some of the cost of this work. The site levels once again were critical and a big challenge, stimulating dissent among residents. The combination of having wheelchair-accessible paths and minimal door thresholds, needing the topsoil to be 225 mm below floor level and sloping away from the houses, and then the overland stormwater system having its own logic with swales 200 mm below ground level at the top end, sloping away from that at 1:200 mm absolute minimum, meant that in some places the swales ended up very deep indeed.

We spent every second weekend for more than a year shaping the channels, concreting rocks against the bank of the channel beside the path, placing soil and planting over ninety metres of swale. It was dirty, hard but enjoyable work, and created a great sense of camaraderie. The whole mood of the community was gradually lifting as things were finished, with a sense of togetherness growing as people became involved and worked together.

Residents completing swales

By April, I was fast running down again. I was still waking in the night worrying about the zinc issue and the earth issue, and the emotional strain of keeping relations good with the builders and architect while also heading for arbitration to resolve liability. I was setting up excavation of the last swale, construction of the last paths and the concrete swale bridges, organising working bees to rock the swales, planning the concrete driveway installation, as well as a myriad of smaller details – thinking ahead, strategising, organising materials, planning the timing and sequence, keeping people's spirits up.

Thirty-two households were living at Earthsong, settled into their homes, using the common house, being neighbourly. Development had become much more peripheral to life at Earthsong, and only the four of us in the CT – Gary, Lippy, Bryan and I – still had our attention on the unfinished aspects of the project. In May, I ground to a halt again and spent time with friends near a beach to recover enough to carry on. But I also had a sense of guiding this ship into harbour, journey nearly over, adventure nearly complete.

David M and Helen H had brought their legal and mediation expertise in behind the scenes to advise and mentor Gary and me in our dealings around the zinc and earth issues. We engaged a barrister and I wrote a summary of the rammed-earth-wall issue for him, collating many documents to back up our case. I repeated the process, though in much more detail, with the common-house zinc issue, writing a detailed summary of information and events for our barrister and collating relevant documents. The architect's insurers contested liability, so we decided to go to arbitration, and many weeks of work went into compiling evidence and answering the other party's claims.

With construction so nearly finished we were focused on wrapping up the accounts, but there remained several variables and complications. Obviously, we needed to complete the driveway and hard landscaping. We also needed to complete the swale rock walls and other stormwater works so we could finally claim the IA grant of $93,000. We were calculating the members' interest on the money early members had paid in 1999 to finance the project and debating whether or not to pay this out in full, or even with an allowance for inflation. We still had one unit to sell, rented out in the meantime. We still had to pay back the council loan of $300,000. We had estimated over $100,000 in costs from the earth-wall issue, and up to $175,000 claimed for the zinc issue. It looked like we might have a loss of up to $130,000 at the end of the project, and there was anxiety in the group about how we would pay for that.

We were debating how much to put aside every year for our Body Corporate Maintenance Reserves Fund. We had also been reassessing the Focus Groups needed to take Earthsong forward post-construction. At a Full Group meeting in July, we brainstormed all the tasks that needed to be handled collectively to maintain our neighbourhood and clumped them into areas of work. This was summarised as a diagram by one member, Christof, as the 'Brainstormygramme'.[4] New Focus Groups based on this summary gradually came into being, starting with CHuM (Common House Management Team) and MaCL (Membership and Community Life) in November.

In amongst everything else I worked on the finer details of the driveway design and setting up the final siteworks and driveway completions, including driveway lighting, permeable paving and speed humps. By October the last sections of swale had been dug and work was under way preparing the driveway for its final surface. The paving supplier, Stevensons, through their engineer, Danka, offered to sponsor the works with $15,000 worth of permeable paving. This donation, unsolicited by us, was partly so they could return in the future to do permeability tests, but also, as Danka explained, it was in acknowledgement and appreciation for the work that we'd put in to get Earthsong going. She said that we were fifteen years ahead of everyone else.

With the arbitration coming up I felt a huge responsibility to my neighbours. It had been two years of effort, stress and worry, problem solving and negotiating to find a solution to the zinc issue that all parties could agree on. By delaying the finishing of the common house, the issue had had an impact on all residents, but it also delayed my being able to finish the job and move on with my life. Most of my work for the arbitration was invisible to the community because it had to be confidential, and few really understood the stress I was under. As it turned out, the arbitration was all over in one day and we felt it went very well, though we wouldn't know the official results for some time. It was a huge relief to have this over and we felt very positive about the result. Though things were still busy with final site works, that stress was finished, and life could ease up a bit.

Another acknowledgement came in November when I was awarded a Winston Churchill Fellowship to enable me to travel and visit sustainable community and town centre projects in Europe and the UK. I planned to leave in June 2008 to attend the US Cohousing conference on the way to Europe. I felt this departure date should give me plenty of time after the driveway was finished to complete my documentation work and recharge somewhat after the huge effort of Earthsong.

We had had a mountain of topsoil and clay on the front of site for several years, starting with the 'crappy clay' from digging the pond in 2001, and progressively stockpiled as sites were stripped for successive building stages. My first job in 2008 was organising diggers to reposition much of this to create an enormous 'bund', a three-metre-high mound running the length of the site between the newest houses and the road, to give visual and sound protection to those houses. The rest of the clay was removed off site by early January, finally revealing once more the natural ground level of the front of site and taking another huge step towards the completion of the project.

At the end of February, we finally heard that we'd won the arbitration. The arbitrator found completely in our favour and awarded us almost everything we had claimed. It was a huge relief, and made our financial situation look better, with $124,000 awarded plus another $38,600 for legal costs. But worth much more than that was the validation. Our barrister Keith sent me an email saying that it 100% vindicated me and affirmed my work, from finding the problem right through to the arbitration. There was lots of appreciation from members. Another huge chunk had fallen into place.

The paving contractors for completion of the driveway and carparks had been meant to start work in November 2007, then they talked about starting immediately after Christmas, but it was late February 2008 before the last big task of construction commenced. The prices were high, the boss was surly and difficult to deal with, but at last work was under way. Residents were on continual notice to shift their cars at dawn or park in different areas as required, and eventually all cars were banished to the street for the final section of driveway. We were still doing working bees to complete the swales, and I was anxious about everything that had to be done before I could sign off as DC and go on my trip in June.

Gary had stood beside me, without payment, through all the stress and uncertainty of finding solutions to the zinc and the rammed-earth issues, because he believed in what we were doing and was committed to completing Earthsong. He hadn't lived at Earthsong since his relationship break-up in 2003. He'd remained in CT all through the long years since then – for the building of Stage II(a), the common house and Stage II(b). He'd been my right-hand man, and along with Cathy and Peter in Stage I and Lippy and Bryan in Stage II, we had been the backbone of the Earthsong construction phase. In a celebration in his honour in March, the group recognised his contribution with a $5000 gift in appreciation for all the work that he had generously given to this project, in particular over the last two years.

The paving and concrete slowly transformed our muddy gravel driveway into clean, hard surfaces. Work proceeded much more slowly than we wanted, and

Appreciation for Gary's contribution (Gary in yellow shirt in the middle)

like everything else, turned out to be more complicated than expected. I was trying to do the Maintenance Manuals before I left for my trip, and had one more big job to do once the siteworks were completed which required a lot of documentation: to apply for the release of the IA grant, granted in 2000 and largely spent by 2002. It had become clear I wasn't going to get away by June, so I rescheduled my trip to leave in early August.

In early July the work was finally finished. After spending eight years living amidst mud and dust on a construction site and sharing the gravel driveway with trucks and diggers, the bright clean surface of the concrete drive-way signalled the end of the project and a new beginning. The development phase of Earthsong was complete, nine years after we began to plan the construction in earnest, and thirteen years after the birth of the project. Who would have thought, back in 1995, or back in 2000 when we started building, or even in 2004 or 2005 or 2006 that we'd still be building in 2008?

Finished at last

… when you're trying to change a culture, persistence pays off. … you gotta be able to go the distance. In the consciousness movement, the people who can persevere for ten, twenty, and thirty years are the ones who can have a dramatic impact on the culture – because that is the true time horizon of effective action. … you have to enjoy the people and the process, and you need the maturity to work in a longer time frame.   RAY AND ANDERSON (2000, P. 203)

EPILOGUE

15

As I sit at my desk, I can hear two of my neighbours on the path, stopping for a chat as they move between their homes and the world outside. The dappled light of the late afternoon sun comes in the window, and birds warble as they prepare for the night. Soon I will leave my desk and walk up to the common house to eat common dinner with my neighbours.

Tonight after dinner there's a meeting of our other company, Walk to Work Eco-Developments Ltd, to make progress on the eco-friendly commercial development we plan to build on the 1 acre (0.4-hectare) site between Earthsong and the road, to provide work opportunities for both Earthsong residents and the wider community. Hatching projects is easier when you live in cohousing.

It took several more years after 2008 to wrap up the construction phase. We didn't sell the last unit until 2011, meaning our company Cohousing New Zealand Ltd (CNZL) had to remain in existence as owner of the unit, renting it in the meantime. We knew CNZL would end up with a loss but didn't know how big this would be until the various financial and legal issues were resolved. We finally closed down CNZL in 2014 with a loss of around $30,000, paid for by our Body Corporate.

For a $15 million project, budgeted to break even with no profit built in, that wasn't a bad result!

I spent a couple of years putting together a set of six thick Maintenance Manuals, downloading all the information I had in my memory and records about our individual units, common house, materials and site services, including thousands of photos I'd taken throughout construction of locations of pipes and cables in each wall and in the ground. I drew detailed as-built plans of the location of all the services under the ground, diagrams of our water and power systems, and collated warranties and information from manufacturers, so all of this information could be in the group domain. We are like a mini-local-government, with responsibility for our own collective services, so it is vital to have full records for ongoing maintenance.

I also wrote extensive material for our website, kindly supported with funding from Waitakere City Council, to make a range of information available to the public and others who are planning a project like ours.

Most of those involved in the planning and development of Earthsong have now moved on, twenty years after we turned the first sod and twelve years since we completed construction. Our foundational vision is as potent and valid as it always was, and we also recognise the need, as residents change over time, to regularly regenerate our shared understanding of what we value about our life at Earthsong and our relationship with the wider environment.

There is always more to do in the gardens. I had imagined that with thirty-two houses on 3 acres (1.2 hectares), the gardens would be small, productive and very well managed, and sometimes they are. But fertile soil produces abundance and diversity, and the amount of work required and who does it continues to be, and will probably always be, one of the areas we struggle with.

Weeding and maintenance are required also in the garden of our relationships. There are still issues playing out in the group that have their origins in those turbulent years, and new issues arise as residents come and go. We are diverse, complex human beings, and as a community we need to continue to pay attention to the relationships between us, recognising areas that have become stagnant and smelly, bringing them into the light and air, turning them over so they can rot down into nourishing compost that feeds a flourishing garden and allows new growth.

Some years ago, I was invited to Beijing to talk at the launch of a journal on New Zealand intentional communities, including Earthsong, written by Chinese artist and intellectual Ou Ning. It was held on the twenty-eighth floor of a new ultra-shiny high-tech building in the centre of the Beijing business district, rising above motorways amongst a forest of other skyscrapers.

A presenter from another New Zealand community spoke before me; and there on the screen was a photo from 1970s Waitati, of my old friend Bill sitting in a bush bath surrounded by the light, space and beauty of the New Zealand landscape. The contrast with where we were sitting couldn't have been more extreme; and yet this back-to-the-land New Zealand experience was relevant and interesting to the Chinese people in attendance. We really do live on a connected planet, and the ripples from one small place and time can keep moving into the future in ways we can never predict. It does matter what we do and the choices we make in each moment, and the attempts we make to live in connection with ourselves, each other, and earth.

Earthsong is a beautiful place. People come from around New Zealand and the world to visit and feel inspired and hopeful. Earthsong has also become a catalyst in the rejuvenation of our wider suburb. Several residents have been deeply involved in local community development projects, working towards a more socially, culturally and environmentally sustainable suburb of Ranui.

Like a healthy person with healthy organs made up of healthy cells, sustainability needs to operate at all levels: the individual, the household, the neighbourhood, the village and the city. A flourishing, sustainable 'eco-city', would include many flourishing, connected ecovillages and neighbourhoods, of an appropriate scale to encourage cooperation and healthy relationships. It is increasingly apparent that we are all part of one vast, complex planetary system or organism, and eco-neighbourhoods and -villages offer fertile environments to re-learn the skills of interdependence and cooperation that will contribute to the health of our beautiful earth home.

Those of us who live in community continue to do work together that is largely uncharted; we are explorers in the territory of respectful and inclusive human relationships. It's not Utopia, nor Ecotopia. It is much more challenging emotionally and requires us to be constantly self-aware, generous and open-hearted. Being in connection with others requires great commitment. It's an ongoing journey of self-discovery of ourselves as well as of others.

Does Earthsong live up to my vision, my expectations? Oh yes. It feels completely congruent with the vision I had all those years ago, although the journey and the details have been different.

Beginnings are important; and staying the distance through all the challenges and obstacles is vital to achieve change. I also really value the power of completion, of deep acknowledgement and honouring of the journey, learning what we can from it, sharing it and moving on. This story is my completion. Thanks for travelling with me.

APPENDICES: TOOLS AND PROCESSES

APPENDIX 1: PRACTICES FOR VISIONING
(Chapter 3)

There are many exercises, practices and tools that can help you to imagine a reality different from your present situation. Some tools and practices that have worked for me are outlined here.

Clarifying your values

Read, question, stay curious about what you come across and how you feel about it. Have conversations with your family, friends and colleagues. What really matters? When you imagine looking back as you near the end of your life, what are the values that you will judge yourself by? Bringing that awareness to everything you do will inevitably influence how you work and where you put your energy.

Connecting with wildness

Striding along a wild beach with the surf roaring and gulls soaring overhead; a quiet walk through undamaged forest with the rich smells of damp earth and light filtering through the diverse canopy; resting beside a babbling stream mesmerised by the dance of light on the water; these simple and nourishing experiences remind me that I am one small and vital part of the whole. In my experience, it is when I feel grounded in my body and connected with the body of earth that my mind opens, and the flow of energy and ideas comes through. I remember that I am not just 'me', a solitary individual; when I feel connected with the whole of life, I become a conduit for the wisdom and life energy of the whole.

Positive news and inspirational models

There are many inspirational thinkers and stories of positive projects and change happening in the world, but they don't often turn up in the newspapers or on TV. If your values don't match what you are served up in mainstream media, it is important to seek out sources of information and inspiration that open up new ideas and possibilities.

Once you look in the right places, there are many positive stories of people taking action in small or large ways to create the world they want. Paul Hawken, in his book *Blessed Unrest* (2007), talks of the vast number of organisations working towards ecological sustainability and social justice, few of whom have any idea there are so many others.

Writers and filmmakers who imagine alternative or future worlds often describe dystopias, but there are some who let themselves imagine how things might be better. Feminist utopian science fiction often opens a window into positive futures. Starhawk's *The Fifth Sacred Thing* (1993) is a powerful imagining of a post-apocalypse future, in both negative and positive directions.

Strategic questioning

Fran Peavey describes the concepts of strategic questioning and asking 'long-lever questions' (Peavey, 1997). Short-lever questions have yes/no answers; they assume all information is already known, and that there is a right and a wrong answer. Long-lever questions open up space and creativity, generate new information and allow new visions to emerge. Fran Peavey developed a system of strategic questioning, moving through a series of question 'families' designed to help individuals and groups recognise issues that they are concerned about, and move towards taking action.

Briefly, it goes like this.

- *Focus questions*, such as: 'What are you most concerned about in your community?'
- *Observation questions*: 'What do you see, hear, notice about this situation?' 'What do you know for sure and what are you not certain about?'

- *Feeling questions:* 'How do you feel about the situation?' 'How has it affected your physical or emotional health?'
- *Visioning questions:* 'How would you like it to be?'
- *Change questions:* 'What exactly needs to change, and how might those changes come about?' 'Who can make a difference?'
- *Personal inventory and support questions:* 'What would it take for you to participate in the change?' 'What support would you need?'
- *Personal action questions:* 'How can you take action in this?' 'Who can help?' 'What are the first steps?' (Peavey, 1997).

Accessing inner wisdom

Allow space in your life to get in touch with your inner world, that authentic inner self whose voice can so easily be lost in the noise of daily life. Getting in touch with a deeper level of awareness and wisdom and bringing it into outer reality by expressing that inner voice – in writing, drawing, painting, talking or whatever works for you – are ways of gaining access to your inner knowing and help to remind you of what is important.

Articulating your vision is like writing down a dream. I rarely remembered my dreams because they dissolved into mist as soon as I tried to catch them, but for a few years I made the effort to write down whatever fragments of my dreams I could catch as soon as I woke, and this became a discipline that improved my recall over time. Once they were written down, I could re-read and think about them with my daytime mind, and often be surprised at the insights or relevance to my life.

Visual diaries,[1] the practice of reflecting on each day by drawing rather than writing, have worked in a similar way for me. For more than twenty years from the early 1990s, I spent time each evening sitting quietly and feeling into the events of the day. An image or sensation usually came to mind, sometimes pictorial, but more often just colours and shapes that expressed the essence or my strongest feeling of that day. I used coloured pencils to do a very small drawing, only five centimetres square, a quick impression without space for too much detail. Once I expressed this on my page, I could look at the image and learn something more about myself, my reactions or what I was really feeling that I hadn't been conscious of before.

For many years, I also wrote morning pages,[2] which is the practise of writing three pages as fast as you can as the very first thing you do every morning, stream-of-consciousness with no censoring or stopping to think. It is often surprising what comes out: 'Oh, is that what I think? Is that how I feel?' Among the repetition and mundanities can be pearls of insight that wouldn't have had a chance to surface otherwise. I think of it as exercising my writing muscle, as well as letting all the dross in my head come out onto the page, leaving more space to access my deeper thoughts and insights.

Setting intentions

Intentional gatherings or rituals, whether to acknowledge and celebrate the seasonal cycle, or acknowledge some important transition of age or status, have long been an important way of accessing my inner truth, making it available to my thinking and action, and setting intentions for the future. For over twenty-three years I have met regularly with a small group of women to acknowledge the changing seasons as the earth moves around the sun, and to reflect on how the qualities of the season are mirrored in our lives. Often this includes setting intentions for the future, what we would each like to bring into our lives, and what support we need to do that. My fortieth birthday celebration and intention of stepping into my power was a pivotal moment that informed and supported everything that happened afterwards. And the Heart Politics gatherings have always included practices of reflection, visioning and setting future intentions.

Guided visualisation

Taking the time to sit quietly and be guided into imagining a different reality is one of the most powerful ways to get in touch with what you want to help bring into being. Envision your best fantasy about how the world could be: the healthiest, most flourishing planet for all species and systems. None of us can exist in isolation from the rest of the world; our whole world is a living system and all aspects are connected. If some parts of our world aren't thriving it diminishes the extent to which each of us as individuals can thrive.

The following exercise focuses on imagining your ideal home place but can be adapted for other scenarios.

Find a quiet place and 20 minutes of uninterrupted time. Sit comfortably, close your eyes and take time to settle into your body. Notice all the sounds you can hear, both near and far away; just notice them and let them go. Without changing anything, notice your breathing. Scan your body and relax any areas that feel tight. Let your attention sink deeper and deeper into your own being.

Allow yourself to imagine your very best fantasy of a flourishing home place, for you and those around you. Don't limit this to what you think might be possible or practical; really let yourself feel free to imagine the best scenario you possibly can. Imagine yourself there; really be there. Go for a walk around your flourishing home place. What do you hear, what can you smell? How does it feel? What can you see? What do you do over the course of a day? Who else is there, and what are they doing? Spend enough time to really get in touch with this place.

Once you have a sense of your new, desirable reality, use crayons or pens to draw on paper whatever comes up that describes this place and helps you get clearer about what it is like. Write any notes that will help to remind you.

If you are doing this with others, take time to talk in small groups of two to four people about what came up for each of you, and what you learned about your desirable futures.

APPENDIX 2: DEVELOPING A VISION STATEMENT AS A GROUP (Chapter 3)

A 'Vision Statement' is a powerful, succinct statement that expresses the essence of what you want to achieve. Ideally it is articulated and agreed by the founding members of the group, is agreed to as a condition by all subsequent members and guides the development of the group endeavour at every level.

The following process can be used to help a small founding group articulate and agree on a Vision Statement.

- Start with some individual quiet time, perhaps with a guided visualisation as above, to allow individual minds and hearts to open to the best outcome you can each imagine.
- Take time to each share those imaginings with the group.
- Brainstorm and record words and phrases that articulate what is most important to your collective project.
- Collectively identify which of those words and phrases best describe your shared vision using a preference process (see Appendix 6).
- Wordsmith those words and phrases into a short, concise statement that encapsulates the essence.
- Fine-tune, agree and adopt the statement as a group.

APPENDIX 3: COMPLEMENTARY PROCESSES TO AID DECISION-MAKING (Chapter 5)

Many other processes can be used within or alongside consensus meetings to move issues forward, shift the energy or free up creativity to consider something different.

Here are some processes to try.

- *Rounds* – Everyone gets a chance to speak to the issue, one after another going around the circle. This can elicit the full range of responses that exist in the group – including from people who don't often speak – but of necessity, a round takes time. A 'popcorn' round is similar, but people speak when they choose (but only once) rather than following the person beside them.
- *Brainstorm* – People offer ideas freely without discussion or evaluation by others until later. These ideas are written up on a board for all to see and consider.
- *Continuum* – Two alternatives are presented, and members are invited to place themselves along the line between them in relation to how much they support either alternative. People are then invited to speak to the group about why they have placed themselves in that position. This gives a quick readout of how those in the group feel about the issue. (Explained more fully in Appendix 6.)
- *Hand signals* – Another way to get a quick readout of how close the group is to agreement. Members are asked to raise a hand high to indicate agreement,

hold it level if they feel neutral, or low to indicate they don't agree with the proposal. This can also be done with a thumbs-up, thumbs-sideways, or thumbs-down.

- *Fishbowl* – A small-group discussion, but within and witnessed by the larger group. Four or five chairs are placed in the middle of the meeting circle. When someone would like to say something about the issue under discussion, they join the conversation in the middle by taking a turn in one of the middle seats. They might stay for some discussion, then rejoin the outer circle, leaving room for another to take their place and have their say.

- *Sharing circles* – A meeting specifically convened to give space to people to 'talk from the heart' and share deeper aspects of themselves or their attitudes to an issue. There are many indigenous and/or spiritual traditions that have a form of this, including Māori, Native American and Quaker. The quality of the listening is at least as important as the speaking. Sharing-circle culture often includes guidelines such as not interrupting or responding to another speaker with discussion, only speaking once, and only when feeling 'moved' to do so. A talking stick or talking bowl may be held by the speaker and laid down when finished, and in some traditions a small song or poem may be offered by the speaker at the end of their sharing. A sharing circle can be a powerful community bonding experience that gives space to understand one another in a more profound way, and often results in a shift in the group energy that allows a collective solution to arise.

- *Online decision making* – There are various online tools available, and Loomio – developed in New Zealand (www.loomio.org) – is one that has its origins in the coloured card system. There is no substitute, however, for sitting together, looking people in the eye, feeling their humanity and being immediately accountable for what you say.

- Many other small-group and large-group processes can be used to get a sense of where the energy is in the group, by allowing each member to have their own response, and seeing how well these correlate and whether it gives a clear direction. *The Zen of Groups* (1992), by Dale Hunter, Anne Bailey and Bill Taylor, is an excellent resource.

APPENDIX 4: AGREEING ON KEY SITE CRITERIA
(Chapter 7)

As a group, and with your Vision Statement in mind, brainstorm the attributes and criteria for a site that group members consider important, and write them up on a large piece of paper on the wall as they are stated. Include issues of size; cost; availability; appropriate planning controls; anything about the location or topography that is important, such as unshaded solar access or walkability to local facilities and public transport; as well as more subjective issues such as 'feel', privacy or connectedness, vegetation, etc.

Once the initial ideas are on the page, spend some time together explaining and discussing the attributes proposed, before using a simple process, such as preferences using coloured spots (see Appendix 6), to get a feel from the group about which are the most important attributes for this project. Check whether there are any attributes that anyone doesn't want to include, and why. At the end of this process, collate those criteria for which there is general agreement, and use your group's decision-making process to approve this document.

A Site Feasibility Check Sheet based on your site criteria is useful for assessing each of the sites you look at, to remind you of what you have agreed is important, and to help you measure each site against your vision.

APPENDIX 5: GROUP SITE ASSESSMENT AND MAPPING (Chapter 7)

Once you have your site, the following group process is a useful way to start thinking together as a group about the design of your future neighbourhood and beginning the design-brief process.

The group first meets on the site. Each person is given a small site plan and a Site Observation Check Sheet similar to the one shown on p. 261. People spend time by themselves walking around the whole site and marking their personal responses to the questions on the plan.

After reconvening at an appropriate venue where you can work together, do a group mapping process by collating people's responses on a large site plan drawn to scale and with contours marked. To save time on the day, the plan could be marked up beforehand with all the information you have previously found out about sun

Site Observation Check Sheet

Part of feeling at home on a particular piece of land involves developing a relationship between you and that place. This relationship, like any between people, starts with sensory impressions and intuitive feelings when you are physically present on the land. As well as factual information about the site, it is important to access and include these personal emotional responses, as they form the basis of an ongoing and deepening relationship with the site you choose.

Here are some questions to prompt you in observing, listening to and sensing the land. They are given as a guide only, and the invitation is to record on your site plan any significant places or aspects that you notice (including the obvious).

What sounds do you notice, and where?

What can you smell, and where?

Where are the views that you like, or don't like?

Which areas feel exposed, or sheltered? Sunny or shaded?

Where might you feel overlooked, by whom and at what times of day?

Where on the site do you feel most peaceful? Most energised? Perhaps unsettled?

Are there special or sacred places that you are drawn to?

What places feel like a focal point? Where do you feel is the centre of the site?

Are there areas with a microclimate or vegetation that feels particularly important, or significant trees that you think should be kept?

Any other aspect that is significant for you on this site?

and wind directions, access, location of existing services (power and water supply, sewer, etc.), overland flow path of water, etc. Discuss areas of views, vegetation, etc. and mark them on the plan. Each member gets small coloured spots to mark their sacred places, focal points, centre and any other significant aspect on the large plan.

If there is general agreement from those in the group about which areas of the site are special, this would indicate they should be kept as common areas, not privatised into an individual house or yard.

If you have access to a solar modelling programme, it would be very valuable to check the solar access and potential shading to different areas of the site at different times of the day and year. This may give you a clear directive as to how far apart the houses or house rows need to be and where the buildings need to be on the site to avoid shading in winter.

APPENDIX 6: PROCESSES FOR PARTICIPATORY DESIGN (Chapter 7)

There are many processes that can be used to facilitate participatory design. Here are some processes that we found useful at Earthsong.

- *Guided visualisations* – As described in Appendix 1. These help members imagine their life in the completed neighbourhood, and therefore the spaces to be incorporated.
- *Brainstorm processes* – Members are invited to offer ideas on a topic, and these are written up without editing on a large sheet of paper visible to all. Words and phrases may be clumped together if they are similar. Discussion or evaluation of these ideas does not happen until after the brainstorm.
- *Preferences* – Each member is given a certain number of choices, usually around 20% of the total items, to indicate the ideas most important to them. If there are twenty-five ideas written up from a brainstorm, each person can place five coloured spots, or simply be asked to put their initials, alongside the five ideas they most align with. This gives a quick readout of the most important items for the whole group.
- *Continua* – A continuum is quick and fun, and accesses feelings and intuition as well as thoughts by asking people to physically move and find the place that feels right for them. The facilitator indicates a line between two aspects, for

example this end of the room is this aspect, and the other end of the room is that aspect. Everyone present stands somewhere along that continuum to indicate their preference and talks with others nearby to check they are in the right place relative to each other. A few people, including those at the extremes and others in the middle, are asked to explain to the group why they have placed themselves at that point. It is okay (in fact encouraged!) for people to change their position based on what they've heard from others. A record can be made of the continuum on a sheet of paper by asking people to initial the appropriate place on the line where they stood, with any comments. A two-dimensional continuum with two axes can also be useful. (See photo on p. 122.)

- *Prioritisation* – This is useful when you have identified a list of wants, such as a list of the rooms you would like to have in the common house. It is unlikely that you will be able to accommodate everything on everybody's wish list, so prioritising together helps to avoid arguments later when you need to make budget cuts. One way to do this is to work in two or three groups to discuss and arrange the places in order of priority. Make a set of places for each group by writing each identified place on a separate slip of paper. Each group works to arrange these places in a list, from the highest priority to the lowest. The groups then compare their lists, discussion ensues and the group works towards agreement on the priority order.[3]

- *Questionnaires* – These can be useful, giving more time for members to think about and fill in their responses. Results are collated and feedback is given to the whole group. However, what you are building is not just a collection of individual homes, but one neighbourhood to accommodate the range of needs as well as possible. Having gathered the individual responses, the next step is to see how that works collectively and make consensus decisions in the best interests of the whole. A word of caution on questionnaires and surveys: they very easily end up reinforcing the assumptions or expectations of those who write the questionnaire because that is how they are written: a questionnaire's structure, questions and focus often develop from the author's assumptions/expectations. *'The act of looking for certain information evokes the information we went looking for'* (Wheatley, 2006, p. 65).

APPENDIX 7: COMPILING MAINTENANCE INFORMATION (Chapter 9)

- Take photos of all underground services as they are being installed, including permanent reference points in the photo that will remain visible (buildings, significant trees, manhole lids, etc.) to help identify the location later. Identify the pipes or services on or with the photos.

- Measure and record distances and depths of pipes and cables from permanent points such as adjacent buildings or manhole lids before the service trenches are filled in.

- Collect documents during construction such as product brochures, material data sheets, installation instructions, warranties, etc.

- After construction, draw up accurate and detailed as-built plans of all underground services, including depths below adjacent floor levels or manhole lid levels. They are a vital record of what is no longer visible.

- Write up instructions on the operation and maintenance of all systems, equipment and materials that are specific to your neighbourhood, such as water tanks, photovoltaic systems and common house equipment and including a maintenance log to be filled in as required.

- Similar records can be made for each house. Take photos of wall framing with all the pipes, wiring and other services installed before the wall linings go on, with appropriate notes to identify each. Compile these with details of materials and systems into a House Manual for each household.

- Compile all of this information to make Site, Common House and House Maintenance Manuals for the neighbourhood so that all the relevant information is easily accessible to future residents. They will be consulted often.

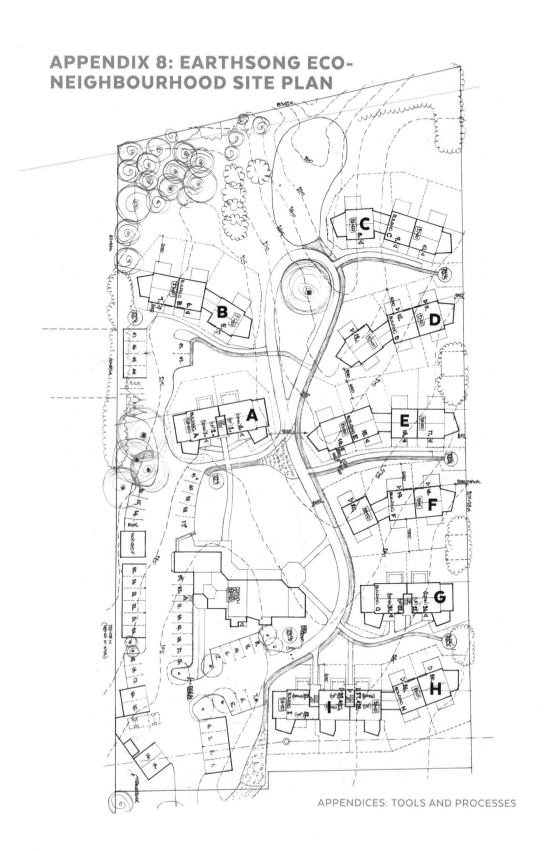

GLOSSARY

AGSAP – Agreement for Sale and Purchase of property

bach – simple holiday cottage

BRANZ – Building Research Association of New Zealand

Building Consent – local council approval for the architectural and structural design, materials and details of a specific building project

Code Compliance Certificate – Council's final sign-off that a building has been constructed as required under the Building Consent

chooks – chickens (colloquial)

CHuM – Common House Management Team (Stage II)

Cohousing Agreement – the legal agreement between Earthsong members and CNZL

CNZL – Cohousing New Zealand Ltd, Earthsong's development company

CT – Construction Team (Stage II)

DPC – damp-proof course, the waterproof layer between concrete and timber construction

DC – Development Coordinator

didgeridoo – wind instrument of the aboriginal peoples of northern Australia

DT – Development Team (Stage I)

Ecowater – the water management division of WCC

ET – Employment Team (Stage II)

FG – Full Group of Earthsong members

fourplex – Earthsong apartment block (Buildings A and G) with two units downstairs and two units above

GE – genetic engineering

GST – Goods and Services Tax

hui – meeting (Māori)

IA – Infrastructure Auckland, a regional funding body charged with solving Auckland's transport and water problems

IOA – Initial Organising Agreement, Earthsong's first membership agreement

iwi – tribe (Māori)

kaitiakitanga – stewardship, 'looking after that which nourishes' (Māori)

kaumātua – elder, a person of status within the whānau (Māori)

kete – Māori woven basket (Māori)

koru – unfolding fern frond (Māori)

kōwhai – *Sophora* spp., small endemic tree (Māori)

LIM – Land Information Memorandum, a summary of information held by Council on a property, including details of drains, rates, potential erosion, subsidence or flooding and possible presence of hazardous substances

MaCL – Membership and Community Life Group (Stage II)

Māori – first peoples of Aotearoa/New Zealand

matai – *Prumnopitys taxifolia*, endemic black pine tree (Māori)

Mātāriki – Pleiades star cluster (Māori). The reappearance of the seven Mātāriki stars in late May or early June signals the beginning of the Māori New Year

maunga – mountain (Māori)

MOU – Memorandum of Understanding

MT – Management Team (Stage II)

pākehā – non-Māori (Māori)

papakāinga – village on communal Māori land (Māori)

Papatūānuku – Earth mother and wife of Rangi-nui (Māori)

PT – Personnel Team (Stage II)

PKA – Promanco Kenman Auckland Ltd, Earthsong's project managers for Stage I

PVs – photovoltaic cells for generating electricity

QS – Quantity Surveyor

Rangi-nui – Sky father and husband of Papatūānuku (Māori)

Resource Consent – local council planning approval for projects that have an impact on the environment or could affect other people

rimu – *Dacrydium cupressinum*, endemic podocarp tree (Māori)

SEF – Social Entrepreneur Fund run by Community Employment Group of the Department of Labour to encourage social innovation

sixplex – Earthsong apartment block (Building I) with three units downstairs and three units above

te reo Māori – the Māori language

topo – topographical survey

tuatara – small endemic reptile, the only living dinosaur (Māori)

tūī – indigenous songbird (Māori)

valuation – the current market value of a property (known as appraisal in the USA)

W2W – Walk to Work Eco-Developments Ltd, the company set up by a group of Earthsong members to buy and develop the front of site as eco-commercial premises

wānanga – learning community (Māori)

WCC – Waitakere City Council in west Auckland, now incorporated into Auckland Council

WENCP – Waitakere Eco-Neighbourhood Cohousing Project, as Earthsong was called in 1998 and 1999

WENT – Waitakere Eco-Neighbourhood Trust, as Earthsong was called in 1996 and 1997. It was never formally registered as a trust

whakataukī – proverb or significant saying (Māori). In this case it was used to mean a statement of one's personal intent as an architect

whānau – extended family group (Māori)

whenua – placenta (*also* ground, country) (Māori)

NOTES

Preface

1. Attributed to Zev Pais, Cohousing US.
2. See Lovelock (1979).

Chapter 1

1. The cohousing model was developed in Denmark in the early 1970s. The Danish government was supportive and helped the concept to thrive. Now Denmark, with a population of 5 million, has over 700 communities, and there are many others throughout Europe and the world. This resident-led housing model was introduced to the English-speaking world with the publication, in 1988, of *Cohousing: A Contemporary Approach to Housing Ourselves* by two US architects – Kathryn McCamant and Charles Durett. This book is now into its third edition with the title *Creating Cohousing: Building Sustainable Communities*. It seeded a strong cohousing movement in the USA and other networks all over the world, many of which generously share systems and learnings to encourage the establishment of more cohousing neighbourhoods.
2. See Durett (2005).

Chapter 2

1. McCamant and Durett, 1988.
2. Peavey, 1986.
3. See Appendix 1: Strategic Questioning on p. 254.
4. Attributed to Margaret Mead.

Chapter 3

1. From the song 'Dreams and Visions' by Kate and Ini, aka Kathryn McMillan and Ineke Veerkamp, Australia.
2. Robin Allison, personal journal.
3. Notes taken during a talk by Fay Weldon (Auckland).
4. Robin Allison, personal journal.
5. As told by Wolfgang Hiepe. Original source unknown.
6. Murray, 1951.

Chapter 4

1. Robert Gilman, see www.context.org/bfnow/
2. The Timeline Game was developed specifically for cohousing groups by architect Bruce Coldham in the late 1990s.
3. The Building Biology and Ecology Institute (BBE). www.bbe.org.nz

Chapter 5

1. *The Concise Oxford Dictionary.*
2. I acknowledge my yoga teacher Margaritha for this concept.
3. See Chapter 13 for discussion about leadership in an empowered group.
4. Shaffer and Anundsen, 1993, p. 31.
5. Described as 'Colours of Empowerment' in Hanson, 1996, p. 27.
6. Laird Schaub, notes taken during a workshop on Power and Leadership at USA National Cohousing Conference, Nashville, 18–21 May 2017.
7. Adapted from Leafe Christian (n.d.)

Chapter 6

1. Robin Allison, personal journal.
2. The Building Biology and Ecology Institute (BBE). www.bbe.org.nz

Chapter 7

1. Paul Downton, notes taken during a presentation in Christchurch, 2013.
2. McCamant and Durett, 2011, p. 249. Medium size is sixteen to twenty-five households – large enough for extensive common facilities, small enough for direct democracy. Large is twenty-six to thirty-five – more diversity and common facilities, spread costs, but can fracture.
3. Known as Design Program in the USA.

Chapter 8

1. Not their real name.
2. See Appendix 8: Earthsong Eco-Neighbourhood site plan on p. 265 for house and building numbers.
3. Macrocarpa, *Cupressus macrocarpa*.

Chapter 9

1. From Earthsong Eco-Neighbourhood Vision Statement, see p. 16.
2. 'Earthsong land use and usual land use'. Unpublished study for Bachelor of Planning, University of Auckland by Peter Scott 2003.

3. World-leading comprehensive Earth Building Standards have been available in New Zealand since 1998. They are accepted by local authorities throughout New Zealand as a means of compliance with the New Zealand Building Code, making the process of getting Building Consent for earth construction considerably easier. These valuable standards have been updated as NZS 4297:2020 Engineering Design of Earth Buildings, NZS 4298:2020 Materials and Construction for Earth Buildings, and NZS 4299:2020 Earth Buildings not Requiring Specific Engineering Design. Available from https://shop.standards.govt.nz/catalog/ics/.
4. Tung tree, *Vernicia fordii*.
5. Mainly macrocarpa (*Cupressus macrocarpa*) and Lawson cypress (*Chamaecyparis lawsoniana*).
6. CD50, with copper quinolinate, made by Churton Pacific.
7. PVC, polyvinyl chloride, a known carcinogen.
8. In New Zealand over 80% of electricity is generated from renewable sources, mostly hydro and geothermal.
9. 'Home Energy Comparison'. Unpublished study of Earthsong by Peter Scott 2003.
10. 'Earthsong Eco-Neighbourhood Water Supply System Performance 2005–08' by Mark Essex of Qmex Ltd for Waitakere City Council, July 2010.
11. Analysis of Earthsong Eco-Neighbourhood Refuse by Jennifer Chenery for Waitakere City Council, April 2010

Chapter 10

1. Not their real name.
2. Alan Drayton Builders is now Biobuild Ltd.
3. See Appendix 8: Earthsong Eco-Neighbourhood site plan on p. 265 for house and building numbers.

Chapter 11

1. The Timeline Game was developed specifically for cohousing groups by architect Bruce Coldham in the late 1990s.
2. Ann Zabaldo, notes taken during a workshop on Resales at USA National Cohousing Conference, Nashville, 18–21 May 2017.

Chapter 12

1. North American Cohousing Conference, 19–22 June 2003.
2. See Appendix 8: Earthsong Eco-Neighbourhood Site Plan on p. 265 for house and building numbers.
3. Alan Drayton Builders is now Biobuild Ltd.

Chapter 13

1. Laird Schaub, notes taken during a workshop on Power and Leadership at USA National Cohousing Conference, Nashville, 18–21 May 2017.
2. Laird Schaub, personal correspondence.
3. Williamson, 1992.
4. Anecdotal; source unknown.
5. *The Concise Oxford Dictionary.*
6. See Greenleaf (1977).

Chapter 14

1. Neil and Tim Finn, 'Won't Give In', from the Finn Brothers album *Everyone is Here.*
2. Waitangi Day is a public holiday to commemorate the signing of the Treaty of Waitangi, New Zealand's founding document, in 1840.
3. Robin Allison, personal journal.
4. Brainstormygramme, see p. 80.

Appendices

1. See Batten (1997).
2. See Cameron (1992).
3. Acknowledgements to Charles Durett for this process.

REFERENCES

Batten, Juliet. *Releasing the Artist Within: The visual diary.* Auckland: Tandem, 1997.

Block, Peter. *Community: The structure of belonging.* San Francisco, CA: Berrett-Koehler, 2008.

Cameron, Julia. *The Artist's Way: A spiritual path to higher creativity.* New York, NY: Tarcher Putnam, 1992.

Campbell, Joseph. *The Hero with a Thousand Faces.* New York, NY: Pantheon (Bollingen series), 1949.

Durett, Charles. *Senior Cohousing: A community approach to independent living.* Berkeley, CA: Habitat, 2005.

Gilman, Robert and Diane. *Ecovillages and Sustainable Communities: A report for Gaia Trust.* Langley, WA: Context Institute, 1991.

Greenleaf, Robert K. *Servant Leadership: A journey into the nature of legitimate power and greatness.* Mahwah, NJ: Paulist Press, 1977.

Griffin, Susan. *Woman and Nature: The Roaring Inside Her.* London: The Women's Press, 1984.

Hanson, Chris. *The Cohousing Handbook: Building a Place for Community.* Vancouver, BC: Hartley and Marks, 1996.

Hawken, Paul. *Blessed Unrest: How the largest movement in the world came into being and why no one saw it coming.* New York, NY: Viking Penguin, 2007.

Hunter, Dale, Bailey, Anne and Taylor, Bill. *The Zen of Groups: A handbook for people meeting with a purpose.* Auckland: Tandem, 1992.

Janov, Jill. *The Inventive Organization: Hope and Daring at Work.* San Francisco: Jossey-Bass, 1994.

Leafe Christian, Diana. 'How the "N Street Consensus Method" Helps N Street Cohousing Thrive', *Ecovillages*, Issue 157, n.d. DianaLeafeChristian.org.

Lovelock, James. *Gaia: A new look at life on Earth.* Oxford: Oxford University Press, 1979.

McCamant, Kathryn and Durett, Charles. *Cohousing: A contemporary approach to housing ourselves.* Berkeley, CA: Ten Speed Press, 1988.

McCamant, Kathryn and Durett, Charles. *Creating Cohousing: Building sustainable communities.* Gabriola Island, BC: New Society, 2011.

Meltzer, Graham. 'ESD and "Sense of Community"' in Birkeland, Janis, *Design for Sustainability: a sourcebook of integrated eco-logical solutions.* London: Earthscan Publications, 2002.

Meltzer, Graham. *Sustainable Community: Learning from the cohousing model.* Victoria, BC: Trafford, 2005.

Mollison, Bill. *Permaculture: A Designers' Manual.* Tyalgum, NSW: Tagari, 1988.

Mollison, Bill and Holmgren, David. *Permaculture One: A perennial agricultural system for human settlements.* Melbourne: Corgi, 1978.

Murray, William Hutchinson. *The Scottish Himalayan Expedition.* London: Dent, 1951.

Peavey, Fran. *Heart Politics.* Gabriola Island, BC: New Society, 1986.

Peavey, Fran. *Strategic Questioning: An approach to Creating Personal and Social Change,* Vivian Hutchinson (Ed.), 1997. www.jobsletter.org.nz/pdf/stratq97.pdf

Ray, Paul H. and Anderson, Sherry Ruth. *The Cultural Creatives: How 50 million people are changing the world.* New York, NY: Harmony, 2000.

Sandelin, Rob. 'Optimizing the Group Design Process', *CoHousing Journal,* Fall 1998.

Shaffer, Carolyn and Anundsen, Kristin. *Creating Community Anywhere: Finding support and connection in a fragmented world.* New York, NY: Tarcher/Putnam, 1993.

Starhawk. *The Fifth Sacred Thing.* New York, NY: Bantam, 1993.

Wheatley, Margaret J. *Leadership and the New Science: Discovering order in a chaotic world.* San Francisco, CA: Berrett-Koehler, 2006.

Wheatley, Margaret J. *So Far From Home: Lost and found in our brave new world.* San Francisco, CA: Berrett-Koehler, 2012.

Williamson, Marianne. *A Return to Love: Reflections on the principles of A Course in Miracles.* New York, NY: HarperCollins, 1992.

IMAGE CREDITS

Front cover   Site plan: William Algie, architect, re-drawn by Bryan Pulham; theme and story symbols: concept by Amanda Garland, re-drawn by Anna Egan-Reid; spiral garden photograph bottom row: Margaret Duncan

P. 12   Karen Meikle

P. 15   *The New Zealand Home* television series

P. 17   William Algie, architect

P. 24   David Allison

P. 25   David Allison

P. 81   Table decoration by Chris Free

P. 99   Cathy Angell

P. 101   Cathy Angell

P. 105   Cathy Angell

P. 116   Auckland Council, https://geomapspublic.aucklandcouncil.govt.nz

P. 124   Geoff Ball

P. 133   Illustration by JJ

P. 140   Bevin Fitzsimons

P. 178   Cathy Angell

P. 179   Cathy Angell

P. 243   Christof Schneider

P. 247   Gary Stewart

P. 265   William Algie, architect

Back-cover flap   Amanda Garland

ACKNOWLEDGEMENTS

My deep gratitude to all past and present members of Earthsong who believed in the vision and gave their energy, creativity and love, for short or long periods, to bring Earthsong into being. Every contribution has helped to shape Earthsong, and many continue to be part of our collective evolution.

Particular thanks to Helen Haslam for wise, loving and consistent support; to Gary Stewart for steady, caring friendship and strategic thinking; and to Cathy Angell and John Hammond for coming on board at the first public meeting in 1995, being active participants through the long development phase, and enduring some very tough times to remain committed residents today.

Loving thanks to those fierce friends who listened to my tales and always had my back: Rosie Kaplan, Lewis Williams, Jenny Allison, Lesley Brokenshire, Judith Ackroyd and Karen Stacey. Deep gratitude to Ank Mellema and Margie Pearl for support and wisdom through many years. My grateful thanks to those who gave me sanctuary to rest, recharge and start writing this story: Barb Baragwanath, Juliet Batten, Charmaine Pountney and Tanya Cumberland.

Deep respect to my friend and mentor Vivian Hutchinson, a kauri of community regeneration and empowerment in Aotearoa. Acknowledgements and gratitude to all my Heart Politics whanau for inspiration, support and accountability, without which this story may not have happened.

Huge acknowledgements to Katie McCamant and Chuck Durett for observing, analysing and introducing the cohousing concept into the English-speaking world, starting a movement and inspiring so many people to take that journey. The Cohousing Association of America has fed this movement for many years and continues to support the ongoing development of the cohousing model.

Thanks to my readers Niki Harre, Helen Haslam and Helen McNeil for very helpful feedback on my manuscript, and to Juliet Batten as both reader and wise mentor during the writing process. Anna Egan-Reid and Sophia Egan-Reid have been a joy to work with in the publishing stages.

Enduring love and thanks to my two sons, Willow Allison-Maxwell and Erin Allison-Maxwell, for gracefully coming along on this ride and growing into thoughtful, aware and caring men. And deepest love and gratitude to my wife Amanda Garland, who arrived when space opened up after the events of this book, has helped me think about and process the journey while writing, and is a loving and supportive partner in our flourishing life.

INDEX

PRAISE FOR COHOUSING FOR LIFE

Robin Allison is a pioneer in cohousing and has written a thoroughly engrossing book about her experience of designing and co-founding the Earthsong community in Auckland. Robin's is a story of struggle and success, cooperation and conflict; highs and lows; and, most important, a story of absolute determination needed to make this ambitious project work. Her tale of overcoming the hurdles she and the project faced during the decade it took to bring Earthsong to life is deeply compelling. Cohousing enthusiasts will love this book, but so will anyone with an interest in community building and staying true to your principles during a complex, long project.

– Niki Harré, School of Psychology; Associate Dean Sustainability, Faculty of Science, University of Auckland

In her book *Cohousing for Life*, architect Robin Allison documents the extraordinary achievement of co-founding and building Earthsong community. Her moving account describes the loving and dedicated creation of an environmentally friendly village as a working community, with all the struggles that such communities inevitably endure along the way to becoming rooted, diverse, complex and democratic, in the true sense of the word. We badly need such communities, especially in urban environments, at this turbulent time in the world. Projects like this are clearly the way forward for building resilience, offering low-carbon living and a life which is close to the earth, bringing old and young back together. I hope this readable and accessible personal account will inspire others to do the same.

– Mary-Jayne Rust, ecopsychotherapist, author of *Towards an Ecopsychotherapy*, Confer Books, 2020

In the face of the climate emergency and with youth taking to the streets in protest against inaction, communities and ecovillages around the world are instigating real positive change. Robin Allison is one such community leader who decided to become part of the solution. In this book she shares the story of how her love for life and her intelligence helped to propel her forward. Today, the Global Ecovillage Network reaches out to over 6000 sustainable communities such as Earthsong. This is no longer an isolated phenomenon. Be inspired by Robin's seemingly ordinary, extraordinary story to transform your own life – and help chart a pathway to a regenerative future for all of us.

– Kosha Anja Joubert, Executive Director, Global Ecovillage Network